This book explores how a variety of social groups – women, African-Americans, and political radicals – create their own "public spheres," parallel to the mainstream public arena. Because such groups have historically been excluded from conventional public discourse and activity, they build their own unique infrastructures for opinion formation and expression. The book draws upon theory in a variety of disciplines – sociology, philosophy, political science, and communications – in order to understand communication patterns among the politically marginal at different points in history. Three diverse historical case studies (female-operated salons of eighteenth-century Paris, the black press of the 1930s, and the creation of *The Masses*) and a contemporary analysis of the Libertarian party illuminate the experiences of those who live on the fringe of the public sphere. Through synthesis of existing scholarship and original archival research, *Politics at the Margin* demonstrates the centrality of political communication to the study of social action.

POLITICS AT THE MARGIN

Politics at the Margin
Historical Studies of Public Expression Outside the Mainstream

SUSAN HERBST

Northwestern University

CAMBRIDGE
UNIVERSITY PRESS

Published by the Press Syndicate of the University of Cambridge
The Pitt Building, Trumpington Street, Cambridge CB2 1RP
40 West 20th Street, New York, NY 10011-4211, USA
10 Stamford Road, Oakleigh, Melbourne 3166, Australia

First Published 1994

Printed in the United States of America

Library of Congress Cataloging-in-Publication Data
Herbst, Susan.
   Politics at the margin : historical studies of public expression
outside the mainstream / Susan Herbst.
      p.   cm.
   Includes bibliographical references and index.
   ISBN 0-46184-7 (hc)–ISBN 47763-8 (pb)
   1. Marginality, Social–Case Studies. 2. Communication in
politics–Case studies.   I. Title.
HM136.H454   1994
320–dc20   93-41566
                                                   CIP

A catalog record for this book is available from the British Library.

ISBN 0-521-46184-7 hardback
ISBN 0-521-47763-8 paperback

For My Parents

Contents

Acknowledgments

Scholars who conduct interdisciplinary research are usually indebted to an eclectic group of colleagues, since this sort of work leads one far from his or her area of expertise. The list of people who reacted to my ideas at conferences (across several disciplines), explained the genesis of certain concepts or theories, or listed books and articles I couldn't ignore, is very long and difficult to compile. I hope that they know who they are, because I am grateful for their contributions. My analyses of two cases in this book (Chapters 2 and 4) were inspired by, and are dependent upon, the careful archival research of scholars in French history and early twentieth-century American history. Works by these very imaginative researchers are noted in the text, endnotes, and bibliography, but I'd like to underscore my appreciation of their writings here.

I am indebted to a variety of people – scholars and informants – who either read chapters of the manuscript, or helped me to clarify my ideas upon hearing me discuss the themes of the book: Jim Beniger, Henry Binford, Daniel Dayan, Jim Ettema, Elihu Katz, Sarah Maza, John H. Sengstacke, and Sue Walton. Kathy Kendall read the entire manuscript, and gave me some very sound advice, as well as some much-appreciated encouragement. Scores of Libertarian political activists took the time to explain their philosophy to me, and many sent newsletters, books, political tracts, cartoons, and other useful materials for Chapter 5.

Hiram Sachs and Bo Penh provided expert research assistance, while Mike Hostetler and Pat McGrath cheerfully assisted with a variety of mundane clerical tasks associated with completing the manuscript. Jill Edy and I collected the data for Chapter 5 and she patiently and skillfully transcribed all of our interviews. I'd also like to thank the reference librarians at the Chicago Historical Society, the Northwestern University Library, and the Newberry Library, who helped me track down a multitude of obscure citations and images. A grant from the Office of Research and Sponsored Programs at Northwestern was critical to the completion of the ethnographic work in Chapter 5.

My editor at Cambridge, Alex Holzman, recognized the value of a pretty odd, interdisciplinary book. I am grateful for his support and enthusiasm. Many thanks also to Helen Wheeler for her skillful copyediting.

I am indebted to my husband, Doug Hughes, for his unwavering support, and the fact that he rarely lets me get away with an illogical or unsubstantiated argument. Finally, I dedicate this book to my parents, Rose and Adolph Herbst, who inspired me in so many ways.

Introduction

To be in the margin is to be part of the whole but outside the main body. As black Americans living in a small Kentucky town, the railroad tracks were a daily reminder of our marginality. . . . Living as we did – on the edge – we developed a particular way of seeing reality. We looked both from the outside in and from the inside out. We focused our attention on the center as well as on the margin. We understood both.

bell hooks, "Marginality as a Site of Resistance"

Since the advent of the civil rights and feminist movements of the 1960s and early 1970s, individuals inside and outside of academe have given considerable thought to the idea of political marginality. Although we may use different approaches and different jargon to pursue this idea, we are all acknowledging the same phenomenon: the barriers faced by social groups who are trying to "break into" mainstream political dialogue. Some recent cases of marginality have been especially compelling – gay rights protesters angrily demanding research funds for the study and treatment of AIDS, for example. With the most cursory glance at the past, we can find countless instances where individuals, inhabiting the far edges of the conventional public sphere, struggled to express their views about politics, religion, and social life.

Academics have studied these marginal groups seriously but unevenly. A variety of researchers from a variety of disciplines have turned their attention to what I call "political outsiders" – especially during the last two decades.[1] Despite this large collection of cases, however, we still lack theoretical perspectives that might help us pull together these cases. This book is an attempt to do just that: to understand the common threads that run through the experiences of outsiders. In particular, I am interested in the style, structure, and content of alternative political discourse. How do outsiders express themselves? What sorts of channels do they create in order to voice their concerns, and how do these media – in turn – change the nature of marginal groups themselves? Finally, why are certain channels meaningful or useful to particular groups? I believe that the most interesting aspect of marginality is how groups, acting outside of the mainstream, actually create alternative discursive "space" for themselves. Sometimes this space coincides with geography: Marginal people may occupy certain neighborhoods of a city, for example. Usually, though, the space is linguistic and not physical. It is created through publications (e.g., books or periodicals) and interpersonal communication (e.g., correspondence or conversation). Political outsiders who find each other tend to create interesting and innovative networks for expression, leaving behind a legacy of fascinating documents and artifacts.

In communications and political science, the two disciplines that should be most concerned with public expression, marginal political discourse is largely ignored. New case studies appear every year, but we still lack tools for understanding the overarching structures of marginal expression. In my own subfield – public opinion research – political outsiders are almost completely neglected. "Public opinion" has come to mean the aggregation of individual opinions, with a disregard for smaller groups who compose the public. Groups, be they political, religious, or social, are washed over by journalists who report on polls in search of the ever-elusive "public mood." Even when a survey, published in a newspaper or academic journal, breaks out opinions into groups (e.g., women's versus men's opinions, or blacks' versus whites' opinions), these groups are large, artificially created ones: The women or men interviewed for the typical opinion survey do not have relationships with each other, and do not necessarily share a coherent group identity.[2] Public opinion research never captures the textured, complicated modes of expression among the marginal. To think that we can understand the *structures* and *styles* of alternative public opinion – opinions outside of the mainstream – through surveys, is naive.

Within marginal publics, community building is critical. Groups on the political and social fringes of a society often, either consciously or unconsciously, build collectivities that bind together their members. In this book, I demonstrate how communities are formed through discourse – through the spoken word and the written one. In the case of Chicago's African-

American neighborhood in the decades before the civil rights movement (Chapter 3), for example, a lively community newspaper was established by a man who understood the relationship between communication and solidarity. In another case (Chapter 5), contemporary political activists use computer networks, newsletters, and social gatherings to strengthen their community, support each other, and publicize their ideas.

As I noted earlier, portrayals of marginal groups and their ideas abound in the academic literature. Anthropologists and sociologists have long studied them, and literary critics have also begun to analyze and publish works by blacks, Hispanics, women, homosexuals, and others.[3] Social historians have conducted research on marginal groups for years now, attempting to understand the lives of those traditionally left out of national historical accounts.[4] My purpose here is not to explicate or critique these numerous studies, but to develop theory about marginal discourse using concepts and approaches from political communication. I do add several new cases to the existing literature on minority discourse, but I do this with the intention of developing a more general, interdisciplinary theoretical perspective.

I chose to study three historical instances of minority political expression, and one contemporary one. The historical cases are extremely useful, because they allow me to trace the entire lifespan of particular groups and their politics. In my study of the early twentieth-century radical magazine, *The Masses* (Chapter 4), for example, I am able to explore both its origins and the reasons for its demise. If we analyze a marginal group's activities, from beginning to end, we gain perspective on their impact, their effectiveness, and their problems. In addition to the three historical cases, I have chosen to study a current group – the Libertarians – because their situation sheds light on the abstract issues surrounding marginality. The Libertarian activists are true political outsiders, since many of their beliefs are dismissed almost instantaneously by mainstream politicians and by citizens. Their advocacy of drug legalization, or their desire to eliminate the personal income tax, get very little attention from the mass media, and are viewed as absurd by most Americans. The Libertarians make much of their own marginality, often calling themselves "the politically homeless."

The cases I discuss in this book are diverse, and were selected in order to sample – although not systematically – different periods in political history. When I began this work, I searched for groups that were marginalized because of gender, race, or political ideology. All of the groups I chose desired (or still desire, in the case of the Libertarians) a place in mainstream political dialogue. It isn't that they sought assimilation, as much as they wanted attention and respect. Most important, all of the groups developed their own unique sets of communication channels, and repertoires for public expression.[5] Outsiders' communicative innovations are engaging from several standpoints, because they reveal many things: how minority group members reach each other, how they influence – or fail to influence – societal politics, and why they do what they do.

Before I take up these case studies, however, I lay out some perspectives and concepts that will serve as useful analytical tools in subsequent chapters. Chapter 1 briefly examines a variety of ideas about political discourse and action, such as Jürgen Habermas's writings, and theories about community building. My central focus here is on what I call *parallel public space* – the arenas that marginal groups develop in order to voice their opinions.[6] In building these forums, minority factions generate alternative media (mass and interpersonal), which they hope will further their political or social agendas. I use this first section of the book to develop some new ideas about communication *backchannels*: the "behind-the-scenes" routes people use to send messages to each other, or to those outside of their circle. And I also discuss the idea of communication *environments*, building on recent political theory about power. Some writers have defined power as the ability to shape the rules and boundaries for political dialogue, and this sort of conceptualization helps us to understand the position of marginal groups in relation to mainstream institutional politics.

Chapter 2 is the first of four case studies of political marginality. In this section, I discuss the Enlightenment salons of Paris – most of which were created and maintained by women. Although a variety of successful authors, philosophers, statesmen, and businessmen attended these drawing room gatherings, women decided on the composition of the salons and the topics for discussion. This is a particularly interesting case of marginality, because the women who ran the salons were elites in one sense: They were wealthier than most Parisians, and mingled with very rich, influential men. Many of the salonnières were themselves from the middle classes and had worked their way into the salon culture by marrying or befriending wealthy men. Despite the privileged surroundings inhabited by these bourgeois women, however, they were marginal political actors.

Women in prerevolutionary France were second-class citizens, with no real political rights or voice. Most men – even those who respected the salonnières – thought that women should remain in the domestic sphere, since they were incapable of rational thought or argument. After the revolution, with its rhetoric of equality, women and their problems were still largely ignored by the patriarchal French government. In Chapter 2, I describe some typical salons of the period from 1730 through the early years of the revolution. Drawing upon accounts of salons, and some excellent new work by French historians, I show how women, despite their marginal status, were extremely influential in shaping the political dialogue of the period. Most Enlightenment writers dismissed women's capacities for political action, and many, like Diderot, were ambivalent. Yet despite barriers to conventional participation, the salon culture reveals how a group of *political* outsiders can actually exercise considerable force.

For the next case study, we move to early twentieth-century America. The focus of Chapter 3 is the South Side of Chicago, from the First World War through the beginnings of the civil rights movement. Early in this period, a son of former slaves named Robert Abbott established a newspaper called *The Chicago Defender*. *The Defender*, which is still published as a community paper, was one of America's preeminent national black weeklies. This chapter details how Abbott, and the community, used the newspaper to create a parallel political sphere on the South Side. Because white Chicago – its leaders and institutions – was largely unconcerned with the problems of segregation and discrimination, Abbott's paper became the central medium of communication for an oppressed group of Chicagoans. That African-Americans, living in Chicago, were marginal political actors during these years is an understatement: Most white citizens viewed blacks as inferior beings, most valuable as servants and laborers. Yet *The Defender* doggedly insisted that the black community was a thriving and important part of Chicago. The paper even coined a name for its neighborhood – "Bronzeville" – and organized its own mayoral elections from the 1930s through the early 1960s. Chapter 3 analyzes the newspaper, the mayoral race, and the goals of *The Defender*.

Chapter 4 takes up another marginal group living and working in the United States in the early years of the twentieth century: the Greenwich Village radicals who created *The Masses*. Unlike the cases of eighteenth-century women or Bronzeville, this chapter focuses on *deliberate* political marginality. Although women and African-Americans were automatically considered outsiders because of their gender or race, the radicals of lower Manhattan *chose* life on the margin. *The Masses*, first published in 1911, was introduced in order to critique mainstream American institutions and ideals – religion, the press, capitalism, the military, traditional gender roles, and even the Boy Scouts. Through editorials, fiction, poetry, and art, the men and women who sustained *The Masses* risked injury to their careers and imprisonment. Although the magazine, under the editorship of socialist Max Eastman, published work by some of the most talented individuals of the period – John Reed, John Sloan, Floyd Dell, and Art Young – it was forced to close in 1917. The federal government and the postmaster decided that *The Masses* violated the Espionage Act, since it advocated pacifism and stood firmly against military conscription. Five *Masses* contributors were tried and acquitted on sedition charges twice in 1918. Chapter 4 describes the origins of the magazine, its goals, content, and impact.

The last case study concerns a contemporary group of political activists, who have also chosen to live on the fringes of the public sphere – the Libertarians. Libertarians believe that the federal government plays far too large a role in our lives, and propose that we dismantle most of our social programs and regulatory structures. Although they have placed their own candidates on local, state, and national ballots since the early 1970s, the Libertarians feel as though they are badly misunderstood by their fellow citizens and by elected officials. The party also has tremendous difficulty gaining attention from the news media, who often ignore Libertarian candidates, platforms, and ideas. In Chapter 4, I discuss the results of a set of in-depth interviews I conducted with Libertarian activists. My conversations with them covered a variety of topics, including their ideologies, their campaign tactics, and the reasons they stay in the party. The Libertarians, like other political groups, have created an extensive communication network, and in this chapter I describe how these activists maintain a sense of community and purpose.

The final chapter moves beyond these portraits of outsiders, and concentrates on more general themes. Here I take another look at the theories and literature about political marginality by focusing on correspondences across the case studies. What have we learned about the communication patterns and tactics among those who work outside of the mainstream, either because of their gender, their race, or their politics? What sorts of rhetorical and discursive techniques are most effective for these groups? Finally, I am interested in the relationship between two variables – the communication strategies of outsiders and the cohesion of their communities. In cases of political marginality, how do discourse and identity interact with each other?

Although it is fashionable these days to talk about multiculturalism and marginality, those who study political discourse have begun only recently to focus on such issues. Current work in this area is extremely interesting, but also very fragmented. Through archival research, textual analyses, and ethnography, we can start to build theory about political outsiders – how they act, what motivates them, and most interesting to me, how they express themselves. No matter how many barriers to free expression are erected by governments and mainstream institutions, groups with unconventional ideas often manage to build their own infrastructures for dialogue and debate. Although legal scholarship about the protection of free speech is critical, constructing social theory about marginal expression is also extremely important. In fact, as we continue to recognize and respect the differences among social groups, it is imperative that we understand their activities, their perspectives, and their dilemmas.

I

Politics, Expression, and Marginality

In this age of electronic communication, when the media confer status and construct our political environment, public space is a contested arena. Which groups are allowed to speak through the mass media, and how their interests are "framed" by newspapers, television broadcasts, and magazines are among the most divisive issues in American politics. Journalists, working for profit-driven news agencies, have become very powerful, because they often determine which voices we hear, and which we don't. Public officials also wield this sort of power, highlighting particular groups and their goals. Some members of the U.S. Congress, for example, are dependable spokespeople for certain ethnic or religious groups that are part of their constituent base.

Each year, the media pay increasing attention to minority groups and the issues surrounding multiculturalism. Most newspapers, newsmagazines, and television networks have – in one way or another – described aspects of life outside of the mainstream: We have all read or viewed accounts of immigrants' economic problems, discrimination against African-Americans, and the devastating effects of AIDS on the gay community. Despite this slowly growing recognition of minority groups, however, it is still extraordinarily difficult for these groups to command the kinds of media attention they feel they need. As a result, complaints about lack of access to the media, from a variety of groups, abound. Ironically, these complaints are themselves rarely heard, since the media do not feel the need to publish or broadcast stories about dissatisfied customers.

Any thoughtful person who reads or watches the news understands quite a lot about the plight of the politically marginal. Yet there is a substantial amount of theoretical and empirical work in the academic literature that sheds light on important issues related to marginality. My intention in this chapter is to introduce some of these theories, debates, and research paradigms. Although the number of books and articles on the subject, published in the United States and abroad, is large, particular ideas have greatly enriched our understanding of outsiders. The first, and perhaps the most relevant, is the notion of "public space." I focus on the German social theorist Jürgen Habermas, and his extremely influential writings about the emergence of the "public sphere" in Western nations. In this section I'll also discuss the work of a few other writers – from philosophy, sociology, and other disciplines – who have elaborated or taken issue with Habermas's ideas. In the interdisciplinary field of Cultural Studies, several scholars have concentrated on marginality and public space, so I'll discuss some of their ideas here as well.

Related to the public sphere debate is the notion of "public opinion." Habermas, for example, has argued that rational, critical public opinion can emerge only where there is an open, thriving public sphere. I will argue that the literature about public opinion in the social sciences has essentially ignored marginal communication, despite its many interesting faces. Current research on public opinion is fascinating, from the perspective of this book, mostly because of what it *omits*. Yet the idea of public opinion – broadly conceived – is still very useful to us.

The next section concerns the much-debated concept of "community." Many groups of political outsiders, especially the ones described in this book, build collectives outside of the mainstream. By emphasizing a sense of community and solidarity, such groups are able to mobilize their members, cope with discrimination, and express themselves more effectively. Finally, I spend some time in this chapter discussing power and influence. How do theories about power help us to understand the efforts and problems of marginal groups? And how is it that some groups, although they lack the conventional skills and resources associated with power, are able to gain influence nonetheless? Here I introduce two concepts that reappear in the case studies: "communication backchannels" and "communication environments." These notions, which draw upon traditional perspectives in communication studies and political science, are very useful in mapping the expressive repertoires of political outsiders.

A prefatory note about definitions: One phrase used throughout this book is "outside the mainstream." Although no dominant culture is completely hegemonic or monolithic, I use the word "mainstream" to signify the norms, conventions, and values held by the vast majority of individuals living in a particular cultural setting. Also implied by this word are a society's popular styles of public discourse, and its most widely used communications media.[1] It is difficult to draw a clear line around "the mainstream," because its boundaries are usually in flux, so this book focuses on groups that were not (or presently are not) very close to the conventional public sphere at all.

"Marginality" is a relatively new concept in the academic literature, and there is little consensus about its meaning. For the purposes of this book, I use a rather broad and very simple definition of marginality. Social groups are marginal, from my perspective, when conventional institutions (or individuals associated with those institutions) attempt to *silence* them. These attempts at silencing aren't always effective. And such groups are not necessarily resource-poor or small. Also, feeling marginal doesn't necessarily make one marginal: There must be some significant or compelling evidence that the language and ideas of a group are systematically excluded from the mainstream public sphere, because of group members' ethnicity, gender, or beliefs.[2]

OUTSIDERS AND THE PUBLIC SPHERE

Since the publication of the English translation of Habermas's *Structural Transformation of the Public Sphere* in 1989, a lively debate about the nature of public discourse has occupied scholars across the social sciences and the humanities. Scores of historians, sociologists, anthropologists, philosophers, and media critics have begun to think about public space, and also to use Habermas's ideas as tools in their empirical research. The breadth of Habermas's scholarship, his provocative view of Western history, and his critical approach to classical texts all account for his wide interdisciplinary appeal. Oddly, although so many scholars have found his work useful, those who study American politics (past and present) often neglect it.[3] We can ascribe this negligence to several factors. First, Habermas's work is difficult to penetrate because his dense writing draws on concepts from so many different disciplines. Second, neo-Marxist aspects of his theorizing dissuade some scholars, who assume Habermas's studies are dogmatic in the manner of more traditional Marxian analyses. Third, the concept of public sphere is vague and as yet underdeveloped, since empirical work on the subject has only recently begun. The abstract nature of some Habermasian debates is difficult to grasp, because those involved in these dialogues often neglect to provide empirical illustrations of their arguments. Finally, Habermas's oeuvre has a strong normative component: He is interested in the empirical nature of the public sphere, but has also described the nature of *ideal* public space. In debates about the public sphere, writers often shift quickly between normative and descriptive language, which makes for perplexing reading.

Habermas is one of the last members of the Frankfurt School, a group of neo-Marxist scholars who established an institute for social research in the years before the Second World War. As a student, Habermas worked with the social critics Theodor Adorno and Max Horkheimer. Long before Habermas became his student, Adorno had written extensively about a phenomenon he called "the culture industry." Adorno argued that the mass media in the United States (but also in any advanced capitalist society) were in thrall to corporate interests: The media perpetuate the social and political status quo by destroying our critical abilities. In hopes of entertaining us, and thereby turning a profit, mass media outlets deliver mindless, inane, and trivial sorts of programming. The media corrupt the public sphere, according to the first generation of Frankfurt School theorists, and make rational discourse impossible. Many of the Frankfurt School thinkers fled Nazi Germany in the 1930s, and so were particularly concerned with the dominance of conservative "propaganda" they discovered in American political discourse.

Horkheimer and Adorno argued that media industries control the public sphere via the minds of uncritical audiences, who have lost the ability to imagine a world different from the one they live in. In their most vehement, and most compelling essay about the culture industry, written in 1944, they noted the insidious roles of marketing and market research in the broadcast industry:

Marked differences such as those of A and B films, or of stories in magazines in different price ranges, depend not so much on subject matter as on classifying, organizing, and labeling consumers. Something is provided for all so that none may escape; the distinctions are emphasized and extended. . . . Everybody must behave (as if spontaneously) in accordance with his previously determined and indexed level, and choose the category of mass product turned out for his type. Consumers appear as statistics on research organization charts, and are divided by income groups into red, green, and blue areas; the technique is that used for any type of propaganda.[4]

In his early work, Habermas used the Frankfurt School critique of the mass media to put forth his own argument about the disintegration of the contemporary public sphere. Although published just a few years ago in English, Habermas's *Structural Transformation of the Public Sphere* was originally his *habilitationsschrift* (graduate thesis), and reflects – to some extent – the pessimism of his teachers.

In *The Structural Transformation,* Habermas argues that the public sphere first emerged in late seventeenth- and early eighteenth-century Europe. Prior to that period, he posits, citizens did not distinguish their own interests from those of the state, and rulers claimed to represent the masses. Before the emergence of the public sphere, European monarchs would use public forums to parade the trappings of their authority before the people. Yet with a variety of changes in international commerce, and the development of the press, a public sphere began to emerge. Salons, coffeehouses, newsletters, and books became plentiful, and people began to converse about state affairs: For the first time, upper-middle-class men and aristocrats began to think critically about the government and its actions. Salons in Paris, the focus of the next chapter, were particularly important arenas for evaluating state policy and the activities of the king.[5] Though the public sphere thrived for a while, and though its growth instigated events like the French Revolution, it began to disintegrate in the late nineteenth century, according to Habermas. Because of the state's increased intervention into the economy, and escalating state bureaucratization, it became increasingly difficult to distinguish the private and public spheres. With the economic upheavals after 1870, competition among social groups and classes became more serious, and resources became more scarce. The state stepped in to become the mediator among these contending groups, and has maintained that role ever since the late nineteenth century. The institutions that had always stood apart from the government (e.g., the press) began to work *for* the government bureaucracy. The media, in particular, became an agent of capitalist ideology, and a supporter of the state.[6] As a result, forums for free and critical discourse disappeared. The culture industry, as described by Adorno and Horkheimer, dominates the public sphere in Habermas's early conceptualization.

In this historical study, Habermas described what a rational, critical public sphere was like, in its earliest incarnations. Yet one of his most concise definitions of the public sphere can be found in an article published in 1974. He wrote:

By "the public sphere" we mean first of all a realm of our social life in which something approaching public opinion can be formed. Access is guaranteed to all citizens. A portion of the public sphere comes into being in every conversation in which private individuals assemble to form a public body. They then behave neither like business or professional people transacting private affairs, nor like members of a constitutional order subject to the legal constraints of a state bureaucracy. Citizens behave as a public body when they confer in an unrestricted fashion – that is, with the guarantee of assembly and association and the freedom to express and publish their opinions – about matters of general interest. In a large public body this kind of communication requires specific means for transmitting information and influencing those who receive it.[7]

There are several important aspects of this definition. First, the ideal public sphere or public space enables all citizens, regardless of race, gender, ethnicity, sexual preference, or political ideology, to engage in political dialogue. Second, it is *conversation* that gives public space its vibrancy and its true value. These conversations do not necessarily entail face-to-face interaction, but they are reciprocal: They evolve because two or more parties have an interest in the dialogue. Third, freedom of speech is a critical part of the public sphere. Corporations and governments certainly have the right (and indeed, the duty) to engage in public discourse, but individuals should not feel compelled to maintain loyalty to these institutions. Citizens, debating in the ideal public sphere, should not fear for their careers, or their lives because of utterances made in the heat of rational debate. Finally, information technologies are an inherent part of the public sphere. Habermas emphasizes the fact that media – no matter how rudimentary – are crucial if debate is to develop properly. Although Habermas lists magazines, newspapers, radio, and television as the information technologies that dominate the political public sphere, we can expand the notion to include newer, more innovative ones: computer bulletin boards, electronic mail, personal video cameras, cable access television, and the like.[8]

The nature of public space changes with historical circumstance. Economic downturns, political upheaval, class division, war, technological changes, and other occurrences can all cause the boundaries and contents of the public sphere to shift dramatically. For example, the definition of who is a citizen has been modified considerably since the days of the ancient Greek democracies. Then, women, foreigners, and slaves could not participate freely and equally in political discourse, despite the existence of a very lively public sphere for male citizens.

Public space changes as time passes, shrinking and expanding to meet the needs and desires of institutions and individuals. Yet Habermas's conceptualization of the public sphere is a normative one. He has outlined what public space *should* look like, not how it actually appears. Because Habermas's empirical work on the subject was mostly synthetic (*The Structural Transformation* relies heavily on published works, and not on sustained archival research), there is considerable work to be done on the reality of public space – how and why this space is constructed. Several scholars, mainly historians, do use the public sphere notion to guide their research.[9] In these empirical studies, historians explore how the public sphere – during a particular era – deviates from the ideal type. Such comparisons can be extremely provocative, since they force researchers to evaluate the content of political discourse *as well as* the missing elements. Having an ideal typical model of the public sphere prompts one to ask some interesting questions – whether certain actors are absent from the public sphere, or why particular issues are avoided. Without a normative template, such queries might be less obvious and could conceivably remain unasked.

Feminist scholars have been among the most appreciative and the most critical of Habermas's ideal public sphere. Nancy Fraser, in particular, has used his theory as a starting point for a more realistic and inclusive conceptualization of public space. Because a variety of social groups are trying to break into the public sphere, and have difficulty doing so, perhaps it is best to think of multiple public spheres instead of a large, all-consuming one. Fraser proposes a new concept, "subaltern counterpublics," in order to go beyond the notion of one public/one public sphere. Counterpublics are "parallel discursive arenas" where oppressed or minority groups "invent and circulate counterdiscourses to formulate oppositional interpretations of their identities, interests, and needs."[10] Instead of thinking about a lone public sphere, where all groups do rhetorical battle, Fraser argues for many public spheres. She makes a compelling case against Habermas's sole public sphere:

Public life in egalitarian, multicultural societies cannot consist exclusively in a single, comprehensive public sphere. That would be tantamount to filtering diverse rhetorical and stylistic norms through a single, overarching lens. Moreover, since there can be no such lens that is genuinely culturally neutral, it would effectively privilege the expressive norms of one cultural group over others. . . . The result would be the demise of multiculturalism (and the likely demise of social equality).[11]

The literary critic Rita Felski has argued that the American feminist movement, which began in the 1970s, is an excellent illustration of alternative public space.[12] She believes that the movement enabled women to oppose the rhetoric and institutions of the mainstream, and at the same time develop a new arena for discourse. Feminists, through books, journals, consciousness-raising groups, and other media, have been able to create a thriving parallel public sphere. This counter-public of female activists has developed what Felski calls a "counter-ideology," which challenges the values of the hegemonic culture industry. In the new public space created by the women's movement, feminists can use their preferred lens of gender to view the world around them. Although the women's movement pressures the mainstream from outside, feminist thought has certainly affected the contours of the conventional (male-dominated) public sphere. That the movement has changed mainstream thinking about gender is obvious: Sexual harassment, wife beating, and sexual assault, although still commonplace, are not socially acceptable. Even the culture industry, with its allegedly sexist biases, has been forced to recognize the importance of so-called women's issues.

Scholars who study social movements have recently become very interested in the development of counter-publics, where outsiders are bound together by communication infrastructures. Some of these sociologists argue that the establishment of parallel public space is a prerequisite for the development of a social movement. When people who hold similar ideas, or share particular social characteristics form communities, they sometimes develop what Aldon Morris has called "oppositional consiousness" – an understanding of the flaws in mainstream social life, and a shared approach to challenging conventional politics.[13]

In the chapters that follow, I will explore how different social groups – some cohesive, some not – create parallel public space for themselves. These arenas for discourse and social action in some ways mimic the ideal Habermasian public sphere, because they are characterized by vibrant forms of mass mediated and interpersonal communication. Like the contemporary mainstream public sphere, however, these parallel public spaces are far different from Habermas's ideal model.

MARGINALITY AND CULTURAL STUDIES

Those scholars working in the interdisciplinary field of Cultural Studies support the notion that there are a variety of social groups, counterpublics, or subaltern publics that try to influence the mainstream, but also construct alternative public space. Cultural Studies is an extremely diverse field, which draws upon a variety of methodologies and theoretical approaches – feminism, psychoanalysis, semiotics, ethnography, and Marxism, among them – in order to understand historical and contemporary cultures. Although very few people believe that the large Cultural Studies literature has a coherent focus or a theoretical core, it usually (although not always) displays a leftist political slant. As Tony Bennett puts it, Cultural Studies is a field whose borders "which, however widely divergent they might be in other respects, share a commitment to examining cultural practices from the point of view of their intrication with, and within, relations of power."[14] A very recent collection of essays, published in a volume entitled *Cultural Studies*, seems to capture the essence of the new field. It includes a variety of essays on gender, race relations, AIDS, popular culture, literature, and art using historical analysis, ethnography, and textual analyses of various sorts.[15]

Although Cultural Studies is far from achieving disciplinary status, and seems to avoid the coherence and shared perspectives such a status might imply, it has produced a number of interesting empirical portraits of contemporary marginality. One goal of the field is to collect alternative voices, and map parallel public spheres rarely acknowledged by the mass media. These scholars focus on marginalization – the way that some groups and their ideas are either ignored or de-legitimated by mainstream leaders and institutions. Most of these researchers concentrate on groups that they believe are oppressed by the social and political status quo. And those working in Cultural Studies feel strongly that pressure on mainstream dialogue by homosexuals, women, African-Americans, and others is critical in a democracy such as ours. As these groups assert their identities, however, they do become a threat to American middle-class values and ideals, argues Russell Ferguson: "The relaxed self-confidence of a TV patriarch like Ward Cleaver now seems to have slipped out of reach, replaced by the increasingly hysterical and ruthless campaigns of the last ten years to *enforce* 'traditional family values.'"[16]

Cornel West calls the project of Cultural Studies "the new cultural politics of difference." This new approach challenges the mainstream, questions the rules of conventional political discussion, and at the same time articulates new arenas for marginal expression. West acknowledges the difficulties faced by this project, which is at once very specific (e.g., homoerotic art), and also very vague in its intentions. For one thing, West wonders how artists and intellectuals can best carry out their strategies for upsetting the comfortable, mundane, and oppressive value systems that dominate the culture. He summarizes the fundamental goal of the new politics this way:

In the recent past, the dominant cultural identities have been circumscribed by immoral patriarchal, imperial, jingoistic and xenophobic constraints. The political consequences have been principally a public sphere regulated by and for well-to-do White males in the name of freedom and democracy. The new cultural criticism exposes and explodes the exclusions, blindnesses and silences of this past, calling from it radical libertarian and democratic projects that will create a better present and future.[17]

The diverse works in Cultural Studies about marginality and the politics of difference, although nebulous, are helpful in that they underscore several important ideas. First, marginality is expressed through art and through the written word.[18] Artistic media are particularly useful to groups who find themselves on the fringes of the public sphere, because these media are so malleable. One can express an infinite number of concepts and emotions through paintings, drawings, performance art, cartoons, and the like. In Chapters 3 and 4, we shall see how blacks and political radicals used drawings and political cartoons to express their dissatisfaction with the status quo. Second, Cultural Studies scholars point out that marginal groups are not simply frustrated outsiders. They are oppressed by a mainstream population that holds stereotypic and dangerous impressions of them. This feeling – that most people have a lack of respect for their ideas and lifestyles – is universal among the political outsiders described in this book. From the Parisian women who struggled to join the intellectual dialogue of the eighteenth century, through the Libertarian activists working in contemporary America, we can detect exasperation, disappointment, and even depression. More than any other field, Cultural Studies highlights the cruelty and ignorance with which marginal groups must contend as they attempt to live their own way.

PUBLIC OPINION AND MARGINALITY

I mentioned in the introduction to this book that public opinion research has ignored marginal social groups. Survey research, which is the dominant methodology in public opinion research, is oriented around the idea of a single (although complex) public. Pollsters, journalists, political leaders, and citizens commonly describe an entity called public opinion, using terms like "divided," "strong," or "influential." When an issue, such as the civil war in the former Yugoslav republic or the Clarence Thomas Supreme Court nomination hearings, gains public attention, many of us automatically ask: "What does public opinion say?" Because this book is about public expression, it seems natural to ask where marginal social groups stand in relation to this monolithic public.

The first problem we face in trying to position marginal groups with respect to public opinion is that public opinion itself is a reification. The notion that one can – through survey research or any other methodology – capture the subtlety and complexity of Americans' beliefs, and speak about them succinctly, is somewhat naive. This is *not* to say that we cannot evaluate public opinion at all: In some cases, consensus about a government policy or action seems widespread. During the late 1960s and early 1970s, there *was* an obvious diffusion of anti-Vietnam War sentiment.[19] Similarly, during the recent Persian Gulf conflict, a majority of people clearly supported President Bush's policies.[20] Yet to speak too freely or authoritatively of a "public mood" or public opinion, on the basis of data collected at one moment in time, is to grossly simplify political attitudes.

Several critics have argued this same point, noting that public opinion is an artifact of research methodologies, since polling (in particular) forces people to speak their minds within a fairly narrow framework.[21] Others, like Walter Lippmann and Pierre Bourdieu, contend that the average citizen cares very little about domestic or foreign affairs, so his or her opinions are not always intelligent or thoughtful ones. Both wonder whether public opinion is a meaningful construct, when it simply reflects superficial reactions to pollsters' queries.[22]

Even pollsters, when they break the public into statistical clusters by gender, race, education, or social class, are admitting the obvious: that the public is made up of a large number of groups. Yet this recognition, in the reporting of survey research, isn't quite satisfactory, because these "groups" are statistical categories and not cohesive communities. The idea that public opinion is actually a compilation of groups was first noted by Arthur Bentley in 1908, who argued that

There is no use attempting to handle public opinion except in terms of the groups that hold it and that it represents. Public opinion is an expression of, by, or for a group of people. . . . When we examine this public opinion with its onward tendencies, we find that, besides being borne in a group, or given differentiated expression for a group, it always is directed against some activities of groups of men.[23]

Forty years later, the sociologist Herbert Blumer would argue much the same thing, in an attack on survey research. Society, Blumer noted, is not simply an aggregation of citizens. A society is composed of "diverse kinds of functional groups."[24] In politics, especially, *groups* are the powerful actors, since it is impossible for individuals to act without alliances and constituencies. How can one begin a social movement, or even stay in power, without the coordinated effort of a group or groups? From Blumer's standpoint, polling data about public opinion are not very informative, since they wash over group differences in favor of aggregating disparate, isolated individuals.

In this book, I assume that public opinion is created within publics (just as do pollsters), but that we must recognize multiple publics and multiple public spheres. Each public sphere, although it overlaps with many others, has its own infrastructure of public opinion. This infrastructure includes the techniques citizens use to express their opinions, their institutions and publications, as well as the issue debates they generate.[25] Thinking about the public as a conglomeration of groups is not only more sophisticated than treating the public as a mass. It also helps us explain and understand social conflict (groups clashing with each other) and hegemony (groups overwhelmed by more powerful groups). Marginal groups, I argue here, are interesting and worthy of study, even if they aren't large enough in membership to appear in opinion poll reports. In fact, one of my goals is to reintroduce groups into the study of public opinion. Even though minority group numbers may be small, their opinions are often so divergent that they greatly affect the culture and political discourse of a nation: One need only think about the burgeoning gay rights movement, which is tiny but vigorous.

MARGINALITY AND COMMUNITY

Although all marginal groups are different, some are particularly interesting because they also represent dense social networks. Scholars often refer to the entire black community or gay community as marginalized groups, but this book is concerned with outsider groups that subsume many interpersonal, social ties. Since I am concerned with groups where the members know (or at least know of) each other, I am able to draw on the insights of sociologists who study community. Community studies is an extremely large field because the concept is such an old and compelling one. Community membership helps us to figure out who we are, and also enables us to locate ourselves in the larger configuration we call "society." Over the last few decades, "community" has become a fundamental concept in empirical and theoretical social research.[26]

One benchmark in the study of community was the publication of Ferdinand Tönnies's *Gemeinschaft und Gesellschaft* (*Community and Society*) in 1887.[27] In this seminal work, Tönnies contrasted traditional communities with modern, industrial ones. Gemeinschaft was characterized by close, personal relationships, like those one finds within extended families. Inside communities, people view each other as ends in themselves, and respect each other as part of a close-knit social network. Individuals living in a community stay put, seldom venturing outside of the locale, or interacting with those outside of the region. In communities, people also "know their place," and live in a harmony of sorts. Tönnies describes the typical gemeinschaft as a place where people care deeply about one another, and where a strong sense of morality pervades all relationships. Gemeinschaft is contrasted with gesellschaft or "society." With the advent of industrialization, Tönnies argued, this new type of social organization grew and began to replace communities. A society is characterized by impersonality: The central ties that bind people together are commercial and contractual. In a gesellschaft, people treat each other quite intentionally as means to ends. Tönnies, like other early sociologists (e.g., Max Weber), believed that the shift from community to society was dangerous – that it would lead to growing alienation and disenchantment. Gemeinschaft and gesellschaft are ideal types, but they have been very useful to those who study community, because they richly describe two polar ends on the continuum of social organization. Emile Durkheim, for example, wrote in the same tradition as Tönnies, describing the shift from mechanical to organic solidarity with increasing population growth.[28]

Even though Tönnies inspired considerable work on community in sociology, researchers have yet to agree on a definition of the concept. Over thirty years ago, one researcher found ninety-four definitions of community in his review of the literature.[29] Since then, scores of other sociologists have offered their own definitions, although there is still no consensus about the meaning of the term. In their very popular book, *Habits of the Heart*, Robert Bellah and his colleagues proposed this definition of community: "a group of people who are socially interdependent, who participate together in discussion and decision making, and who share certain *practices* . . . that both define the community and are nurtured by it."[30] This is a good definition, because it speaks to the network aspects of community: People in a close-knit community tend to have interlocking relations and interests. The definition also underlines the importance of conversation and communication, and thereby parallels Habermas's ideal public sphere. Discussion – speaking and listening – helps a community to develop, expand, and to attract new members. Finally, this definition hints at the role of information and expression technologies, by arguing that community members share certain important practices with each other. Practices are activities, as well as norms, values, and means to achieve certain goals. The problem with Bellah et al.'s definition is that it fails to highlight the *boundaries* of community – the fact that one is either on the inside of such a social formation, or on the outside.[31]

If we use Bellah et al.'s definition, and supplement it with another offered by Anthony Cohen, we begin to capture the rich essence of community. Cohen acknowledges the definitional quandary faced by sociologists, but believes that the following meaning of community is particularly useful for empirical research. Community members, he says

(a) have something in common with each other, which (b) distinguishes them in a significant way from the members of other putative groups. "Community" thus seems to imply simultaneously both similarity and difference. The word thus expresses a *relational* idea: the opposition of one community to others or to other social entities. . . . It seems appropriate, therefore, to focus our examination of the nature of community on the element which embodies this sense of discrimination, namely, the *boundary*.[32]

Cohen argues forcefully that the "consciousness of community" is related to the boundaries it draws between itself and other communities. In the case of marginal communities, members establish boundaries between themselves and the larger society, or are *drawn out* of conventional society by members or institutions of the mainstream. For example, during a campaign speech before a conservative audience in 1992, U.S. Vice President Dan Quayle argued that homosexual activity challenged "traditional family values." By using this rhetoric, Quayle sought to marginalize the homosexual community by drawing a clear boundary around it.[33]

Another interesting set of issues about the nature of community was raised by C. J. Calhoun in an essay about community and history. Calhoun underscores an important distinction – that communities are experiential *and* structural at the same time. In other words, strong communities generate feelings of "belonging," but are composed of what he calls "relations among relationships." He argues that the structural connections among community members – their bonds – reflect a kind of "multiplexity:" Members are linked to each other, for example, because they live in the same areas, have similar values, and face the same economic difficulties. There are multiple *layers* of connection among those in a bounded community. Calhoun posits that among the different types (or "orders") of community bonds (e.g., kinship, obligations), *familiarity* is a very powerful sort of linkage that should not be overlooked. He notes that

We have a certain investment in the familiar, even when it is not what we might choose. Thus simple frequency of interaction and the built-up familiarity and predictability which it entails can be a major fact in strengthening a social relationship.[34]

In this book, I describe communities where familiarity is indeed the central type of bond linking individuals – not kinship or contracts. Participants in the Parisian salon culture, black citizens of Chicago, socialists in Greenwich Village, and current-day Libertarian activists, were linked by an awareness of each other and by habit to some extent. Communication is central to the establishment of such bonds, regardless of where community members live.

Of all the functions of community, perhaps the most meaningful is the way it strengthens one's sense of identity. We know who we are, in part, because of the groups to which we "belong." In everyday life, when we meet new people, they may give us clues about the communities to which they belong – a church, or a profession, for example. This information helps us to discern the identity of individuals, because we are able to draw upon reserves of knowledge about the goals and values of those particular communities. How exactly does membership in a community give us identity? For one, community membership tells us who we *are not*, eliminating scores of possible roles and activities from our universe of experience. Through community membership, we learn values, norms, ways of speaking, of thinking, and of behaving. On a more concrete level, belonging to a community serves an information processing function that enables us to develop identity. The values one learns in a community help one to deal with the flood of information that characterizes this age of electronic communication. If a woman is a member of a staunch antiabortion group, for example, she is likely to see the world through a particular set of lenses. She might view a presidential campaign, the actions of city council members, and the public school curriculum as they relate to abortion rights. This "schema" for processing information is efficient, since we have limited time to think about current affairs. Membership in the antiabortion group strengthens one's beliefs (and therefore one's identity), because it provides an extremely useful interpretive framework for viewing the world.

Some thinkers regard community as a state of mind, more than an interlocking social network, or a shared neighborhood. Benedict Anderson, in his influential book on national identity, writes that "all communities larger than primordial villages of face-to-face contact (and perhaps even these) are imagined. Communities are to be distinguished not by

their falsity/genuineness, but by the style in which they are imagined."[35]
Key to this "imagining" process is the notion of collective consciousness:
We shall see in the case studies that follow just *how* members of marginal
communities portray themselves and their goals. Some groups, like the
political activists of Chapters 4 and 5, actively seek to explain and depict
their differences from mainstream society. In contrast, the women and
African-Americans of Chapters 2 and 3 are also part of imagined communities, but worked to de-emphasize such differences: It was difference that
led to their oppression.

One of the most important ways that people build community is
through symbolic action and the creation of rituals. Symbols are generated
constantly within vibrant communities. These symbols are often inscribed
on buttons or bumper stickers, or take the form of slogans or key words.
Symbols help to broadcast the ideas and goals of a community beyond the
boundaries of that community, and are often used rhetorically in interactions with mainstream individuals and institutions. Returning to the abortion controversy, for example, we discover a variety of symbols. Proabortion
rights activists in the United States have recently begun to use the symbol
of a hanger on their signs at protests and demonstrations. The hanger,
meant to symbolize a technique for performing illegal abortions, communicates the danger of such abortions to the life of a pregnant woman
unable to take advantage of safer methods. Symbols are often embedded
in larger rituals. The hanger symbol, for example, is usually part of stylized, ritual protest activity on the part of activists. Abortion rights groups
(like antiabortion groups) are highly organized, and orchestrate their
major demonstrations in order to present a compelling, unified front to
the public. These groups have chants, slogans, and practices that they
teach to each other, so that their performance in the public sphere will go
smoothly.

In each of the case studies that follow, symbols and rituals enable marginal communities to maintain solidarity, while also sending a message to
the mainstream. The salons of Enlightenment Paris were brimming with
ritualized activity, since women carefully orchestrated how these gatherings would proceed. Even clearer instances of ritual action are found in the
other cases described here. In Chicago, during the decades before and
after the Second World War, black citizens created their own set of elections for a symbolic mayor of the African-American community. And in

the case of Greenwich Village, the socialists and pacifists of *The Masses* engaged in numerous rituals of critique: Regardless of how effective they were, almost every issue of the magazine published after the war included rhetorical rituals of dissent. Cartoons poking fun at the mainstream press or the military, anticonscription petitions, and antiwar slogans were printed regularly. The sociologist Steven Lukes has provided a particularly useful definition of "ritual" that captures the regularity and power of these practices in historical and contemporary communities. He argues that ritual is "rule-governed activity of a symbolic character which draws the attention of its participants to objects of thought and feeling which they hold to be of special significance."[36] I employ Lukes's definition throughout this book to describe the rituals of dissent and assimilation created by four marginal groups.

We shall see that each group – from the women of the salons to present-day Libertarians – take the idea of ritual very seriously, even if they don't use this label to describe their actions.[37] Not only are symbolic action and ritual part of their practices: Their rituals are extremely innovative, sometimes mocking mainstream rituals, and sometimes celebrating their own identities and values. One reason that these rituals are so creative is related to marginality: Groups outside of the conventional public sphere have a kind of freedom that those inside lack, because if one is "different," one is empowered to use unorthodox means of expression. Sometimes this expression takes the form of artwork, other times it is embedded in conversational techniques, fiction, or speech making.[38]

By way of summary, then, communities have several characteristics. Their members share a set of values, practices, and symbolic repertoires that they use to maintain solidarity. While communicating to each other, and building alternative public space, members of communities also try to reform mainstream discourse. The feminist movement in America, for example, provides a space for women to share experiences, but also aims a series of critiques against society's institutions – businesses, schools, government agencies, and the like. Finally, communities help their members to develop their own identities, and draw clear lines between themselves and those with whom they disagree. These boundaries – sometimes drawn by communities themselves, and sometimes drawn for them – distinguish enclaves from each other in a meaningful (although not always beneficial) manner. Some marginal groups, like the ones studied here, were particularly small and close-knit, since they were not seen as viable or important political actors. It is this political de-legitimation that forces marginal groups to generate creative rituals, symbols, publications, and art.

POWER, INFLUENCE, AND MARGINALITY

The phrase "marginal groups" connotes powerlessness. When we consider gay rights organizations or radical feminist groups, it is difficult to think of them as powerful in any conventional sense of the word. Political scientists have traditionally defined power as the ability of Person X to make Person Y perform some activity that Person Y might not otherwise do.[39] But this definition has come under attack by a variety of scholars from different disciplines. Here I borrow two sets of insights about power, one from Michel Foucault and the other from Steven Lukes. Both theorists' views are complex, and explications of their works abound, but I single out their writings on power because they are central to understanding marginal communities.[40]

Power, for Foucault, is inextricably intertwined with the ability to create knowledge, and to control what is "true" or "false" for an entire community or society. This emphasis on discursive action leads him away from the idea that power is a commodity, held by particular parties or classes. For Foucault, power is an assortment of practices woven into the activities of institutions, and into the fabric of social life: Sometimes these practices are obvious and therefore easily recognized, but often, they are subtle and difficult to trace. Foucault wrote

By power, I do not mean "Power" as a group of institutions and mechanisms that ensure the subservience of the citizens of a given state. . . . It seems to me that power must be understood in the first instance as the multiplicity of force relations immanent in the sphere in which they operate and which constitute their own organization; as the process which, though ceaseless struggles and confrontations, transforms, strengthens, or reverses them.[41]

Foucault's notions of power underscore the importance of discourse, conversation, and media, but also highlight local struggles against power. He has even argued that manifestations of power rarely go unchallenged: For Foucault, "where there is power, there is resistance" to the exercise of that power.[42] That struggles against power are constant, not uniform, and embedded in historical circumstance is extremely relevant to the analysis of all types of marginal behavior. Political outsiders engage in power struggles, but in innovative ways that they themselves do not (or can not) always articulate. The ritual of "shadow" mayoral elections, described in Chapter 2, is a good example of carefully constructed, subversive dissent.

Steven Lukes has suggested another means of conceptualizing power, which steps away from the traditional behavioristic and individualistic definitions of the term. He sees power, in part, as the ability to control a nation's or a society's political agenda.[43] Lukes believes that institutions and individuals who have power are able to shape the nature of the public sphere, and thereby dictate (in a subtle, indirect manner) citizens' interests and needs:

To put the matter sharply, A may exercise power over B by getting him to do what he does not want to do, but he also exercises power over him by influencing, shaping or determining his very wants. Indeed, is it not the supreme exercise of power to get another or others to have the desires you want them to have – that is, to secure their compliance by controlling their thoughts and desires?[44]

Put another way, power is the ability to shape the *communication environment* through persuasion, force, manipulation of symbols, or any other means. Person A can *withhold* certain types of information from Person B, and shape his desires that way. Or, a powerful person can make available particular channels of communication, which may limit the ability of other citizens to persuade and to mobilize. If one's communication patterns are so limited, then that person is unlikely to set ambitious goals for changing the status quo, and will never gain much influence.

The operation of the contemporary American news media provides numerous illustrations of Lukes's conception of power. Editors and journalists, taking cues from others (e.g., the public or public officials) dictate the content of political discourse by highlighting particular events and interpretations of events and downplaying or ignoring others.[45] A recent example, from the 1992 U.S. presidential campaign, helps to elucidate this agenda-setting power. Journalists spent considerable time and effort during the campaign talking and writing about Governor Bill Clinton's alleged adulterous liaisons. In fact, at the time of the New Hampshire primary, rumors about this insufficiently documented affair nearly destroyed Clinton's well-funded campaign. The woman who claimed to have had an affair with the governor held a news conference, confirming a story she had provided to a tabloid newspaper describing the romance. It is safe to say that the American media were obsessed with the issue of the affair, and often framed it as a "character issue." Over the course of just a few weeks, the media repeatedly highlighted the question, "Could voters trust a man who cheated on his wife?"[46] Although Clinton did address these charges continually after the New Hampshire primary, his campaign struggled constantly with these allegations of infidelity. George Bush certainly had his battles with a critical media, but journalists did not use the "character/ trust" news frame to discuss his presidency or problems.

Media have the ability to tell us what to think about, as so many scholars have noted, but they also have the ability to tell us *what* and *how* to think.[47] Media influence public dialogue and public attitudes through framing issues, and interpreting them for us. In this sense, media are powerful shapers of the communication environment: They provide the language, symbols, and tools that we employ to think about and discuss political and social matters.[48]

The idea that power is the ability to dictate the bounds of the communication environment, and therefore, the public sphere, is helpful in the study of marginal groups. Because they are marginal, they usually lack power in the traditional sense: They can rarely force people or institutions to do things they might not normally do. Yet marginal groups can obtain power and influence through creative political expression. In the case of the Enlightenment salons, women were able to dictate both the form and content of these high-brow discussions. So we can say, using Lukes's conception of power, that they had an enormous amount of influence. This communication-oriented definition of power can also reveal the ways that marginal groups *lack* power. Often, their ideas are ignored or de-legitimated, so such groups never gain the kind of influence they seek. A rather complicated case of this kind of power-seeking is discussed in Chapter 4, where I describe the struggles of *The Masses*. If we think about power as the capacity to shape public communication, we can track the subtle successes and failures of marginal groups, instead of just dismissing their efforts as totally ineffectual.

In this book, I also introduce another way to think about power in relation to the activities of marginal groups – the notion of communication *backchannels*. Communication backchannels are the behind-the-scenes routes people use to send messages to each other, or to those outside of their circle. In several places, I note how a particular group is able to influence men in power by using unorthodox or unconventional means to make their desires known. The most obvious cases of communication backchannels are found in Chapters 2 and 3, since both the salonnières and the mayors of Bronzeville managed to catch the attention of mainstream leaders through the use of unusual media. In fact, the salonnières, by creating new communication environments, and using these environments to establish backchannels, were particularly effective in this respect.

We talk about and create communication backchannels constantly, in our personal relationships and our professional ones. In the typical corporate office, government bureaucracy, or academic department, for example, some employees may use backchannel communication to express their opinions to high-level managers in private. Instead of using communication media that were designed for such exchanges between employees of different rank (e.g., monthly reports, working with one's immediate supervisor, meetings, etc.), users of a backchannel can sometimes exert a more effective form of influence on their superiors. These same communication patterns are also found in the highest reaches of government, although Americans read about them only in the memoirs of former White House officials. During the Reagan administration, for example, there was evidence that the president's wife, Nancy, used her direct backchannel with her husband quite often. Instead of lobbying members of Congress about issues, or writing long position papers, presidents' wives can often circumvent these routes in favor of the backchannel.[49]

Some scholars who study organizational behavior and communication have written about the ways that individuals, working in bureaucracies, "bypass" formal channels of communication. In his classic study of bureaucracy, for example, Anthony Downs notes that employees rarely find formal channels of communication alone to be adequate, so they create unconventional networks for exchanging information. He calls these innovative, often hidden, routes "subformal" channels.[50] Although research in the field of organizational behavior is relevant to the study of backchannels in general, this book focuses on loose social networks, and not formal, hierarchical organizations. Backchannels, as described here, are communication routes established to circumvent the structures and rules in political communities of various sorts – neighborhoods, cities, and nations.

THE CASE STUDIES

In order to explore issues of political marginality, community building among outsider groups, and the notions of communication environments and backchannels, I have chosen four cases that illustrate these ideas. I selected the cases quite intentionally, because they highlight the connections between marginality and political expression so well. Although there are commonalities among the cases, which I'll evaluate in Chapter 6, they are different enough to reveal the unusual, culture-specific characteristics of marginal public opinion expression. The three historical cases are useful because we can trace the invention of strategies for opinion expression among these groups, as well as the disappearance of these groups and strategies. Also, because so much time has passed since the time the salonnières, the *Masses* writers, and the mayors of Bronzeville lived, we are able to view these groups and their activities a bit more thoughtfully and with greater perspective. The contemporary case of political activists, on the other hand, uncovers much about the current situation of outsiders, and the difficulties they face in communicating their ideas to the media and other mainstream institutions.

I use a variety of methods to analyze the different cases. In all three historical chapters, I rely upon secondary and primary sources – memoirs or correspondence of the central figures, their artistic and literary works, or accounts of their actions published during the periods in which they lived. In Chapters 3 and 4, I concentrate on the publications of marginal groups – a black newspaper and a radical magazine. In Chapter 2, I discuss the very interesting memoirs of salonnières, the fictional or quasi-fictional works of the philosophes, as well as the letters between male intellectuals and their female confidants. Chapter 5 is a study of the contemporary Libertarian party, so I have used the ethnographic method of in-depth interviewing to draw out some important aspects of their political behavior. By speaking at length with twenty of these committed men and women, I was able to obtain a solid understanding of what they do, and why they do it. Over the past few years, I have also accumulated a large number of documents distributed by the party – outlines of their platform, ideological statements, newsletters, and recruiting material. Although a quantitative content analysis of these documents is inappropriate, they are quite revealing from an interpretive standpoint, so I weave them into the story of the Libertarians. Unlike some of the other activist groups I have studied in the past, the Libertarians I interviewed for this book were extremely cooperative and helpful.[51] Almost all of the informants went out of their way to illuminate for me the nature of their ideas, their political tactics, and their rhetoric.

There are, undoubtedly, many different ways to understand marginal public opinion expression. One might rely entirely on published texts – the literary, artistic, and polemical documents created by political outsiders. This is useful, because such documents help us piece together the actions and ideas of groups of outsiders that no longer exist. Yet ethnographic work (e.g., the in-depth interviews of Chapter 5 and the shorter oral historical ones in Chapter 3) helps us to probe marginal actors more directly and pointedly about their work. Survey research with political activists was one option with which I considered and experimented, but I found in-depth interviews to be far more revealing. Closed-ended questions or short open-ended ones – administered by mail, phone, or in person – are not particularly useful in the study of marginal activists: It seemed entirely inappropriate to squeeze their ideas and their explanations into the narrow dimensions of a survey form.

Regardless of the methodologies employed, however, one must approach the analysis of marginal groups with caution. In studying political outsiders, and making generalizations about them, it is easy to gloss over the profound differences among them. It is important, therefore, to maintain a delicate balance between the broad analysis necessary for theory building and a preoccupation with the specifics of each group – their origins, members, and cultural products. This book is an attempt to walk that fine line by discussing each group's actions in some depth, yet evaluating them in light of certain theoretical notions. Each group considered here deserves extended study, and in one of the cases – the Enlightenment salonnières – social historians have begun to do such work.[52] The radicals of Greenwich Village have also received attention from historians and literary critics, although some of their ideas, battles, and publications rarely receive close scrutiny. In the other two cases, empirical research is still very sparse. Very few academics have written about the history of the black press in America, preferring to focus on mainstream newspapers. And the Libertarians have been almost completely ignored by researchers. The few political scientists who study contemporary activists gravitate toward those individuals working for the Democratic or Republican parties.[53] None of the case studies are meant to be comprehensive descriptions or analyses of social groups, since my goal is to elucidate a few important aspects of marginality.

I have three primary goals, which are reflected in the case studies. The first is theoretical: How can the experiences of marginal groups help us understand alternative political discourse, public opinion communication, and power? My second goal is to create templates for future case studies of political outsiders. Scholars in Cultural Studies, in particular, have recently begun to publish volumes about marginality, with all sorts of autobiographical and theoretical contributions. Yet this literature, some of which is cited here, is diffuse and fragmented, because the field is so new and the writers often have disparate goals. One of my intentions is to provide a model for work that analyzes a variety of cases, but views them from a narrow set of theoretical perspectives. Even if we undertake scores of case studies of marginal political groups, they won't add up to much if we do not develop guides for understanding the empirical data we collect.

Finally, I believe that academic work on political marginality can (and sometimes does) have practical implications. The Libertarians, for example, have had tremendous difficulty getting the sort of attention they deserve from the mainstream mass media. Although they often have candidates on the ballot for local, state, and national elections, the media rarely comment on how difficult and time-consuming this petitioning process actually is. Many of the activists I spoke with were surprised that the media focused so much attention on the 1992 candidacy of Ross Perot, who began to run for the U.S. presidency without an established party infrastructure. Journalists spent considerable effort writing about, and discussing, the barriers that Perot supporters faced in achieving ballot access, when the Libertarians (and other third parties) have faced these same hurdles for decades. Perhaps more descriptive and analytical investigations of groups – especially contemporary ones – will alert journalists and others to the problems of political outsiders.

2

Backchannels of Communication: Salonnières of the French Enlightenment

Women have always had difficulty breaking into mainstream political discourse. During most eras in Western history, they faced social, religious, and economic discrimination, and their lack of status in politics seemed appropriate and natural to most. As so many contemporary social historians and theorists have pointed out, women's speech has traditionally been trivialized or ignored altogether.[1]

This chapter is not about the lengthy history of female oppression, or the various barriers women have faced in achieving political recognition or equality. For the purposes of my argument here, I will assume that women – with some important exceptions[2] – have been marginalized in European and American politics until the very recent past. Instead, I document one important case in which women were able to shape political discourse, and mold the public sphere to their own purposes. By exploring how women influenced literary, philosophical, and political dialogue in Enlightenment France, we can gain some insight into backchannels of communication – the behind the scenes character of women's expression. Elite women of Paris could not hold public office, find many open avenues to voice their concerns and ideas, or receive a decent formal education. Nevertheless, many women managed to help shape the communication environment *and* the content of political discourse in the last century of the Old Regime.

To understand the ways women have influenced the environment in which political debate occurs, I have chosen to concentrate on the salons of mid-eighteenth-century Paris – those exclusive gatherings where philosophers, statesmen, writers, clergymen, musicians, and artists came together to discuss important issues of the day. Women established and maintained almost all of the influential Parisian salons. I draw upon accounts of the salons by attendants, the many Victorian-era histories of the salons published in America and Great Britain, and work by contemporary social historians writing about the Enlightenment – particularly the fascinating research of French historians like Dena Goodman. After a description of the functions of salons, and the sort of dialogue one found in these forums, I'll focus specifically on the roles of women during and after the period of the great literary and philosophical salons. Did the presence of strong women in the salons enable them to achieve a legitimate voice in political affairs? In other words, did the type of influence one gained by establishing a salon translate into broader political influence or recognition? I conclude this chapter with some thoughts about marginality and communication strategies, underscoring interesting patterns that have been largely neglected in the study of political expression.

Some might argue that salonnières of the Enlightenment were not marginal at all, since they were financially and socially superior to the large majority of Frenchwomen. This is undoubtedly true, although some of the most influential salonnières came from the middle classes, and were not born into wealth or nobility (e.g., Suzanne Curchod Necker or Madame Geoffrin). Indeed, one of the most interesting characteristics of the salons was their mixture of social classes.

Regardless of their position in the *social* hierarchy, however, women certainly qualified as *political* outsiders. As a group, they could rarely participate freely and openly in French politics.[3] In general, women did not receive equal protection under the law, and so were discriminated against in almost all arenas – work, education, and marriage. Female participation in public affairs was not expected or approved, so few women even attempted to take part in politics until the revolution drew near.[4] Writers of the day thought women to be obsessed with the trivial, and therefore distinctly unable to participate in important public debates. As Nina Gelbart puts it, "the majority of writers treated the female as a subhuman species."[5]

THE EMERGENCE OF THE SALON

The salons – exclusive gatherings held in the drawing rooms of the Parisian bourgeoisie – were sites for conversation.[6] Men and women convened at these regular meetings to discuss politics, history, religion, literature, and philosophy. Most of the attendants were either statesmen, scholars, writers, or businessmen with intellectual aspirations. The salonnières occasionally planned agendas for discussion, but most often the conversations were spontaneous. Much of the talk was driven by passion and impulse, although some salons were more stifling and formal than others, depending upon the wishes of the salonnière. Some philosophes, such as Rousseau and Montesquieu, attended the salons regularly, but had mixed feelings about the domination of these forums by women. Others, like Diderot, felt much differently:

Women accustom us to discuss with charm and clearness the driest and thorniest subjects. We talk to them unceasingly: we wish them to listen: we are afraid of tiring or boring them. Hence we develop a particular method of explaining ourselves easily which passes from conversation into style. When women have genius, I think their brand is more original then ours.[7]

Diderot's comments highlight one great achievement of the salons: As media of communication they forced intellectuals to express themselves in ways that the public (represented by women) might understand.[8]

My focus in this chapter will be on the salons of the eighteenth century, although one of the earliest and most famous female-operated salons – the hôtel de Rambouillet – was established in 1617.[9] Carolyn Lougee studied lists of "illustrious women" appended to various seventeenth-century French documents, and hypothesized that several hundred Parisians attended the early salons. She found that although the women who frequented the salons were largely from noble families, this group of guests was more heterogeneous than historians had assumed: Almost half of the women's fathers did not possess noble titles, and derived income from a wide range of occupations. Lougee concluded that, "When contemporaries wrote, with praise or blame, that women in the salons were 'mixing the orders,' they apparently accurately perceived the phenomenon of social fusion occurring there."[10]

The hôtel de Rambouillet was established by Catherine de Vivonne Rambouillet, a wealthy woman of Italian descent who was disgusted by the rituals of court life. She decided to simulate the court in her own home by inviting "people of intelligence, breeding, and fashion" for regular meetings.[11] Although Madame de Rambouillet attempted to avoid what she believed were the vulgar manners of the court, it's not clear that her salon was any different from those gatherings. Part of the problem was that seventeenth-century women who attended the salons *were* consumed by the petty and the trivial. As Jacques-Joseph Duguet noted:

Gradually, the court where [women] have power, as serious as it may have been originally, degenerates into a court full of amusements, pleasures, frivolous occupations. Luxury, revelry, gambling, love, and all the consequences of these passions reign there. The city soon imitates the court; and the province soon follows these pernicious examples. Thus the entire nation, formerly full of courage, grows soft and becomes effeminate, and the love of pleasure and money succeeds that of virtue.[12]

Although women of the eighteenth century would be perceived differently by their male contemporaries than were those of the seventeenth, Madame de Rambouillet's gatherings were prototypes for the more serious salons of the next century. Chauncey Tinker, writing in 1915, believed that Rambouillet's salon had five characteristics that made it typical of the Parisian literary and philosophical salon:[13]

1. The large reception area was broken up into a sequence of tiny rooms and alcoves, which enabled a warmer, more intimate atmosphere for conversation;

2. Merit – as a writer, poet, musician, or wit – allowed one to gain entrance and success in the salon. Nobility was not necessary if one were to open or visit a salon;[14]

3. Conversation was the salon's raison d'être. Attendants read poems, essays, or plays that they wrote, and their audience participated in these readings and evaluated the work. Critique was the dominant mode of discourse, and one's style of expression mattered very much: Clever, witty, and incisive comments were those valued most;

4. Great friendships developed in the salons among influential women and their favored male intellectuals. These were deeply sentimental attachments (many of which were documented by the philosophes), which evolved only occasionally into passionate romances;

5. The salonnières themselves were celebrated by participants. As Tinker puts it, "The hostess of the salon is invariably the subject of ideal descriptions, 'tributes' which recite her charm as a hostess, her merits as a patron, and her general superiority to the Muses."[15]

Although the salons of the eighteenth century would share these characteristics with their predecessors, they became far more popular and serious. The most effective way to illustrate Parisian salon activity in the decades before the revolution is not to generalize about them, however, but to describe a few of the most famous salonnières and their salons.

PARISIAN SALONS OF THE EIGHTEENTH CENTURY

Scores of bourgeois women organized salons from the early decades of the eighteenth century through the start of the revolution. At some of these gatherings, literature and art were at the center of the dialogue, whereas at others, conversation about politics or religion dominated the discussions. Some of the salonnières sought to create an intellectual atmosphere in their homes, but others were much more interested in games, music, and flirtation. The vast majority of Parisian salons combined the trivial and the intellectual.

Perhaps the best-known salon of the period was that of Madame Geoffrin. Her salon met on Mondays and Wednesdays: On Mondays, artists and architects were invited to her house, and on Wednesdays, she entertained a literary crowd including Diderot, Marmontel, and d'Alembert. The suppers she arranged, where attending philosophers and writers discussed books and ideas, were famous throughout elite European circles. Many foreigners – David Hume and Ben Franklin among them – paid their respects to Geoffrin while in Paris. Unfortunately, most of Geoffrin's letters have been lost, so portraits of her salon must be drawn by sewing together the comments and descriptions of her contemporaries.[16] These fragments indicate that her salon was central to intellectual life during the Old Regime. As one attendant, Sainte-Beuve, put it:

[Madame Geoffrin's] salon was the best regulated, best conducted, and most firmly established, of any salon in France, since the days of the famous Hôtel de Rambouillet. It was, in fact, one of the institutions of the eighteenth-century.[17]

Like many salonnières, Madame Geoffrin (Marie Thérèse Rodet) was born to a middle-class family in Paris. When her parents died shortly after her birth in 1699, she was raised by her grandmother who – by most

accounts – was uninterested in education or affairs of the mind.[18] Yet the
older woman did, despite her deeply held religious beliefs, encourage her
granddaughter to think somewhat critically. In a 1765 letter to Catherine
the Great, Geoffrin wrote that, "My inner life was as visible to [my grand-
mother] as my outward life; everything was a subject of instruction; my
education was continual."[19] In 1713, at the age of fourteen, Marie married Monsieur Geoffrin, a wealthy manufacturer of glass and mirrors. He
was not particularly disposed to intellectual matters or the arts, and never
supported his wife's growing interest in literature or philosophy. Stories
about his stupidity and boorish behavior abound in the literature, but
these are only rumors that were undoubtedly embellished as they spread
through Geoffrin's social circle. Supposedly, Monsieur Geoffrin sat
silently at the end of the supper table, and rarely spoke during meetings
of his wife's salon.[20]

Madame Geoffrin, like several other salonnières of the period, learned
about arranging and managing these gatherings from an older woman who
served as a mentor to her. Dena Goodman has demonstrated that many
daughters who grew up in their mothers' salons eventually established
their own such gatherings. In addition, older women often adopted younger women in quasi-familial relationships, instructing them on how a salon
was run. Madame Geoffrin had such an adopted daughter in Suzanne
Necker, but also had a "real" daughter – Madame de la Ferté-Imbault –
who became a salonnière. De la Ferté-Imbault wrote in 1772 that,

I took my course in philosophers and philosophy in my mother's home from my
earliest childhood until my marriage. I have always loved my mother and will be
grateful all my life that she was forced in her youth to keep me with her. . . . My
mind and my reason were formed by the conversation of the great minds of that
time, of which her house was always full.[21]

Figure 2.1. This 1812 painting of a salon, by Anicet Charles Gabriel Lemonnier, depicts
hostess Madame Geoffrin (third from the right, front row) in the company of several nota-
bles, including Fontenelle, Montesquieu, Diderot, and Marmontel. The painting is not a historical document, but an imaginative reconstruction of Geoffrin's salon. Lemonnier captures
some key elements of the eighteenth-century gatheringss – in particular, the elegant surroundings and the large number of male attendants. Several guests gaze in the direction of
their hostess or at the elevated bust of Voltaire. For further discussion of the painting, see
Lough (1991). Musée National des Châteaux de Malmaison et Bois-Préau. © Courtesy of
the Réunion des Musées Nationaux, Paris.

Geoffrin's mentor was Madame de Tencin, a neighbor whom Geoffrin met when she was a young woman. After Tencin invited Geoffrin to her own lively salon, Geoffrin decided to establish one in 1737. When Tencin died, almost all of her guests were invited to Geoffrin's salon. Tencin was an intellectual in her own right, and entertained luminaries such as Montesquieu and Lord Chesterfield.[22] Unlike most of the salonnières, she was a successful writer, and published a melodramatic novel about a doomed romance titled *Mémoires du Comte de Comminge* in 1735.[23]

It is unclear why Geoffrin's salon became so famous in later years. Unlike Tencin, she was not a writer or intellectual. And she was said to lack the physical beauty of some of the other salonnières (namely, Mesdames Necker and Récamier). Supposedly, the food at her suppers was mediocre. However, from accounts of Geoffrin's salons, it is clear that she was a good listener and an excellent facilitator of discussion. Once certain men became regulars at her salon – d'Alembert, Grimm, Morellet, the Abbé Galiani, and Hume among others – there was a snowball effect: Madame Geoffrin's salon was clearly "the place to be" among intellectuals, statesmen, writers, and artists living in Paris at mid-century. In a letter to Madame d'Epinay (another salonnière), Galiani made Geoffrin's name into a verb when describing the differences between Italian and French salons: "There is no way to make Naples resemble Paris unless we find a woman to guide us, organize us, *Geoffrinise* us."[24]

Madame Geoffrin's salon may have been one of the most famous in mid-eighteenth-century Paris, but there were many other salonnières whose gatherings competed with hers. Suzanne Necker, wife of Director-General of Finance Jacques Necker, maintained a salon as did Mesdames Du Deffand, De Staël, and Mademoiselle de Lespinasse.[25] One of these women, Madame d'Epinay (born Louise Florence Pétronille d'Esclavelles), was not only a great hostess to the intelligentsia, but a well-respected mind in her own right.

Like many of the salonnières, d'Epinay did not come from a rich family. There were some traces of nobility in her background, but she and her mother were left with very little money after her father's death when she was ten in 1736. Since her mother could not support them, she and Louise lived with wealthy relatives. After these arrangements proved problematic,[26] d'Epinay moved to a convent where she was raised and educated.

A few years after her marriage to a cousin in 1745, d'Epinay established her salon. Among the regular attendants were her close friends – diplomat and author Friedrich-Melchior Grimm, the writer and Italian ambassador to France Abbé Ferdinando Galiani, and the philosophes Rousseau, Diderot, and Voltaire. The historian Evelyn Beatrice Hall (who wrote under the pseudonym S. G. Tallentyre) studied a variety of Enlightenment salons, and described d'Epinay's charms as a salonnière:

After the *ivresse* and folly of the Regency, gravity had suddenly become the mode. The most frivolous women were profoundly absorbed in political econ-omy and philanthropy. Philosophic ideas were daily gaining ground. One day one was evolving a new religion – some fine religion of Humanity, which worked out beautifully in talk or on paper, and in practice led to Candeille, Goddess of Reason. To this Salon came almost the whole diplomatic corps. . . . Louise lis-tened equally charmingly to them all. . . . When this man was talking philosophy to her she was an impassioned philosopher. With a theologian she had a *culte* for religion.[27]

As d'Epinay's salon became increasingly successful, she became the inti-mate of several regular attendants. Two of her most passionate friendships were with Rousseau and Galiani. Her relationships with these two men are well documented in her own memoirs, as well as Rousseau's *Confessions* and Abbé Galiani's correspondence.

D'Epinay's relationship with Rousseau is interesting to social and intel-lectual historians, because she clearly had an enormous amount of influ-ence on his life. Although her impact on his ideas is difficult to trace, she served as something of a sounding board and patron for Rousseau during critical periods of his intellectual development. Early on, d'Epinay recog-nized that Rousseau was gifted. In a diary entry from 1746 she wrote about a play that she and her friends staged – Rousseau was its author:

We started with *L'Engagement Téméraire*, a new play by M. Rousseau, a friend of Francueil's [a well-known artist and one of d'Epinay's lovers], who introduced him to us. The Author took one of the parts in the play. Although it is only a society comedy it was very successful. I doubt whether it would succeed on the stage, but it is the work of a very able man, perhaps an unusual man. I cannot tell, however, whether it is what I have seen of the man, or of the play that makes me think so. He pays compliments without being polite, or without seem-ing so. He seems ignorant of the ways of society, but it is clear enough that he is exceedingly able.[28]

Figure 2.2. Madame d'Epinay, who became one of the most famous salonnières in Paris.

After their first meeting, d'Epinay and Rousseau became close friends, although he felt as though she was a little too interested in his romantic affairs, attempting to manipulate his behavior and affections. There was speculation that Rousseau might have been in love with her at one point,

Figure 2.3. Jean-Jacques Rousseau attended a variety of salons, but was a favorite guest of Madame d'Epinay. From the painting by Angélique Briceau, 1791. Courtesy of the Bibliothèque Publique, Geneva.

although from most accounts, he tended to fall in love often and easily with women in his social circle. Rousseau worried about d'Epinay achieving emotional control over him, yet upon her invitation, he did move into the guest house of her estate outside of Paris. At first, he was happy in the cottage at Montmorency, but eventually (as he predicted) he had a falling out with his patron. By the time he wrote the *Confes-*

sions, he had some unkind words for d'Epinay – a reversal in his thinking about her:

> I probably loved her too well as a friend to be able to do so as a lover. I felt pleasure when I saw her and chatted with her. Her conversation, though pleasant enough in company, was dull in private; and mine, which was no more brilliant, was of no great assistance to her. . . . I was very glad to show her little attentions, and to give her the most fraternal of little kisses, which seemed to arouse her sensuality as little as they did mine; but that was all. She was very thin, very fair, and with a chest as flat as my hand.[29]

D'Epinay's association with the Abbé Galiani, on the other hand, was a strong friendship that lasted for years, sustained by salon visits and extensive correspondence.[30] Galiani, who was officially assigned to Paris as a representative of the Italian government, was a man of great intellectual breadth – a classics scholar, an economist, and an archeologist.[31] Perhaps he is most famous for his work on the importance of trade restrictions, an attack on the *économistes* titled *Dialogues Sur le Commerce des Bleds*. Until 1769, when he was recalled to Naples by Ferdinand IV, Galiani visited the salons of women like Madames Geoffrin and d'Epinay. He became a central figure in the *coterie holbachique*, a group of philosophers, writers, statesmen, and scientists that met regularly at the home of Baron d'Holbach.[32] Galiani's friendship with d'Epinay and her influence on his work are revealing to social historians because their relationship was ideal-typical for the period: A variety of extremely successful men maintained long-running patterns of correspondence with salonnières. D'Epinay advised Galiani on many of his published works, and was responsible for extensive editing on his *Dialogues*. She also oversaw proofreading of the manuscript, fought with censors (the book criticized government policy), and even aided in distribution of the book.[33] Upon her death in 1783, Galiani wrote: "Mme d'Epinay is no more! And thus I too have ceased to exist. . . . My heart is no longer among the living: it is completely entombed."[34]

Like many salonnières, d'Epinay had little formal academic training. She did, however, take great pains to make sure that her own children (a son and daughter) were properly educated by tutors. As d'Epinay explained in her memoirs:

Figure 2.4. The Abbé Galiani, economist and man of letters.

When I was a child it was not the custom to teach girls anything. They were more or less inoculated with their religious duties, to prepare them for their first communion: they were given a very good dancing-master, a very poor music teacher, and in rare cases a mediocre teacher of drawing. Add to this a bit of history and geography, devoid of any incentive to further learning: it was merely a question of memorizing names and dates, which were forgotten as soon as the teacher was let go. Such was the extent of what was considered a superior education. Above all, we were never taught to think; and any study of science was scrupulously avoided as being inappropriate to our sex.[35]

Under the influence of Grimm, Rousseau, and the other men she would meet through her salon, d'Epinay educated herself. By 1754, she would write to Rousseau, "If you could lend me the fourth volume of Plutarch's *Lives* you would give me great pleasure."[36] During her years in Paris, she kept a rather detailed diary that was published in 1818, thirty-five years after her death. In addition to a series of essays published in the *Mercure de France*, she also wrote a book on education titled *Les Conversations d'Emilie*. The book, a series of Socratic dialogues between a fictional mother and child, won an academic prize. Referring to her intense interest in educational matters, E. G. Allingham argued that d'Epinay "out-Rousseaued Rousseau."[37]

In a recent monograph, Ruth Plaut Weinreb has argued that d'Epinay was more than a salonnière, that she was a *philosophe* in her own right, and has been unfairly ignored by historians in part because of Rousseau's harsh words about her in his *Confessions*. According to Weinreb, d'Epinay was central to intellectual life in the mid-eighteenth-century: She was an intelligent essayist, a talented novelist, and incisive critic. In fact, d'Epinay did produce scores of book reviews, theater reviews, and essays for the *Correspondance littéraire, philosophique et critique*, the influential journal of the philosophes. Weinreb demonstrates that d'Epinay contributed to the *Correspondance*, collaborated on articles with Diderot, and edited the journal during Grimm's trips to England in the late 1760s.[38]

Both Geoffrin and d'Epinay were typical of the best-known salonnières: They were intellectuals, yet had almost no decent academic training. Both had mastered the womanly art of entertaining early in life, but later learned to manipulate, encourage, and argue with men. In many ways (as I discuss in the next section), Geoffrin and d'Epinay effectively used their femininity to enter and alter the world of ideas. At a time when the political discourse of a nation was greatly influenced by drawing room discussion, successful salonnières were formidable indeed.

THE NATURE OF SALON DIALOGUE

Even though a variety of eighteenth-century salonnières and their guests left behind memoirs and letters, evidence documenting salon conversation

is scanty. There are several reasons for this. First, conversations are difficult to recount and transcribe. These days a variety of machines allow us
to record meetings of all types, but remembering what was said during a
raucous gathering at a salon was undoubtedly difficult for attendants. Second, from most accounts, salon conversation did not unfold in a linear
fashion: Topics were introduced, but often changed quickly depending on
the whims of participants and salonnières. Third, and most important,
what salon attendants valued most was *process*. The function of salons as
forums for conversations – places for the free exchange of opinions and
ideas – mattered more than the content of discussions.

Fortunately, we have been able to document some of the characteristics
of salon dialogue through the analysis of texts like Madame d'Epinay's
memoirs.[39] At her salon, and at most of the other famous gatherings (those
of Geoffrin, Necker, de Lespinasse, and Du Deffand), participants discussed politics, religion, the economy, art, music, and literature, among
other things. Singing, dancing, reading, and acting in short plays were also
popular activities, although conversation seemed to dominate the meetings. In the following extended excerpt from her memoirs, d'Epinay
describes a conversation about religion in the salon of Mademoiselle Quinault in 1751. It was here that d'Epinay first learned about such gatherings. The dialogue is worth quoting at length, because it is one of the few
"transcripts" available:

Saint-Lambert, whose brain was fired, started it [the conversation] afresh: I
[d'Epinay] was shocked by his comparison of paganism and our own religion. "But
you see," I said to him, "how powerful must be the influence of our own religion,
since the very philosophers are stirred by the spectacle of a multitude upon their
knees in prayer." "Quite right," said he, "but hard to understand."

Duclos: "Where does this nation keep its reasoning capacity? It scoffs at people
of other lands, and yet is more credulous than they."

Rousseau: "I can pardon its credulity, but not its condemnation of those whose
credulity differs from its own."

Mlle Quinault observed that in religious matters everyone was right, but that all
people should stick to the religion in which they were born.

"No, by God," returned Rousseau warmly, "not if it is a bad religion, for then
it can only do much harm."

I bethought myself to say that religion did much good as well, in that it was a
curb upon the lower classes who have no other standard of morality. But this they

all cried down, and refuted me with arguments which did, as a matter of fact, appear to be better than mine. Someone said that the lower classes were more afraid of being hanged than damned. Saint-Lambert added that it was the business of the Civil and Criminal Code to regulate manners and morals and not that of religion, and that religion, though it took good care to restore a crown at Easter to its servant, had never caused ill-gotten gains to be refunded, nor an usurped province to be restored, nor a calumny atoned for. [Here d'Epinay notes that dinner was served]. . . .

When the servants had gone and the door was shut, Saint-Lambert and Duclos went at it so vigorously that I feared they were for destroying every form of religion: I therefore begged grace for Natural Religion.

"Not more than for the others," said Saint-Lambert.

Rousseau replied that he did not go that far, and that he said with Horace, *Ego sum paulo infirmior,* and that the morality of the Gospels was the one thing in Christianity that he retained because all the ancient religions were based on natural morality.

Saint-Lambert argued the point with him a bit. "Well, leave it at that – but what about a God who gets angry and relents?"

Mlle Quinault: "But tell us, Marquis, are you an atheist?"

His answer annoyed Rousseau, who muttered something: they laughed at him [As the conversation progressed, Rousseau got increasingly angry and threatened to leave, but was distracted by the arrival of a visitor].[40]

This passage exemplifies the nature of salon conversation on several levels. First, religion was a typical focus for such drawing room discussions. Most salon attendants were themselves deists or extremely conflicted about the usefulness of religion, so it was an ideal starting point for social critique. Questioning or dismissing religion was so common in these circles (despite the presence of many clergymen), that Madame Geoffrin's ties with church leaders were thought bizarre by her acquaintances.[41]

The conversation in Mlle Quinault's salon was typical in style as well as in content. The participants move freely from one aspect of the topic to another, with little transition or logical segue. Often speakers interrupted each other, shifting the focus of the dialogue either intentionally or unintentionally, and thereby reorienting the conversation. In addition to the lack of linearity, reciprocity was a key element in the discussions as speakers taunted, prodded (and on occasion), agreed with each other. In this excerpt – and in the longer diary entry from which it is drawn – we can recognize the discursive equality of the salon: If you had the energy and desire to enter the conversation, you were free to do so. Although it is always dangerous to place too much faith in the veracity of a memoir or diary entry, it seems from this passage that Madame d'Epinay was able to express her thoughts freely. She was not ignored and her comments were taken as seriously as were those of the other participants. We get the feeling that Mlle Quinault, as hostess, tried to keep the conversation from getting too heated or personal, but she herself couldn't resist a barb or two. In the full text about this meeting, we can tell that Quinault had much to juggle that night: She had to help maintain the cordiality of the conversation, greet additional visitors as they arrived, confer with servants, and coordinate the timing of the meal.

The literary critic Chauncey Tinker has argued that the mid-eighteenth-century salons of Paris gave birth to a new sort of expressive freedom. Since he wrote in 1915, a number of theorists and historians have concurred that critical public discourse expanded (albeit temporarily) during these years in part because of the salons. We can think of salons as new media of communication, which complemented other existing channels – books, journals, theatrical productions, and public speeches. There was a loose, careless style of talk in the salons that enabled participants to speculate in ways that were inappropriate in written work. The Abbé André Morellet, an economist and member of the *coterie holbachique,* noted that:

Conversation is the great school of the mind, not only in the sense that it enriches the knowledge gained with difficulty from other sources, but in making it more vigorous, more accurate, more penetrating, more profound. . . . In the majority of men, reading is not accompanied by this strong attention that is precisely the instrument of all our knowledge. . . . This attention becomes easy in conversation.[42]

The philosophes saw salons as forums where the Republic of Letters – a phrase used to describe the intellectual community of Enlightenment Paris – could achieve some sort of coherence and order.[43] Intellectuals, statesmen, and clergy felt a need to discuss written work in public either before or after publication, so the salons were ideal places for elaborating and debating theories. Before the mid-eighteenth-century, the philosophes had difficulty influencing the content of salon dialogue. But beginning in the 1760s, they were able to turn the more formal salons into useful and exciting arenas of their own.[44]

Women were critical to the salons, as moderators and as participants.

Many of the philosophers and writers who attended the Parisian salons spoke highly of female participants – some even claimed that stimulating conversation would have been practically impossible without women. As Morellet put it, "To be frank, I have never seen consistently good conversation except where a salonnière was, if not the only woman, at least a sort of center of the society."[45] The Scottish philosopher David Hume, who attended many of the Parisian salons, argued forcibly for meaningful communication with women: "I am of Opinion that Women, that is Women of Sense and Education . . . are much better Judges of all polite Writing than Men of the same Degree of Understanding."[46]

One reason why women were important to intellectual dialogue (although they themselves were rarely writers) was that they represented "the public" to male intellectuals. As Goodman has pointed out, men assumed that if they could make their ideas palatable to women, their books, plays, and poems might gain popularity with citizens outside of the rather exclusive salons. The very presence of women stimulated philosophes to express their ideas clearly, since female participants made excellent audiences: They were interested in learning, patient, and enjoyed the highly charged (sexual and intellectual) atmosphere of the salon. Morellet argued that sociability between men and women was closely linked to dialogue: "The free commerce of the two sexes [is] one of the most powerful principles of civilisation, and of the improvement of sociability. This effect occurs by means of conversation."[47] Even Rousseau, not known for holding favorable or progressive attitudes toward women, recognized the role of women in the culture of conversation. He wrote in *La Nouvelle Héloise* that "A point of morals would not be better discussed in a company of philosophers than in that of a pretty woman of Paris."[48]

Despite Rousseau's choice of words, prettiness actually had very little to do with successful salon management. In fact Madame d'Epinay was, by most accounts, charming but rather plain. Women seemed to have certain interpersonal communication skills that men lacked, and as we know from contemporary research on gender communication, this is still often the case: Researchers find that women tend to be more "cooperative, prosocial, and more concerned with including all of the group members [in small group discussions]."[49] An ability to make intellectuals express themselves in clear terms, a desire to listen, and a talent for encouragement characterized the best salonnières. It is said that Madame Geoffrin could time her questions in a manner that stimulated conversation, and that she would add supportive comments as her guests worked to state their arguments properly.[50] The salonnières were themselves quite conscious of, and shrewd about, the amount of intervention necessary to keep a conversation running properly. Suzanne Necker took her job so seriously that she could say, "The government of a conversation very much resembles that of a State."[51] Perhaps the poet and playwright Jean-François Marmontel's memories of the salons best capture the value writers placed on communication with intelligent women:

> The conversation [in the salons] was a school for me, not less useful than agreeable, and I profited by their lessons as much as possible. He who only wishes to write with precision, energy and vigour, may mix with men only; but he who wishes to have a style which is supple, pleasant, attractive, and with what is called "charm," will do well, I believe, to live among women. When I read that Pericles sacrificed all his mornings to the Graces, I interpret it as meaning that he lunched every morning with Aspasia.[52]

Beyond the salonnières' gifts for starting and maintaining conversation, Goodman believes that women were especially skilled at controlling philosophical egos.[53] In the previous excerpt, for example, Mlle Quinault takes the opportunity to gently tease Saint-Lambert as he and Rousseau sparred heatedly over the nature of God.

Despite their popularity, the salons were often a focus of critique among some of the intellectuals who attended them. On occasion, a writer would complain about the way a certain woman ran her salon. Several philosophes complained of Madame Geoffrin's uncritical attitude toward the state and prudish demeanor. Some, like Duclos, believed that the salons encouraged the diffusion of inferior literary products. He called the salons "factories of cleverness," arguing that mediocre ideas and thinkers often got too much attention in the salons.[54] Yet it is clear that the most important philosophers of the period (e.g., Rousseau, Montesquieu, or Condorcet) achieved great influence in the salons, despite the presence of less dazzling intellects. The most damaging critique of the salons was that they sometimes stifled intellectual freedom. Although all the salons were somewhat different in their focus and tone of discussion, a few narrow-minded salonnières would discourage conversation on topics they found offensive or threatening. This seemed not to dissuade the philosophes from attending the salons, though, since they flourished throughout the Enlightenment.

FUNCTIONS OF THE
ENLIGHTENMENT SALONS

Gatherings at the salons were highly ritualized, and one usually knew what to expect: lively and well-orchestrated conversation, a chance to meet like-minded others, and an audience for one's work. The major salonnières scheduled gatherings twice or three times a week, always on the same day at the same time. The regularity of the salons was important to writers who needed to talk about or present their work. Important relationships developed in the heady social environment of the salons, and attendants could expect to meet their friends at the appointed time and place. Finally, many of the salonnières served lunch or dinner to those who visited, so one could count on a regular (albeit usually simple) meal as well.

Some historians and literary critics – Goodman in particular – have argued that the salons provided "workspace" for Enlightenment philosophers.[55] Writers used the salons to experiment with alternative conceptual frameworks for their arguments, or used these gatherings to see whether or not their ideas would persuade. Salons occupied the space between writers and the mass public: They were workshops of a sort, which provided a relatively supportive atmosphere for intellectual trials. As Chauncey Tinker put it

Like the modern critical review, it was at once feared and courted by authors who affected at times to despise its pronouncements but never ignored them. The salon mediated between the author and the public. It aimed, like a true critic, to correct both the conceit of the author and the indifference of the world.[56]

Not only did the salons provide an environment for discussion of work in progress, but often completed work would actually imitate (or simulate) the discursive style of the salons. Two well-known examples are Bernard le Bovier de Fontenelle's *Conversation on the Plurality of Worlds* and Denis Diderot's *Dialogues*.

Fontenelle's very popular *Conversation on the Plurality of Worlds* (*Entretiens sur la pluralité des mondes*), first published in 1686, was a meditation on the universe. In this set of dialogues, Fontenelle argued for (among other things) the infinite nature of the universe, voyages to the moon, and the possible existence of intelligent life on other planets. Two characters – a philosopher (the author) and the Marquise (his female companion) – explore these issues on several consecutive evenings while they gaze upon the stars. On the first evening, the philosopher says some provocative things about other worlds, and the Marquise shows a keen interest in his remarks. But the philosopher is skeptical of her ability to comprehend his ideas and says, "It will never be said of me that in an arbor, at ten o'clock in the evening, I talked of philosophy to the most beautiful woman I know. Look elsewhere for the philosophers."[57] Yet he quickly gives in and finds her, over the course of the dialogues, to be an excellent audience: astute, curious, and argumentative. Fontenelle's intention was to make the Marquise a representative of the unsophisticated public, interested in science yet without formal education. She was, like many of the salonnières, his ideal of the imaginary reader. The reader (male or female) is asked, by the literary form, to identify with her. A sample from the first evening's dialogue:

[The philosopher]: "Nowadays we no longer believe that a body will move if it's not affected by another body and in some fashion pulled by wires; we don't believe that it will rise or fall except when it has a spring or counter-weight. Whoever sees nature as it truly is simply sees the backstage area of the theater."

"In that case," said the Marquise, "nature has become very mechanical."

"So mechanical," I replied, "that I fear we'll soon grow ashamed of it. They want the world to be merely, on a large scale, what a watch is on a small scale, so that everything goes by regular movements based on the organization of its parts. . . ."[58]

It was no coincidence that Fontenelle chose a woman to serve as a sounding board and intellectual comrade for the philosopher. Women were often asked to play this sort of role during the Enlightenment, and much literature of the day contains traces of these relationships.

Diderot's dialogues – imaginary conversations with a variety of his contemporaries – were an attempt to entertain, and also to pontificate on some important philosophical matters of the day. Although Diderot was not considered to be a particularly original thinker (he is most famous for his role in organizing the *Encyclopédie*), he was a great stylist and educator of sorts: He could grasp the interesting debates on science, cognition, and aesthetics, and synthesize this discourse for a wide audience. In one of his more imaginative dialogues – "D'Alembert's Dream" – Diderot reflects on the nature of matter, being, and God by orchestrating a lively discussion among four people. The characters are himself, the philosopher

Saint-Lambert, Dr. Theophile de Bordeu (a well-known physician), and the salonnière Julie de Lespinasse. That he used Lespinasse as a central character is interesting to us, because it reveals how Diderot viewed such women. Not only is Lespinasse intelligent, if somewhat naive, in the "Dream": She is also quick-witted and careful in her thinking. Lespinasse does a great service to the other characters in that she moves the conversation along smoothly. At one point, she is a recorder of d'Alembert's nocturnal mumblings (he is dreaming about philosophical matters), and interprets his ideas for Dr. Bordeu, making a house call to see d'Alembert. Lespinasse communicates with ease, displays her ability to translate for d'Alembert and, at the same time, enhances the discussion with her own comments.

Beyond the "workspace" function of the salons, and their role in inspiring literary dialogues, was the capacity of salons to shape public opinion. As Habermas and others have argued, the salons provided an arena where people could gather to discuss politics and criticize the state. Public opinion was formed in the salons, although the "public" was, of course, quite small and narrow in composition. In fact, the term public opinion was popularized by Jacques Necker to describe the talk of the salons.[59] There were several ways that salon conversation influenced public opinion and perceptions of that opinion. First, the court often monitored the political dialogue of the salons by sending emissaries who reported back to the king. The court thought of the salon conversation as public sentiment. Second, ideas first elaborated in the salons found their way into important works of literature and political philosophy, since so many productive writers frequented these meetings. Third, many of the salons actually published newsletters that were distributed far beyond the Parisian living rooms in which they were created. Although women had less of a role in the production of newsletters than men, women were still critical to the diffusion of these publications since they originated in salons. The newsletters were distributed locally, but also carried outside of the country by diplomats and foreign visitors to the salons. As Lionel Gossman explains,

[These ledgers of unofficial news provided] something like the "inside story" behind official announcements and official silences. They undermined respect for the Court by revealing or insinuating frivolous motives and causes behind important policy decisions, fostered disrespect and skepticism concerning official dogmas of all kinds, animated the spirit of criticism and inquiry, and contributed to the formation of a public opinion. Madame Doublet's newsletter seriously embarrassed the King on occasion.[60]

In fact, Madame Doublet's newsletter was so threatening and humiliating to the king, that he even had the police threaten her with imprisonment in 1753.[61]

Salons may have influenced literary and political thought during the Old Regime, but they also had more practical and immediate functions for their participants. Writers needed the salons, because they enabled them to penetrate an entire network of patrons. Although the practice of patron-age – where one artist or writer has one patron – had slipped somewhat by the mid-eighteenth-century, salons assumed such functions.[62] The salonnières helped writers and artists directly or indirectly. Direct help consisted of stipends, payment of bills, and gifts of food or lodging. Mad-ame d'Epinay gave Rousseau use of a cottage house on her country estate, for example, and others sent him chickens or butter.[63] Also, as mentioned earlier, a writer who was barely making ends meet could count on a filling meal at a variety of Parisian salons.

Another form of direct help was the securing of academic posts. Such chairs were filled upon the recommendation of those with high status, so salonnières could determine which of their favorite writers should have these positions. As Kingsley Martin reports,

[Madame Tencin's] greatest triumph was to arrange for an Academic Chair for her friend Marivaux in a year when Voltaire failed to obtain one. Montesquieu's elec-tion was due to Madame Lambert, who, said d'Argenson, had at one time created half the living Academicians. D'Alembert owed his Secretaryship of the Academy to Madame du Deffand. A few years later Madame Geoffrin and Mademoiselle de Lespinasse were close rivals for the honour of dispensing the greatest number of academic chairs.[64]

Though significant, these forms of direct aid were usually not enough to sustain the struggling philosophe. Academic chairs existed, but the sum of qualified writers far outnumbered the number of positions avail-able. Pensions, food, and lodging could also provide relief, but were often dispensed in an uneven – and therefore undependable – fashion. More important to writers was the fact that fame was *manufactured* in the salons. If an author's ideas were lauded in the salons, and he gained a reputation as an important author, his books were more likely to have large readerships. If he avoided the salons, he might not benefit from the positive word of mouth so critical for book sales during this period. Even Rousseau, whose allegedly foul manners were far from acceptable in polite company, knew that he could benefit from visits to salons and close relationships with salonnières like Madame d'Epinay. His disdain for the salons (and for D'Holbach's coterie) did not keep him from these important forums.

Salons were critical, then, for public opinion formation and communication during the Old Regime. Many philosophers and writers – with varying degrees of talent and status – found the salons useful for meeting patrons and for "floating" their new ideas. Salonnières, on the other hand, also derived benefits. They could boost their own social status, expand their circle of friends, and meet potential companions or lovers. Yet there was another value to organizing and maintaining a salon that has received far less attention in the secondary literature. These gatherings were akin to informal schools for the salonnières, who knew very well that the salons would grant them exposure to some of the most important and exciting ideas of the Enlightenment. Beyond their contact with writers through the salons, some of the women engaged in extensive correspondence with these men in order to keep up the literary and political dialogue. Madame d'Epinay's long correspondence with the Abbé Galiani or Suzanne Necker's letters to and from Gibbon are good examples.

Although some salonnières wrote tracts about the importance of educating girls, or mentioned it casually in their correspondence, they did not normally characterize (or advertise) the salon as a place for females to receive an education. Similarly, male writers of the period failed to mention this crucial function of the salons. Yet the value of the salons from a pedagogical perspective cannot be overemphasized. As Evelyn Gordon Bodek explained in her study of English and French salons:

The salon was really an informal university for women – a place where they could exchange ideas, avail themselves of some of the best minds of their time, receive and give criticism, read their own works and hear the works of others, and, in general, pursue in their own way some form of higher education. The English and French are important in the history of female education because they illustrate the ingenuity of women, *who when excluded from the educational mainstream created an alternative route* which satisfied their desire to learn, while at the same time camouflaged their activities behind the acceptable female role of hostess [my emphasis].[65]

The salon, with its ritualized structure and fairly regular constituency, was extraordinarily useful to a variety of parties – men of letters, politicians, socialites, and female intellectuals in search of stimulating company. Typical salons were exclusive, since no struggling writer or artist could attend without some sort of connection. Yet there was a certain permeability of the salons, because ideas often flowed from these gatherings into the public discourse. The reverse was also true: Attendants at the salons brought with them news and ideas from the world outside of these bourgeois living rooms. Many of the salonnières cultivated an international clientele by regularly entertaining diplomats. An assortment of British and American visitors made brief or extended visits to the salons when they were in Paris, in order to keep abreast of French politics and ideas.

WOMEN, SALONS, AND MARGINALITY

The experience of women in creating and maintaining the eighteenth-century salons of Paris reveals much about the inventiveness of marginal political actors, the creation of public space, the establishment of communication backchannels and environments, and the expression of public opinion. This section is devoted to a discussion of each of these phenomena, though a few words about marginality itself are in order before I turn to these theoretical notions.

As I argued earlier, it is not difficult to make the case that women – all women – were marginal political actors in eighteenth-century Paris: Females were not viewed as equals by men in any socioeconomic category. Women were bystanders, hostesses, wives, mothers, and daughters. As a group, they were certainly not a force to be reckoned with, since gender was a biological classification and not a political one. Although the women studied here were undoubtedly wealthier and more autonomous than those in lower social classes, their concerns and opinions were most often labeled frivolous. Despite this sort of marginalization, however, bourgeois and upper-class women had enough freedom to carve out some comfortable, intellectual alcoves for themselves. The salon, as an idea and a place, represents the most successful attempt to build this sort of niche.

One important characteristic of the eighteenth-century salonnières was their creativity. These women inherited the idea of the salon from their seventeenth-century predecessors, yet they re-created the salons to suit their own needs and goals. In the seventeenth century, the salons were places to pass time – to play parlor games and to engage in social or sexual intrigue. These elements were still present to some extent in the eighteenth-century salons, but by then the salonnières began to think differently about their roles. Eighteenth-century hostesses experimented with invitations, in attempts to bring together interesting combinations of people. Increasingly, salonnières encouraged the reading of poems, essays, plays, and philosophical tracts in place of games. Most important, strong women remade the salons: They became central information nodes in the communication network that was eighteenth-century Paris. Salons were soon news agencies, workshops for writers, and centers for patronage.

Many of the salonnières worked actively to make their gatherings *simulate* the classroom. Although discussion was the key mode of communication at the salon, lecturing followed by close questioning of the speaker was not uncommon. The form of discourse in the salon made it seem like a school for the sophisticated adult, but the relationships between male intellectuals and female attendants also echoed the educational environment. Many of the philosophes tended to treat women as social equals (or superiors), yet at the same time, prodded them gently to learn. The salonnières themselves seemed not to mind the student role, since their guests treated them with respect and often with great admiration.

Women used the salons strategically to learn, to be entertained, and to escape the boredom that characterized many of their lives. Through their creation of the salons, their organizational innovations, and their high spirit, salonnières were very often able to overcome deeply ingrained doubts about women among the philosophes. Many of these men agreed with Diderot that women were naturally and inherently inferior. In his essay, "On Women," Diderot argues that pregnancy, childbirth, aging, and difficulty in achieving orgasm ("Our organ is more indulgent"), are all a woman's unfortunate lot. Yet instead of advocating schooling or more rights for women, Diderot pitied them:

Woman, how I pity thee! . . . Remember that, owing to her lack of principles and power of refection, nothing penetrates deeply into the comprehension of women: notions of justice, virtue, vice, goodness, or wickedness, float on the superficies of their soul. . . . More civilized than us externally, they have stayed simple savages within, all more or less Machiavellian.[66]

Interestingly, Diderot ends his essay on a rather positive note, arguing that women are the best audiences for intellectuals, and that when women "have genius" they are more "original" than men. Diderot's comments in this essay exemplify the ambivalence among some of the premier intellectuals of the salons: On the one hand, they maintained a certain distaste for and pity of women, on the other, they realized just how valuable women were as audiences.

Another example of this ambivalence about the salonnières can be found in Rousseau's writings on women. Rousseau believed women to be inferior to men, and as Carole Pateman puts it, "naturally subversive of men's political order.[67] Although Rousseau befriended Madame d'Epinay and other women of the salons, and was a regular attendant at these gatherings, he had this to say about salonnières in *Emile*:

I would a thousand times rather have a homely girl, simply brought up, than a learned lady and a wit who would make a literary circle of my house and instal [*sic*] herself as its president. A female wit is a scourge to her husband, her children, her friends, her servants, to everybody. . . . I appeal to my readers to give me an honest answer; when you enter a woman's room what makes you think more highly of her [?] . . . to see her busy with feminine occupations . . . or to find her writing verses at her toilet table surrounded with pamphlets of every kind and with notes on tinted paper?[68]

Salonnières fought these attitudes by expanding their living room forums, instead of organizing a protest movement (this would come later, with the revolution).

Women built salons, and maintained them, in a continuing effort to educate themselves, and also to discover who they were. What did they believe? And where did they stand on critical issues of the day? Women created their own idiosyncratic salons, and the salons in turn *made them*. If her salon became popular, and attracted interesting guests, a woman's status could skyrocket – regardless of her background. Achieving the role of successful salonnière then gave her the freedom to mingle and corre-

spond with leading thinkers and writers. Salons can be viewed as vehicles
for status conferral, since many women derived their legitimacy as social
actors from their experiences in these forums.[69]

One question that scholars ask about the salons of the eighteenth century is whether or not these forums were indicative of an *expanding* or
newly constituted public sphere. In fact, there is a lively debate centered
on this subject among French historians, initiated primarily by the publication of Habermas's *Structural Transformation of the Public Sphere*.[70]
Among the driving queries in this debate are:

1. Were the salons simply extensions of the court – of aristocratic sen-
sibilities and practices? Or did they truly represent a new cultural form,
and the emergence of an independent, bourgeois public sphere?;

2. Were the salons *private* or *public* gatherings? And can we place salonnières – as a class – in either of these realms? Furthermore, is the public/
private dichotomy even appropriate for understanding the role of the
salons in eighteenth-century French culture? Finally;

3. Did conceptions of gender change in any important way, with the collapse of the Old Regime?

These are not questions I can address here, and they are best answered
by historians of the Enlightenment. Yet it seems to me that, regardless of
the relationship between the salon and mainstream French politics, the
salon environment was a *parallel* public space of sorts. The salon did, as
Goodman and others have pointed out, simulate the type of discourse that
characterizes the ideal Habermasian public sphere. Regardless of whether
salonnières could become public figures after achieving success through
the salons, or whether the boundary between some living rooms and the
public sphere was permeable, an alternative place for political communication had developed. The salon discussions were undoubtedly less strategic and tactical than mainstream ones, since policy making did not occur
in these forums. But the discussions were highly politically charged and
motivated nonetheless. An interesting question for students of political
discourse is not whether the salons expanded the public sphere, but how
they made possible *alternative space* for political communication.

Related to the question of parallel political spheres, which somehow imitate an ideal or actual public sphere, is the issue of power. Did women
accrue any sort of power through the establishment of salons? I think it
would be an exaggeration to say that the salonnières – even those as

famous as Madame Geoffrin – had power in the classic sense: It is not clear that they were able to make public men do what they otherwise would not do.[71] What the salonnières did have was influence. Perhaps they could not force particular types of social or political action, but they could certainly direct conversation about it. Through the salons, women were able to set the discursive agenda, steering the conversation to subjects of interest to them. They set agendas by choosing whom to invite to their gatherings, encouraging certain lines of argumentation, and by promoting young men whose thought they favored. Women partially shaped the environment for political discourse in the days before the revolution, and therefore influenced more public forms of social action.

Salons were political communication backchannels. Because women were largely excluded from mainstream political discourse, they were forced to develop their own media for this sort of talk. The salons' guests usually included pivotal figures of the period (e.g., Jacques Necker), so women could influence these public men in subtle (and sometimes profound) ways. This type of influence – hidden from public view – is difficult to uncover, but important nonetheless. We learn of it primarily through fragments of writing by the philosophes and other salon attendants, who on occasion would allude to the enormous role women played in the salon culture of Paris. Though it is difficult to quantify women's influence, or to trace particular public actions of men to certain salon conversations, this should not detract from the significance of the forums: They were, above all, innovative communications media created and sustained by women. Elite women, despite their inferior status, played an important role in what is universally believed to be a critical period in Western history.

Did women affect public opinion? If one thinks of public opinion as the sentiments of those who thought, wrote, and engaged in political action, women had a large role in shaping public attitudes. Jacques Necker had first used the phrase public opinion to describe the talk of the salons. If we accept the narrow, mid-eighteenth-century definition of the public, salonnières were critical to the formation, expression, and assessment of public opinion. And they influenced public opinion in an extraordinarily creative manner, by dictating the style of expression and the forms of debate.

AFTER THE REVOLUTION

Despite some important temporary gains during the period immediately
following the revolution, French women did not achieve political equality
after the events of 1789. On the contrary, as Joan Landes has argued,
women suffered a variety of political setbacks in the years that followed the
revolution. Ironically, the revolution, which embodied an ideology of liberty and equality, hurt women instead of advancing the status of their gender. The patriarchy of the Old Regime did not crumble with
republicanism, as Landes posits, but simply took a different form than it
had previously. After the revolution, the public sphere became almost
exclusively "male," while women were – more than ever – assigned to the
domestic sphere.

In the early days of the revolution, women were involved in popular protests, marching, and petitioning. And the republic made their lives somewhat easier by enabling women to divorce their husbands, by ending
primogeniture, and by protecting the children of unwed mothers.[72]
Increasing demands on the part of women began to threaten men in power,
however, and the attention paid to women's rights gradually began to
recede. Voting, a most basic right of citizens, is one area where women
actually lost ground. Some women had been able to vote *before* the revolution, but were forbidden to do so by 1792. As the statesman and pam-
phleteer Abbé Sieyès had put it three years earlier, "Women, at least as
things now stand, children, foreigners, in short those who contribute
nothing to the public establishment, should have no direct influence on the
government."[73]

Salonnières, like lower- and middle-class women, did not fare well after
the revolution. Some of the more politically oriented salonnières were
forced to leave France or were persecuted as the revolution became more
violent.[74] One of the most famous salonnières of the revolutionary period,
Madame Roland, was executed in 1793 by extremists (the *sans-culottes*) for
her perceived counterrevolutionary activity. She had organized a salon
attended by Robespierre, François Buzot (a deputy to the Estates-General
and National Assembly), and Jérôme Pétion (Assembly member and later
the mayor of Paris), and was believed to hold dangerous ideas and opinions. Roland was much more obviously political than her Old Regime
predecessors, and was caught up in the chaotic and bloody events of the

Figure 2.5. Madame Roland, a salonnière executed by the revolutionary government in 1793. Reproduced with permission from *The Memoirs of Madame Roland*, edited by Evelyn Shuckburgh (Barrie & Jenkins, London).

revolution: Her salon was primarily a place for tactical and strategic planning, since her house was centrally located in Paris. The salon met several times a week, and Roland claimed in her memoirs (written largely in prison) that, "This arrangement suited me very well. It meant that I could keep in touch with public affairs, in which I was so deeply interested; it gave scope to my taste for political argument and for studying men."[75]

As Barbara Pope points out, the communication backchannels of the salons became closed to privileged women with the reign of Napoleon: "The women of the salons were by no means allowed to use their drawing rooms as forums for discussing politics. Napoleon exiled and ruthlessly pursued the liberal Mme. de Staël [Suzanne Necker's daughter] for trying to continue the political role she had playing during the *Ancien Régime* and the early years of the Revolution."[76] Other women who ran salons – even those less politically fervent than Roland and de Staël – could rarely arrange the lively discussions so popular during the mid-eighteenth-century. The Napoleonic codes denied women the opportunity and the right to engage in this sort of discourse, as their proper place was the domestic sphere. Notable literary and political salons after 1789 were usually organized by men.[77]

The decline of the salons, then, was partly due to the falling social status of women during and after the revolution. But this descent was also associated with the collapse of the Old Regime itself: In so many ways, salons seemed to embody the nature and style of the court, and on this ground alone, it was suspect. Salons, as communications media, were common in the nineteenth century, and one finds such gatherings in the twentieth century as well. Yet it was in eighteenth-century Paris that the social, political, literary, and philosophical impacts of salons were most obvious and most interesting.

The eighteenth-century salons of Paris, and the opportunities that they provided for women, exemplify how the politically weak or marginalized can affect public discourse and the climate of opinion. Although this case study of innovative political communication is over two centuries old, it illustrates well some interesting, general behavioral patterns among outsiders: the creation of communication backchannels and the invention of tools for shaping discursive environments. The salons also tell us much about the ways that marginal groups serve themselves through ritualized behavior, since women benefited personally from this social system.

In the next chapter, we turn to a very different historical case of marginal political communication – the nature and effects of black newspapers in early twentieth-century America. Blacks, living in segregated Chicago, were undoubtedly much less privileged than the middle- and upper-class salonnières. Indeed, African-Americans were seen by white Chicagoans as inferior, and sometimes, threatening. Interestingly, however, many of the patterns of communication found in the salons are replicated in the case of the black press. These patterns look somewhat different across the two cases, of course, because the historical circumstances are so dissimilar. Yet both will prove extremely useful as we try to build theory about marginal communication in politics.

3

Race Discrimination, Mass Media, and Public Expression: Chicago, 1934–1960

In 1934 Chicago's foremost African-American newspaper, *The Chicago Defender*, announced the introduction of a contest – an annual election for a "mayor" of the South Side community known as "Bronzeville."[1] Although blacks faced tremendous barriers to participation in the city's mainstream of electoral politics during the 1930s, any black citizen could run for the office of mayor of Bronzeville: Morticians, beauticians, car salesmen, ministers, entertainers, and others sought the post at a time when electing a black mayor of Chicago seemed an impossibility. From the early elections in the 1930s until their decline in the late 1950s, residents of the city's South Side created a lively parallel electoral sphere – complete with coalition building, radio advertising, direct mail, and issue debates. Although Chicago's black citizens did build their own influential party machine to penetrate mainstream city politics, they also elected a nonpartisan mayor of their own community.

This chapter examines the case of the Bronzeville elections from the standpoint of marginal political communication. Whereas the previous chapter documented how women worked to circumvent their inferior political status in the past, this section focuses on race. How did blacks, living in a segregated northern city during the decades before the civil rights movement, engage in political expression and public opinion communication? To answer this question, I'll begin with a detailed description of one prominent black newspaper's attempt to break into mainstream political discourse. Then I will analyze the case from the perspective of communication theory, highlighting backchannel communication, the role of ritual, and the creation of alternative public space for political debate in black neighborhoods.

Unlike Chapter 2, which concentrated on the interpersonal communication of salons, the case of Bronzeville is almost exclusively about mass media. Several black papers circulated in Chicago during the early decades of the twentieth century, and the men who founded them were fierce crusaders against race discrimination. Because blacks could not find employment with white media (e.g., *The Chicago Tribune* or *The Chicago Daily News*), they published their own papers in order to build community and express their distaste for the status quo. Media can, as so many theorists have pointed out, draw people together and create public space out of a geographic area. Media can also aid people in forming their political identities. This chapter describes how the Bronzeville mayoral race was used by *The Defender* to sell papers, but at the same time, to establish a cohesive black municipality within a larger inhospitable city. The mayor of Bronzeville contest was a spectacular ritual designed by *The Defender* to elect a genuine, quasi-official spokesperson for the black community.

THE GROWTH OF BLACK CHICAGO

In the early decades of this century, large numbers of blacks headed toward Chicago seeking better employment and an escape from the overt racism of the south: Between 1910 and 1920, 50,000 blacks moved to the city from southern states.[2] For his famous series of articles about black life published in the *Chicago Daily News* in 1919, Carl Sandburg spoke with a black high school teacher who emigrated from Alabama. The teacher explained that

With many who have come north, the attraction of wages and employment is secondary to the feeling that they are going where there are no lynchings. Others say that while they know they would never be lynched in the south and they are not afraid on that score, they do want to go where they are sure there is more equality and opportunity than in the south.[3]

Although some blacks did fare well upon their arrival in Chicago, discriminatory employment practices posed considerable difficulties for others. Over twenty-five years later, when St. Clair Drake and Horace Cayton conducted the research for *Black Metropolis*, they could still describe grim economic conditions and a slow pace of change in black

Chicago. The "job ceiling" prevented blacks from finding professional or clerical work ("clean work"), so they were disproportionately represented in unskilled and service occupations.[4]

The demographic map of Chicago in the 1930s, as now, had distinct racial boundaries: Blacks lived predominantly on the South Side of the city, in an area referred to by scholars as the "black belt."[5] The area, nicknamed Bronzeville, was like a small town within the city limits. In the course of their study Drake and Cayton were told, "If you're trying to find a certain Negro in Chicago, stand on the corner of 47th and South Park long enough and you're bound to see him."[6] In general, blacks gravitated to Bronzeville because they had few other residential options. As Allan Spear points out, even blacks who did achieve some financial success were unable to move out of the black belt. White Chicago, by threat of violence, simply denied blacks the freedom to settle elsewhere in the city despite the desire of many to move.[7] Since blacks were usually prevented from moving into other city neighborhoods, they established their own businesses, social clubs, churches, and political institutions.

The black belt was soon so densely populated and rich in votes that black leaders were able to build an influential political machine on the South Side in the 1920s. Among the more successful black politicians were Edward H. Wright, Oscar de Priest, Arthur Mitchell, and later, William Dawson. Yet the alliances these men established with the city's white power brokers did not result in improved living conditions for most black Chicagoans. As Ira Katznelson has noted, individual political triumphs failed to help the masses: Essential social services in black neighborhoods did not improve significantly with expanded links to the white machines. In fact, blacks remained on the exterior in city politics, and the African-American community did not always receive assistance in exchange for electoral support.[8] The residents of the South Side *had* political representation, but the need for forceful spokesmen remained.

Besides the church, one of the most important political advocates in the black community was Robert Abbott's *Chicago Defender*. *The Defender*, which first appeared in 1905, began as a slim newsheet and grew to be one of the most influential black newspapers in the country. Although black newspapers had been published in America since 1827, *The Defender* was one of the most popular and most outspoken.[9] Robert Abbott, a son of former slaves who moved to Chicago from Savannah, envisioned a paper that

Figure 3.1. Robert Abbott, who founded *The Chicago Defender* in 1905. Courtesy of *The Chicago Defender.*

"would mirror the needs, opinions and the aspirations" of African-Americans.[10] Abbott found it difficult to finance the paper during the prewar years, and he ran *The Defender* from his landlady's kitchen on a minuscule budget. The paper attracted considerable attention in the black community, though, and by 1925 the circulation of the paper was estimated to be approximately 200,000.[11]

Chicago had several black papers, but *The Defender* may have had reason for brazenly dubbing itself the "World's Greatest Weekly." Besides its popularity in Chicago, a tremendous number of copies were purchased by individuals living outside of Illinois who sought news and editorials about black issues. *The Defender* was a forceful advocate for civil rights since its earliest days of publication, and provided commentary on all aspects of racial discrimination, including prejudice of the white press (see Figure 3.2). One particularly vivid example of the paper's influence was its role in the great migration of blacks to Chicago beginning in 1916.[12] *The Defender* often reported dramatically on violence and poverty in the south, and emphasized the freedoms African-Americans could enjoy if they moved to Chicago. A typical article during this period read:

If you can freeze to death in the North and be free, why freeze to death in the South and be a slave, where your mother, sister, and daughter are raped and burned at the stake, where your father, brother and son are treated with contempt and hung to a pole, riddled with bullets at the least mention that he does not like the way he has been treated? Come North then, all of you folks, both good and bad. If you don't behave yourself up here, the jails will certainly make you wish you had. For the hard working many there is plenty of work – if you really want it. The Defender says come![13]

For Abbott, the drive to bring blacks north was a personal crusade. Although discrimination in housing, the job ceiling, and pervasive racial prejudice characterized black life in Chicago, Abbott still believed life in his adopted city was far superior to life in the south.

The Defender published articles on a broad range of topics, from national politics to local social club activities. New opinion and advice columns by Bronzeville writers were constantly introduced, eliminated, and then reintroduced as the paper grew and changed. *The Defender* was recognized for its news, political commentary, and editorials about black life in America, yet it was also the primary means of communication for a small, densely populated area. As a result, the gossip column, "Everybody Goes When the Wagon Comes," by Ole Nosey, was published with little interruption for many years. In 1943 a journalism student conducted a survey of *Defender* readers, and found that over half of her respondents turned to the gossip column immediately after scanning the front page news items.[14]

Figure 3.2. *The Defender* often included critical commentary about the white press, as in this 1937 cartoon. September 4, 1937, p. 18. Used with the permission of *The Chicago Defender*.

The Defender prospered in the 1920s, and Bronzeville grew in population. As Drake and Cayton put it:

On eight square miles of land a Black Metropolis was growing in the womb of the white. Negro politicians and business and professional men, barred by color from competing for the highest prizes in Midwest Metropolis [Chicago], saw their destiny linked with the growth of Black Metropolis.[15]

During the years between the wars, men like Robert Abbott tried to build black institutions that could provide necessary services to the residents of the South Side. As a result, churches, political discourse, and social life all thrived in Bronzeville. The Defender reported extensively on this local scene, while also providing coverage and commentary about national and international affairs. By the early 1930s, however, the financial hard times that plagued the South Side community began to affect Bronzeville's major news organ. The Defender's circulation started to decline rapidly. Like all newspapers, circulation figures and the advertising revenues they generate were critical to The Defender, so a drop in paper sales was extremely problematic. In the early 1930s, Abbott's newspaper had a substantial deficit for the first time since its inception.[16] It is likely that the mayor of Bronzeville contests, and other such promotional endeavors, were established in part to counteract dwindling sales. Other black newspapers, like the Pittsburgh Courier, also experienced tremendous financial hardship during the late 1920s and early 1930s, and many sought new ideas to boost circulation.[17] Over the years, the annual Bronzeville mayoral race became much more than a promotional tactic for boosting circulation, but it was initiated at a time when many black papers employed contests in their struggle to survive.

THE MAYOR OF BRONZEVILLE CONTEST

In the early 1930s James Gentry, the theater critic of another black paper called the Chicago Bee, introduced the notion that Bronzeville's citizens should elect their own mayor. The contest was not a success, though, until Gentry took a new position on the staff of The Defender a few years later.[18] In 1934, six candidates competed in a mayoral contest conducted simultaneously with a competition for the title of "Miss Bronze America." Although the paper made minor references to the mayor's race, it seemed more interested in the beauty contest. On September 15, the paper asked:

Who will be "Miss Bronze America?" That is what is worrying thousands who are anxiously waiting for Saturday . . . to view the many pretty entrants, each praying and hoping this golden opportunity will be hers. "Miss Bronze America" will be selected from a bevy of bronze beauties and given a chance to be filmed. More than that, thousands of those present [at the show] will also see the mayor of Bronzeville. Candidates will be Jim Knight, Ily Kelly, Levirt Kelly, W. T. Brown, Jr., Tom Smith and Ed Jones. Who will be the mayor?[19]

After this quick mention, the article continued to describe the beauty contest, and listed the various attributes a "Miss Bronze America" hopeful should have if she wanted to compete. The paper announced the results of the 1934 mayoral contest on October 27, although it is unclear why or how the new mayor, "Genial Jim" Knight, defeated his opponents.

Beginning in 1936, both the coverage of the election by its sponsor and its popularity among members of the community accelerated dramatically. Thirty individuals announced their candidacy that year, so a primary was held to narrow the field to four prospective mayors. On August 8, *The Defender* reproduced photographs of the four candidates and provided short biographies of each one. The candidates were all men who moved to Chicago from the south – a doctor, a mortician, the owner of a taxicab company, and a man who worked for a public relations firm. *The Defender* touted the contest as the fiercest to date, although it employed this sort of hyperbole during most elections. A cartoon from the paper portrays the four candidates engaged in a fight, employing the tools of their trades as weapons (see Figure 3.3). One typical article, published on September 12, had the headline "Bronzeville Race Grows in Intensity," and began:

Unaware of their relative standings, four candidates for the Mayor of Bronzeville, fearing they may be outstripped by their rivals are exerting every effort to garner votes before the ballot boxes close next month. Meanwhile every source which is capable of producing votes is being tapped by the four aspirants to Bronzeville's highest office. Churches, lodges, social clubs, fraternities, and civic organizations have all been pledged by the candidates.[20]

Citizens of Bronzeville were encouraged to mark a ballot, printed in the paper each week, and deposit it in one of three voting boxes – at *The Defender*'s office, in a South Side department store, or at the Regal Theater, also in the neighborhood (see Figure 3.4). Balloting was ongoing, and one could vote at any time during an election period that lasted for several months. Apparently, there were no restrictions on who could vote, or how many ballots could be cast. Whether or not candidates' supporters tried to "stuff" ballot boxes, or whether norms dictated a person vote just once,

Figure 3.3. A cartoon from *The Defender*, which depicts the 1936 mayoral candidates fighting over the post, using the tools of their respective professions. October 3, 1936, p. 4. Used with the permission of *The Chicago Defender*.

is unclear because *The Defender* seemed more interested in the horse race than the mechanics of the election. With the exception of a critical letter to the editor in 1940 complaining that most candidates were trying to use the mayor's office as a "one-man business builder," all reports about the election were positive.[21]

Since *The Defender* reported the number of votes received by candidates, it is difficult to estimate how many people participated in the elections. In 1939, the first year *The Defender* reported vote totals, 129,973 ballots were cast.[22] At the conclusion of the 1944 election, *The Defender* tallied 1,323,500 votes.[23] During one of the last elections in

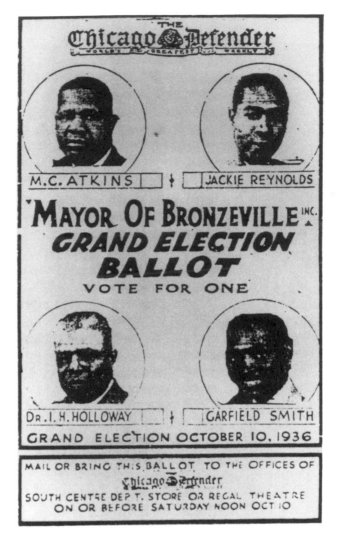

Figure 3.4. A 1936 election ballot for the mayoral race. September 12, 1936, p. 2. Used with the permission of *The Chicago Defender*.

1959, a grocery store owner from Mississippi named Cora Carroll garnered 11,911,250 votes to become the first (and only) female mayor of Bronzeville. She soundly defeated a fireman, a postal employee, and five other candidates, each of whom received over a million votes.[24] Those who ran for mayor needed to mobilize a large number of campaign workers to generate this many ballots, even if those workers voted several times themselves.

We can also get some sense of the contest's popularity from the great number of participants mentioned or depicted in the pages of *The Defender.* In 1936, for example, over 150 people were photographed as they voted, and several hundred people were listed as having reserved advance tickets for the end-of-election celebration ball. During most election years, social events and teas for the candidates were written up in *The Defender.* At one such tea in 1936, over sixty men and women listened to Dr. I. H. Holloway's "very practical address stating what he would strive to do should he be elected," and were subsequently entertained by soloists, pianists, and a monologist.[25]

During the 1936 campaign, there were scores of events organized by *The Defender,* but many were arranged by community groups and other media. Early in the campaign, the four candidates were asked to see the movie "Showboat" as a group and review the film for the public. The mayoral hopefuls spent time meeting with a variety of social clubs and lodges to garner support, and their activities were sporadically reported in the paper. Closer to the election, all of the candidates appeared on the "all-Race" local radio show, "Uncle Joe Dobson's Chili Bowl Hour," to debate the issues of the campaign.

The Defender wanted to keep the campaign as "clean" as possible and published a list of campaign "do's and don'ts" in 1937. Among the list of "don'ts," published for the candidates and their supporters, were the following rules:

1. Don't resort to mudslinging.
2. Don't refer to the present incumbent.
3. Don't mix politics with your campaign.
4. Don't do anything that may reflect on your character during the campaign.[26]

These guidelines highlight the fact that the mayor's position was not a partisan one: Bronzeville's mayor was a community leader allegedly free of ideological biases. All candidates for mayor were assumed to be good "race men," interested in improving the lot of all Chicago's black citizens. In the midst of the 1937 campaign, *The Defender* published an article explaining that the mayor of Bronzeville could do more for the community than most politicians:

It is as if for the first time a huge wave has awakened thousands to the possibility of an immediate solution for many community, social, civic, charitable and even economic ills through the medium of a clearing house which inadvertently forms the nucleus of the governing body immediately surrounding the mayor of Bronzeville after his election. These issues which constitute much of his platform may be solved entirely aside from politics if powers be rightfully vested and delegated to this non-political figure called mayor. . . . [27]

Most campaigns for the mayoralty reflected the nonpartisan nature of the office, although *The Defender* expended considerable effort to characterize the races as close and extremely competitive. It is likely that issue debates and mudslinging did take place, but that *The Defender* chose not publish this sort of news.

Although *The Defender* covered the fanfare of the campaign more diligently than it covered the substantive debates, certain issues came up year after year – housing prices, job and housing discrimination, and juvenile delinquency. The candidates definitely debated the issues, but only an incumbent mayor's opinions were published extensively in the paper. Some of the mayors wrote or edited a weekly column in the newspaper, where they reported on their activities and discussed important race and community issues. The column, "This Week with the Mayor of Bronzeville," was not written by every mayor, and in some years appeared only sporadically.

The traditional links between politics and the church in black Chicago were also present in the Bronzeville mayoral race. In 1936, the Rev. J. H. Lorenzo Smith of the Ebenezer Baptist Church was interviewed by *The Defender* on his "ideal Mayor of Bronzeville." Smith said that election to the office of mayor "constitutes one of the highest honors" in Bronzeville and that

The man who may be thus honored automatically becomes the key man as it relates to the civic, social and economic interests of the members of our particular race group. Such a man must be able to stand in the gap between a less privileged group and a more favored group of people living in the same community. He must be a student of affairs in general and well versed as to the needs of the people whom he represents. He must be a man with an enlarged vision, a man of well founded convictions, charged with an invincible determination to carry on a program that will touch every nook and corner of Bronzeville.[28]

Ministers often announced who their favorite candidate was, and preached sermons outlining that candidate's positive attributes.[29] The ties between *The Defender* and the religious community were many, since the press and church were two institutions that could speak freely about inequality without fear of direct reprisal from the white community. As Drake and Cayton pointed out, in the 1930s the black churches' ministers were expected by Bronzeville's citizens to serve as spokesmen for civil rights: "[Preachers in Bronzeville] were forced to concern themselves with a wide range of secular activities – political action, protest against discrimination, advice on securing jobs and legal aid, and the encouragement of Negro business enterprises."[30]

The climax of each mayoral election campaign was a huge celebration ball in November or December, where the results of the contest were announced. The fête was widely advertised by *The Defender,* and was usually very well attended. At the 1936 inaugural ball, for example, 6,000 people came to dance to the music of Louis Armstrong. Duke Ellington, Ella Fitzgerald, Billie Holiday, and other great black musicians and vocalists provided the music at the yearly dance, and the proceeds from ticket sales went to charity. Some of the artists, like Duke Ellington, were familiar with the contest and the candidates, and publicly praised the mayors. In the weeks that followed the event, *The Defender* reported on the details of the ball – who attended, who wore what, and who came with whom. The newspaper called the dance "the opening of the autumn social season" in their advertising, and reported on the more frivolous details of the event in the social pages. After the 1940 ball, for example, a society reporter wrote a long article listing women who had attended and describing how they looked. LuCretzia Diggs, one of the participants, was described as "beautiful to look at . . . with cerise gloves and a black velvet band around her neck, [and] black frock set off by brilliants and a veil."[31]

The celebration ball was a critical part of the Bronzeville election campaign excitement. The fact that so many famous artists would come to Chicago for the festivities added an air of legitimacy to the Bronzeville contests, making the elections easier to promote. Since so many people voted *and* attended the ball, *The Defender*'s editors felt secure in boasting about the popularity of both the elections and the mayor.

The Bronzeville campaigns differed from mainstream elections in a variety of ways, because there were no voting restrictions and no geo-

Table 3.1. Selected mayors of Bronzeville
and their occupations, 1934–1960[a]

Election year	Winner	Occupation
1934	Jim Knight	Tavern owner/ journalist
1936	I. H. Holloway	Physician
1937	Robert Miller	Businessman/ mortician
1938	Robert Miller	
1939	Joe Hughes	Club owner
1940	Joe Hughes	
1941	William Little	Dry cleaner
1942	C. H. Talley	Store president
1943	James Scott	Physician
1944	James Scott	
1945	R. H. Harris	Gospel group manager
1946	Benjamin Younge	Insurance agent
1948	Al Benson	Radio announcer
1954	John Lewis	Club owner
1958	Cora Carroll	Grocer/Sunday school teacher
1960	Cora Carroll[b]	

[a]During several years *The Defender* did not sponsor the mayoral contest, or chose not to publicize it.
[b]Walter Lowe, an insurance man, is said to be the last mayor, although the year he was elected could not be determined. He is still, officially, the mayor of Bronzeville.

graphic electoral boundaries. More important, the discourse of the campaigns included commentary about racial discrimination, which made the elections unusual in the 1930s. Despite these contrasts, however, the elections were covered by *The Defender* in the style of contemporary, American political journalism.[32] A "horse-race" mentality and an accent on campaign management characterize much of the reporting, especially in the 1940s. Although there were a few references to campaign managers in the late 1930s, strategic actions by the mayors and their staffs to gather support accelerated over time. Mentions were made of social and community groups pledging their support for particular candidates, and often, the candidates were pictured with their backers.[33] In 1948, the paper published photographs of two mayoral candidates consulting with their "boards of strategy."[34] *The Defender* portrayed the 1948 race as a close one and emphasized the differences among the candidates' tactical approaches:

[Mrs. Hughes] has been assured the support of various business leaders in the vicinity of the Monte Carlo at 63rd and Cottage Grove and along State St. Scores of cab drivers have promised to give their support and urge the riding public to help her win. . . . [Candidate Al] Benson has been putting on the heat with his radio programs appealing to listeners to clip ballots from the Chicago Defender and mail them to him. On his battle of the bands show at the Rose Bowl ballroom, Benson has announced that admission is by a ballot from the Defender. Content to remain silent and pile up his votes is Dr. James M. Scott, twice mayor of Bronzeville who is confident he will be the next Mayor.[35]

In a 1955 article about candidates' campaign strategies, the paper reported that

Every possible gimmick in the field of public relations and campaigning has been introduced into the competition. [The candidates] are using every conceivable type of literature – auto stickers, window cards, blotters, pencils, and buttons. . . . Some candidates are making house-to-house canvasses in their neighborhoods soliciting subscriptions to the Defender and asking residents to clip the vote coupons in the paper and send them in to the office of the campaign director. . . . One candidate hired three young ladies who come to his office every evening for two or three hours and who put through a series of calls to a long list of prospective supporters.[36]

The Defender's editors never saw the two types of campaign as equivalent, but they did make occasional reference to national political campaigns when promoting the mayor's race. Early in the 1936 contest a reporter wrote that the four candidates ran their campaigns "with the same care and attention to details which marks a presidential drive."[37] Comparisons between the U.S. presidential races and the mayoral race were natural, from a rhetorical standpoint, since the campaigns occurred simultaneously during the autumn months. By making the connection between the two races, *The Defender* tried to remind readers that the Bronzeville contest was also a legitimate, democratic election, albeit on a much smaller scale.

THE MAYOR AS SOCIAL ACTIVIST

How much influence was associated with the mayoralty? Most of the evidence about the contest is naturally drawn from the pages of *The Defender,* since it had the greatest interest in the event. Because *The Defender* was most concerned with using the contest to boost circulation, the paper tried to make the mayor's races look exciting to the readers. This meant that there was extensive coverage of the horse-race aspect, but very little discussion of what the mayor actually did once he or she took office.

It is difficult to find sources other than *The Defender* that mention the contests. Other black newspapers of the period had no reason to pay attention to the Bronzeville races, since they were conducted by a competitor. I could not find mentions of the contests in white newspapers like the *Chicago Tribune* or *Chicago Daily Times.* This lack of interest on the part of the white press is not surprising, as activities in the black community in the 1930s and 1940s were thought to be trivial and irrelevant. The only mention of the contest in the white press appeared in the *Chicago Tribune* in 1937, when the paper noted:

Robert H. Miller, mortician and garage company executive, prepared yesterday to take over his duties as honorary mayor of Bronzeville, the south side colored district. Mr. Miller was elected in a popularity contest Monday night and will be the official greeter and will preside at social functions in Bronzeville next year.[38]

This note reveals that the *Tribune* knew about the contests, but didn't think much of them. Despite *The Defender*'s contention that the mayor's race was much more than a popularity contest, the *Tribune* editors found this hard to believe. By casting the contest as a social function, the *Tribune* effectively de-politicized the ritual.

Even though there is a distinct lack of documentary evidence about the Bronzeville contests, there are some black men and women who remember the event. Vernon Jarett, now a journalist, thought that the Bronzeville elections were simply popularity contests. He says that the mayor didn't influence anyone, and certainly did not alter the nature of political life at the time.[39] Dr. Clementine Skinner claims that the mayoral candidates were usually community activists involved in organizations like the NAACP and the Urban League. She argues that it was not simply a popularity contest.[40] John H. Sengstacke III, Robert Abbott's nephew and current publisher of *The Defender*, explained that the elections began as popularity contests but changed very quickly into something more. He strongly believes that some of the more active Bronzeville mayors (although not all) were very influential in the community, and had contact with white leaders in Chicago. When asked about the Bronzeville mayors in relation to the local NAACP or Urban League leaders of the 1930s and 1940s, Sengstacke argues that *The Defender* and its mayor were more important and more effectual.[41]

Part of the problem in discerning the influence of the mayor through oral history is that the most interesting contests took place more than fifty years ago. Almost all of the longtime Chicago residents with whom I spoke had trouble remembering life in Bronzeville during that period. Even more problematic is the fact that the Bronzeville elections *did* become popularity contests in the 1950s, so informants may be forgetting the early mayors. None of the mayors from the 1930s or 1940s could be located, and as one of my very elderly informants noted, most of the people who might have participated in the early contests have passed away.

One helpful informant, a successful Chicago businessman named Dempsey Travis, has himself written several books about the history of black life in Chicago. When asked about the mayor of Bronzeville contests, Travis agreed that the influence of the mayor's post was dependent upon the man or woman who held it: Some mayors took the job seriously and others didn't. The potential for great influence or power was low, however, given the general obstacles faced by blacks seeking to change their circumstances. More than anything, Travis argues, the elections for mayor were an "exercise to release frustration." Because it was so difficult for blacks to break into the political process in Chicago, they felt the need for these sorts of events. From a society perspective the mayor was definitely "someone" in the community, regardless of his actions as an incumbent.[42]

Although the search for oral history informants has not been particularly successful, there is a way to get *some* sense of the mayor's influence through the pages of *The Defender*. Instead of concentrating on the paper's rhetoric about what the mayoralty entailed, we can focus on the reported activities of a very dynamic mayor. This way, we can discern (to some extent) the *potential* influence associated with the office. What many mayors *actually* did remains somewhat mysterious, because most of them did not write a column. One mayor who did write a column and appears to have been quite active was Dr. I. H. Holloway, a physician who served as mayor of Bronzeville from 1936 to 1937.

Holloway, who was educated in Memphis and Atlanta before moving to Chicago, took his post as mayor seriously. He spoke out on a variety of national and local issues, such as job discrimination, the importance of indigenous black businesses, and the continuing violence against blacks in the south. Although Holloway made public speeches and organized fund-raising drives in the community, he concentrated on letter-writing campaigns. On January 16, 1937, for example, he published excerpts from his correspondence with the Illinois Bell Telephone Company and the Chicago Park district about their discriminatory employment practices. In a reply to Holloway's letter about the lack of black park police officers, the president of the Park Service explained that such appointments would occur soon – that there were several eligible blacks on a list of recent applicants. These exchanges – where the mayor was clearly being asked to wait patiently for change – are indicative of the general relationship between black community activists and white officials in the 1930s. The message to blacks, in this case as in most cases, was to "sit tight." In that same column, we see hints of Holloway's frustration with white institutions in Chicago. He demonstrated that two members of the local fire department, both of whom served as firemen for over a decade, were due raises and promotions. He asked the community to speak up for these men, because "in union there is strength."[43]

On May 1, 1937, Holloway began to mention the antilynching bill, which was then being considered by Congress. He noted that Chicago's black residents were not behind the bill as strongly as they should have been. In his next weekly column Holloway reported that he and his cabinet met to talk about the bill, and how they could pressure Senator Lewis and others to vote for it. Holloway also encouraged all of the local clubs to send telegrams to their congressmen in support of the measure. In his May 15 column, Holloway reported that his cabinet members sought 50,000 signatures for a petition on the antilynching bill that would be sent to Congress. One cabinet member said he would "contact all ministers of the city" and pay a group of girls to take the petitions "from house to house" for signatures.[44] Holloway asked all clubs that generated petitions to send them to him, so that he could serve as a clearinghouse for the petition drive.

At one point, the mayor organized a letter-writing campaign directed at the Chicago court system administration. He argued that black men should be on more juries, and noted that

We are writing a number of politicians this week asking them to explain why there are not more Race men on the jury in Chicago, especially when it comes to trying Race men for serious crimes. In every such case there should be at least one member of the Race on the jury. We can get it with a little effort. There are many things for us if we go after them.[45]

In this case, as in many others, Holloway was reacting to the absence of blacks in the important arenas of public life in Chicago. Although he knew first-hand the difficulties of penetrating white institutions, he seemed unwilling to give up. In general, his columns alternated between angry frustration and naive optimism.

Since Chicago's white institutions and employers were largely unsympathetic to black concerns, Holloway emphasized the importance of supporting indigenous business enterprises in Bronzeville. If Bronzeville's own businesses were strong, he argued, blacks wouldn't be so dependent on whites for jobs. In his columns he repeatedly urged Bronzeville's citizens to buy from black merchants. His January 23 column included this invective:

We make and spend five million dollars each week. Do we spend it in our community with our business men? If not why? Are we trying to make employment for the young men and women coming out of school? If you are not doing those things who do you expect to do them for you?[46]

Holloway was also concerned with the unacceptably high rents in the neighborhood, which made life very difficult for the average black resident. In his April 17 column, the mayor argued that landlords were taking advantage of blacks, who were unable to move beyond the boundaries of Bronzeville. Although there is no evidence, printed in the paper, indicating that Holloway actually organized local protests, he was clearly in touch with local black leaders, like Alderman (and later Congressman) William Dawson. Holloway wrote:

Wearing apparel, provisions, and rents are all going sky-high, but salaries, in the majority of cases, are remaining the same. . . . Now comes your time to help do what you believe to be just and fair – We have had many strikes in this country, but never before have we had a sitdown strike. If rents keep on going higher, this might fit in well here. . . . [47]

Although Holloway made many attempts to stimulate community interest in political and economic issues, his most obvious contributions involved fund-raising. On occasion the mayor reported news of successful fund drives, such as his efforts to raise money for youth programs or to help flood refugees in the winter of 1937.[48]

Because Holloway was a physician, he occasionally mentioned public health issues in his column. He spoke publicly about the prevention of venereal disease, and pleaded with Bronzeville's residents to take the illness seriously. At times, Holloway addressed the physical condition of the neighborhood, since there were many filthy streets and dilapidated buildings. The mayor advertised and helped to organize a variety of "clean-up" campaigns designed to make Bronzeville a healthier place to live.

Holloway's influence, and the influence of other mayors, was clearly limited. If the mayors had enjoyed enormous success, *The Defender* would have highlighted these accomplishments. In general, the Bronzeville mayors were not as influential as other black leaders, although they often worked closely with the NAACP and Urban League. Any limited influence that the mayor had was most certainly tied to *The Defender*, which was undoubtedly one of the most powerful black institutions in Chicago. For scholars interested in community building, however, one of the most important aspects of the mayoralty was that it established a new, quasi-political *channel* for activism outside of mainstream politics. The mayoralty gave ordinary citizens who had a desire to improve black status in Chicago a chance to hold a potentially influential post.

Even more important than the influence of the mayor, which was entirely dependent on the officeholder, was the symbolism of the mayoral elections. It is clear that the participatory element of ritual action was present during the Bronzeville campaigns: Many individuals took part in the election fanfare, and community involvement was high. Beyond stimulating action, however, rituals also provide opportunities for meaningful symbolic communication. Although it is highly unlikely that *The Defender* planned its use of symbols during the campaigns, the contests should be viewed as a text about the black experience in Chicago.

SYMBOLS IN THE BRONZEVILLE RACE

The Defender's coverage of the mayoral contests, especially in the 1930s and 1940s, was rich in political symbolism. Since its inception, the paper had emphasized the notion of citizenship and the importance of American institutions. Robert Abbott and his successors spoke out fiercely against lynching, job discrimination, and prejudice, and their devotion to democratic institutions, ideals, and symbols was obvious. Two particularly compelling symbols – the ballot box and the idea of Bronzeville as a political entity – were omnipresent in the paper's mayoral election reporting.

Symbolic communication provides us with some cues about emotion: Strong feelings are often so difficult to express that we import symbolic constructs to communicate those complicated feelings. As Durkheim explained in his famous exploration of symbolic communication, *The Elementary Forms of the Religious Life*, a concept, its symbolic representation, and emotion are often closely intertwined:

The idea of a thing and the idea of its symbol are closely united in our minds; the result is that the emotions provoked by the one extend contagiously to the other. But this contagion, which takes place in every case to a certain degree, is much more complete and more marked when the symbol is something simple, definite and easily representable, while the thing itself, owing to its dimensions, the number of its parts and the complexity of their arrangement, is difficult to hold in the mind. . . . The soldier who dies for his flag, dies for his country; but as a matter of fact, in his own consciousness, it is the flag that has the first place. . . . He loses sight of the fact that the flag is only a sign, and that it has no value in itself, but only brings to mind the reality that it represents; it is treated as if it were this reality itself.[49]

During the mayoral campaigns *The Defender* intentionally emphasized the voting process and the idea of "Bronzeville" in order to generate excitement about the elections and the paper itself. Yet these symbols resonated powerfully with critical aspects of the black experience, because blacks lived in America without full citizenship rights for so long. Although social scientists have found ways to measure the impact of symbolic communication through laboratory experimentation, survey research, and ethnographic interviewing techniques, historians do not have the opportunity to engage in these sorts of empirical research projects. In studying the past we can, however, illustrate symbol use and speculate on why particular symbolic repertoires might have been chosen by individuals and institutions.

Since the mayoral race was established to elect a community spokesman, participation of Bronzeville's residents was critical. In nearly every issue of the paper during the fall months, readers were encouraged to cut the ballot out of the newspaper and deliver it to a ballot box. In the 1930s, the paper published a large number of photographs of people voting – wives and friends of candidates, prominent local business owners, and ordinary citizens. Visitors to Bronzeville were often asked to vote or at least have their pictures taken as they dropped a ballot into the box. In 1936, for example, the paper published a large group of photographs portraying a variety of people voting with the headline: "Everybody's Visiting the Polls to Select a New Mayor of Bronzeville." The caption under the group of photos notes that "if you don't believe the citizens of Bronzeville are taking their voting seriously, study these pictures and note the cross-section of Bronzevillians shown here casting ballots for their favorite candidates."[50] That same year *The Defender* reported that heavy voting had created overstuffed ballot boxes, which had campaign officials "worrying."[51]

The Defender's editors probably believed that depictions of people voting would make the practice seem normative to their readers: Portrayals of individuals voting might encourage others to do the same. Yet the fact that voting was unrestricted and casual also had great symbolic meaning for African-Americans during the 1930s. In many of the southern states where Bronzeville's residents were born, poll taxes and a variety of other property and "character" restrictions prevented blacks from voting in large numbers. Indeed, many scholars have documented both the legal and extralegal barriers to voting in the south at this time. Gunnar Myrdal described some especially vivid instances where black voters were terrorized and intimidated, both physically and psychologically, at southern polling places.[52]

Even though Chicago was a hostile environment for black citizens, they voted in general elections. In fact, Harold Gosnell reported that voter registration rates in the largely black Second Ward were higher than those in other, white city wards in 1920 and 1930.[53] Black Chicagoans voted because they wanted to support politicians who represented their interests, but voting was also a meaningful political ritual. Gosnell emphasized the symbolic value of voting:

To some of the race-conscious Negroes the ballot box is the symbol of emancipation, a guaranty of equality and opportunity. In the South the ballot box is a token
of class stratification based on color. . . . When a Negro migrates from the South
to the North, he goes through a transformation. He must find a new job, a new
place to live, new friends, and new amusements. One of the badges of his changed
life is the ballot box.[54]

In addition to encouraging voter turnout for the Bronzeville race, depictions of the voting act highlighted the expanded political freedom African-
Americans found in the North. The image of the ballot box was an
expressive symbol in the case of Bronzeville: Voting was a celebration of
black life in Chicago and an affirmation of the community. The campaign
itself temporarily transformed Bronzeville into an electoral district inhabited by and governed by African-American citizens.

Bronzeville, as a political entity, maintained ambiguous borders during
the 1930s and 1940s. Although Bronzeville was thought by most to be a
narrow geographic area on the South Side bounded by four streets, it
seemed as though any African-American could seek the mayor's office or
vote in the election. In the 1940s, the paper noted that mayoral candidates
came from a variety of different neighborhoods in Chicago. In 1954, the
race was opened even further to allow anyone living within a forty-mile
radius of Chicago's loop to run for mayor.[55] There were no residency
requirements for voting eligibility, so nonresidents often cast ballots – theatrical companies, black celebrities, and visiting friends and family of
Bronzeville's inhabitants were all pictured voting. In a 1938 photograph
from the paper, a court bailiff turned candidate named B. H. Huggins
stood by as his cousin from Wyoming voted for him.[56]

The lack of eligibility rules indicates that Bronzeville's electoral boundaries were not geographic ones, but were determined by membership in
the larger, national black community. According to Benedict Anderson and
other scholars cited in my introductory chapter, nations and other political
communities are real, but are also largely "imagined." Although America
has distinct borders, for example, a variety of "Americas" exist: Cultural
identity often determines how one conceptualizes the political terrain, and
it is through ritual and symbolic communication that an imaginary community becomes an actual one.

Bronzeville, especially in the 1930s and 1940s, was easily defined in one
sense but vaguely defined in another. Even though maps of Bronzeville as

part of Chicago's South Side did exist, *The Defender* and its readership were willing to accept all African-Americans as citizens of the vibrant community known as Bronzeville.[57] Academics, politicians, and musicians wrote about a neighborhood called Bronzeville, but *The Defender* strove to include nonresidents as citizens of the community through rituals like the mayoral contest. *The Defender* encouraged other black communities around the nation to adopt the name "Bronzeville" or devise their own such name, and many did.[58]

Although contests and other such celebrations in secular life are sometimes overlooked by historians, these rituals often serve important *integrative* functions for cultural groups. In the 1930s and 1940s discrimination and exclusion were pervasive elements of black life in Chicago and other segregated cities, so the sense of community fostered by black newspapers, churches, social clubs, and other institutions was crucial. The broadly defined electorate in the original Bronzeville, and the fact that other communities referred to themselves as "Bronzevilles" demonstrate how media can play a central role in promoting cultural identity and attachment regardless of geography. John Sengstacke claims that the Bronzeville contest was introduced primarily to "get blacks together" and to mobilize them politically.[59] *The Defender* repeatedly emphasized the commonalities of blacks' experiences in America, and the establishment of a black mayoralty was an elaborate attempt to realize its goals: The mayor was, more than anything, a symbol of connectedness and community.

THE DECLINE OF THE MAYORALTY

In the early 1950s *The Defender* did not hold mayoral elections, but the paper's editors tried to revive the contest in 1954. In these new elections the mayoralty was described by the paper as a lucrative business opportunity, although the opportunities for community leadership were downplayed. The paper published articles by former mayors testifying to the fact that the office had brought them enormous amounts of additional business.[60] Rules and rewards associated with the election changed as well. *The Defender* offered prizes to the prospective mayor: In addition to becoming the "number one bronze citizen," the mayor would receive a gold badge and a 1955 Ford Thunderbird with a "crest of his office." All mayoral candidates had to be approved by a board of commissioners made up of civic leaders, and one could run for office only if he or she sold $100 in subscriptions to *The Defender*.[61] In the second wave of elections, the mayor was portrayed as a popular figure in the community – a socialite more than a community spokesperson. During campaigns in the 1950s, pictures of candidates were very commonly found, whereas pictures of citizens voting were rare. In 1959, a reporter wrote of the prospective mayor that

He or she will be the most talked about person in Chicagoland. He or she will have gained heights never before imagined – overnight will become one of the city's better known celebrities. He or she will be a person to lead and to be led; to entertain and to be entertained; to glamorize and to be glamorized. In all, this person will be an all around good fellow.[62]

The Bronzeville elections declined in importance by the early 1960s, and were no longer reported on by *The Defender*.[63] It is possible that the appeal of the race faded as *The Defender* established other types of contests and promotional events.[64] Yet the central reason why the elections disappeared is that the position of mayor became superfluous. Increasingly, other established organizations (e.g. the NAACP, the Chicago Urban League, and later, the Operation People United to Save Humanity [PUSH]) and black politicians began to address effectively injustice and discrimination in Chicago. In fact, one of the last mayors, John Lewis, spent much of his energy in office raising money for black organizations like the NAACP. Gradually, issues that the mayors had always addressed were taken on by others. For example, stimulating investment in local black-owned businesses, a priority issue for Mayor Holloway in 1937, was just recently revived by Operation PUSH.[65] By 1960, James Q. Wilson could argue that the black community in Chicago was no longer represented by a single spokesman, because so many interest groups had evolved to address particular policy issues:

The Negro middle class is now producing a collection of would-be leaders who are specialized by area of interest and competence. Housing, health, employment, and education are issues each of which elicits a different group of leaders. No one is or pretends to be a "representative" of the Negro community in all these fields.[66]

One last reason why the contests were abandoned is rooted in the economic history of the newspaper. *The Defender*'s circulation had dropped considerably by the 1960s: The other Chicago dailies and the local television and radio stations began to report on issues of importance to the black community, so *The Defender* was no longer a leading media source for African-American residents.[67] The success of the mayor of Bronzeville elections had always been tied to the popularity of the paper itself. Since the paper could no longer count on a large, loyal readership, the elections may have been impracticable.

FUNCTIONS OF THE MAYORALTY

The contest for the mayor of Bronzeville served multiple functions for *The Defender* during its zenith in the 1930s and 1940s: It probably increased circulation (although this is impossible to determine), and it gave the paper additional influence in the community. The mayor, although in theory an independent actor, was beholden to *The Defender* since the paper controlled the contest and edited the mayor's column. Beyond the benefits to the paper, though, how does the Bronzeville mayoral election illuminate this particular chapter in the history of black marginality?

One important aspect of the mayoralty was that it established an activist role, outside of the party system, which was *construed* as "apolitical" by the paper and the community. Although the mayor spoke out on highly conflictual issues of the day – those debated by Chicago's parties and politicians – he or she was thought to have the best interests of the entire black community in mind. The nonpartisan trappings of the mayoralty, and the fact that anyone could run for mayor, made the post an unusual organ for public opinion expression. Because election to the post was based on popularity and not service to a particular party, and because a new mayor had to prove his efficacy to a skeptical community, the discourse in the mayor's platforms and columns reveal the nature of issues most important to residents of the community. Some of the matters addressed by the mayors affected all of Chicago's residents (e.g., shortages of consumer goods during the war), but others like juvenile delinquency, street sanitation, and job discrimination were most problematic for black residents of the city's South Side. In fact, the political dialogue of the Bronzeville campaigns, as well as the speeches and writings of the incumbent mayors, supply historians with a unique form of public opinion data. Although *The Defender* may have edited the mayor's column, mayors spoke frequently on a wide range of issues. They did not need to concern themselves with party agendas or infighting.

Besides serving as a unique channel for public opinion communication, the mayoralty was an atypical outlet for community action. Common citizens, who did not seek powerful roles in the party machines, could become involved in neighborhood politics through the Bronzeville elections. Although the candidates for mayor were often popular or well-known residents of the community, many other residents worked on campaign staffs or served on the mayor's "cabinet." In 1943 Mayor Willie Little, who was seeking reelection and had a great interest in juvenile delinquency, noted that

[My cabinet] was made up of ministers, school teachers, porters, maids, doctors, undertakers, business men, social workers, stock yard workers, steel mill employees, Pullman and railroad men, city employees and postal clerks; but above all else it contained mothers and fathers.[68]

Political parties and other community groups *structured* public discourse and political action on the South Side, and so did *The Defender.* More than anything, the yearly event compelled Bronzeville's residents to evaluate the state of their community, and express sentiments about problems often ignored by Chicago's white leadership.

A RITUAL OF DISSENT

The mayoral elections established a new forum for public discourse, but were also celebrations of the Bronzeville neighborhood itself. Like other secular rituals, the contests were staged to create a sense of belonging and inclusion among members of the South Side community.[69] *The Defender* described the election as an event designed for everyone: All residents were repeatedly encouraged to vote, to attend the inaugural ball, and most important, to feel some excitement about an upcoming election. Readers were reminded that the mayor of Bronzeville was *Their* most authentic representative since he or she was first and foremost a "race leader."

Even though the mayoral elections were intended to engender cohesion, they can also be viewed as an outlet for political frustration. As Steven

Lukes has pointed out, rituals are employed by marginalized groups to express discontent with the status quo. He notes, for example, that May Day celebrations held in capitalist countries, and the Memorial Day parades held to communicate antiwar sentiment during the Vietnam War, were dramatic forms of protest centered around ritual. If we think about the Bronzeville elections as ritualized channels for frustration, staged by a newspaper known for dissent, they become much more than a yearly celebration of community solidarity. Though Chicago's white residents would come to witness direct, threatening forms of black protest during the 1960s, the Bronzeville elections communicated discord: No matter how sympathetic some of the white mayors of Chicago were to blacks' problems, African-Americans needed their own mayor to work toward change. That Bronzeville could, and indeed *should*, have its own mayor reveals the newspaper's and the voters' dissatisfaction with the political status quo. One Bronzeville candidate even proposed that Bronzeville establish its own city hall, and supposedly had a site in mind.[70] The sheer inventiveness of this campaign proposal, and others like it, echoes Lukes's description of ritual: Rituals, he argues, can "provide a source of creativity and improvisation, a counter-cultural and anti-structural force, engendering new social, cultural and political forms."[71]

Although the mayoral race in Chicago was a unique political ritual, it vaguely resembles the "Negro Election Days" of eighteenth- and nineteenth-century New England. In towns with substantial black populations, like Hartford, Connecticut, blacks would often elect "governors" who served as real and symbolic leaders of the African-American community. Orville Platt, writing in 1898, saw the elections in New Haven as imitations of the white electoral process: "The negroes having no voice in political affairs, naturally enough, fell into the curious habit of holding elections of their own, after the manner of their white masters."[72]

Yet he also noted that the governor was a respected leader in the community who settled disputes and dictated norms for appropriate behavior. Joseph Reidy argues that the elections were not rituals of dissent, but functioned as mechanisms of social control:

Most whites favored Election Day's contribution to social order and stability. The celebration served as a safety valve for the blacks' pent-up frustrations, offering an outlet for the pressure of year-round life and toil. It also supplied the whites in the larger towns with a semiofficial law enforcement apparatus suitable for checking petty crime, insubordination, and rebelliousness. In return, masters often provided the blacks with clothing, horses, and treats for the occasion.[73]

Although Platt and Reidy may be correct in their interpretations of these early gubernatorial elections, the more somber Bronzeville elections were not "safety valves" but expressions of dissatisfaction. Talk of racial discrimination and "Jim Crowism" was pervasive during the mayoral campaigns, and no such dissent was present in the governor's elections. Despite the difference in subtext between the eighteenth-century elections and the Bronzeville races though, both faded as the status of African-Americans changed. As Reidy notes, the New England elections eventually lost favor among influential blacks: "[New England black leaders] saw [Election Day] as an anachronism devoid of any tactical or strategic relevance. In one sense, they had outgrown it; in another sense, the changing nature of black society had simply transcended it."[74]

Similarly, as John Sengstacke argues, the Bronzeville contests were no longer needed as blacks developed other, more effective channels for political expression.[75]

RACE AND COMMUNICATION STRATEGY IN BRONZEVILLE

Like the salons of the Enlightenment, the mayor of Bronzeville contests were a ritualized form of expression. The ritual aspects of the salons were many: People met at a regular time and place, ate meals together, and obeyed the traditional, socially correct rules for behavior. Women created and re-created the salons of the eighteenth century because this innovative forum enabled them to achieve educational, social, and sometimes, political goals.

The mayor of Bronzeville campaigns were also a form of ritualized communicative behavior, although the participants (voters) were far less conscious of strategy than were the women of the salons. The owner and editors of *The Defender*, on the other hand, were well aware of the contest's raison d'être: They constructed the contest with hopes of galvanizing the black community. The campaign and the celebration ball made the ritual lively and entertaining, so participation ran high. The contest occurred on

an annual basis (with some exceptions, see Table 3.1), and people in the
community came to expect it each fall. Because it was instituted by an
already powerful newspaper, the ritual did help to unify the community,
and the idea of Bronzeville was furthered by the mayoralty. The dual goals
of the mayor's race – to bring people together *and* elect a spokesperson –
were achieved through the establishment of ritual.

The mayor's office was meant to be a political communication backchannel in Chicago, although it isn't clear that the mayors of Bronzeville
were particularly successful in this respect. At a time when blacks voted,
but had very little political clout in the city, the mayor's office might have
worked behind the scenes to further civil rights. In his memoirs, Enoch
Waters, a former reporter for *The Defender*, claims that the mayor of
Bronzeville met with white politicians, despite the marginal political status
of blacks in the city. Unfortunately, however, Waters provided no documentary evidence to support his statement that, "The city's political and
business power blocs, as well as the white press, accepted the Mayor of
Bronzeville as the spokesman of Chicago's South Side."[76] Despite
Waters's insistence about the mayor's importance, though, I am skeptical
that the backchannel (once established) was used very often.

More interesting than influence and power backchannels, though, is the
issue of parallel public space. By staging a quasi-political election – complete with balloting and campaigning – the editors of *The Defender* carved
out their own public sphere on the South Side. *The Defender* had, since its
founding, worked on creating an alternative political arena for blacks to
express themselves and engage in political action. The Bronzeville race
accelerated this movement, and enriched the public space by electing a
man (and eventually, a woman) to represent the ideas and values born in
this new arena. If, as Habermas claims, public opinion only can arise
where there is a lively public sphere, *The Defender* and its mayor were creating a place for opinion development and expression. Although white
Chicago was not particularly interested in blacks' opinions, an *infrastructure* for opinion communication thrived on the South Side. Eventually, the
black community would begin to wield real power, enough to elect Harold
Washington as the mayor of Chicago in 1983.

In the next chapter, we turn to another sort of alternative publication,
a radical socialist magazine published before the first World War called
The Masses. Like *The Defender*, *The Masses* claimed to speak for a constel-

lation of groups that were usually shut out of mainstream political and social discourse – anarchists, feminists, socialists, and others on the left. Just as *The Defender* and the citizens of the South Side created Bronzeville, the small crowd of Greenwich Village radicals used *The Masses* to build community, express their opinions, and challenge white, middle-class society.

4

Political Marginality
and Communication in
Greenwich Village,
1911–1918

The last two chapters explored how individuals, marginalized because of race or gender, constructed alternative spheres for political discourse and participation. This chapter, and the one that follows, takes up a different sort of marginality: that of individuals excluded from the political mainstream because of their ideological radicalism. Unlike the cases of eighteenth-century Frenchwomen or African-Americans in the 1930s, the marginality of ideological outsiders is *intentional*.[1] Socialists living and working in the days before the First World War – the subject of this chapter – and contemporary Libertarian political activists (the focus of Chapter 5), chose alternative lifestyles quite deliberately. The fact that both of these groups developed in order to influence the contours of mainstream politics makes them particularly interesting to those who study the changing nature of the American public sphere.

The lives and works of early American socialists, including luminaries such as Eugene Debs, John Reed, and Upton Sinclair, are already well documented by historians. My intention here is not to add to this large biographical literature, but to take a look at one particular aspect of early socialist activity – the creation and distribution of *The Masses,* a literary magazine published from 1911 to 1917 in New York City. The magazine, edited from 1912 through its final issue by the writers Max Eastman and Floyd Dell, was a landmark publication: It was the first sophisticated, intellectual socialist magazine with high production values to appear on the American scene. *The Masses* drew attention for its art, fiction, and its radical editorials about religion, race, and military conscription, but was eventually forced to close after its editors were prosecuted by the federal government under the Espionage Act. A few literary critics and historians[2] have written eloquently about the Greenwich Village intellectual scene in the early decades of the twentieth-century, and about *The Masses*. Leslie Fishbein and Rebecca Zurier, in particular, have conducted pioneering research on the topic. In this chapter, I build upon work by these historians, and reanalyze *The Masses* according to the themes and concepts introduced in Chapter 1. I am most interested in how those who contributed to the magazine formed a communication network, and a parallel political universe of sorts.[3]

Here, I discuss the birth and goals of the magazine, the men and women who contributed fiction, editorials, and artwork to it, and some of the interesting opinions found in its pages. Among my central questions are, first, how did Eastman, Dell, Art Young, John Sloan, and others who sustained *The Masses* use it as an alternative outlet for public opinion expression? Second, what was the character of the parallel public space created by this marginal socialist community? Although socialists were somewhat freer to express themselves before the First World War than they would be later (e.g., during the "red scare" of the 1940s and 1950s), they were still political outcasts – especially in the world beyond lower Manhattan. Lastly, I am interested in how a community gave birth to, and was further solidified by *The Masses*. The magazine, because of its controversial content, forced writers and artists together: Through the journal, their relationships became more serious and more meaningful.

The Masses and its contributors provide the raw materials for an excellent case study of the tactics, strategies, and problems of marginal communities. Unlike many of the citizens of Bronzeville, the intellectuals of *The Masses* were an extraordinarily talented and articulate group: Most were gifted poets, writers, cartoonists, or artists, and most had at least some formal education (unlike the salonnières). Although these Greenwich Village intellectuals were bohemians and radicals, they were well versed in the proper rules of grammar and the "correct" norms of public expression. Their polished prose and witty presentation of ideas are especially interesting, because they used these weapons to communicate rather unorthodox ideas and feelings. John Reed's dramatic reporting of a New Jersey worker's strike, and his subsequent articles on the Russian Revolution, are good examples of the sort of compelling text found in *The Masses*. Despite good intentions and fine writing, however, the magazine was always in financial distress. Even if its publication had not been halted by the federal government in 1917, it would have been a struggle to raise the money needed to continue its operation.

THE ORIGINS OF *THE MASSES*

During the first two decades of the twentieth century, a large number of small, subsidized, art and literary magazines were published in the United States. These so-called little magazines were not profitable, because their limited circulation precluded significant advertising revenues. The magazines were, more than anything, published for a small circle of writers or artists: They served as an outlet for work that did not interest the larger, more financially viable magazines like *The Atlantic* or *Harper's*.[4] The little magazines were controversial, since they sometimes contained poetry or literature that offended private citizens or government officials. The founder of one of these journals, *The Little Review*, was convicted under obscenity statutes for publishing several chapters of James Joyce's *Ulysses*. The little magazines played a critical role in American literary history: They introduced European authors and artists to their American counterparts, and at the same time, provided a lively forum for experimental work in the humanities. Although most of these magazines reached only small circles of intellectuals, they inspired many young writers, since the journals made publication of new or innovative work a real possibility.

The Masses was founded in 1911 by a Dutchman named Piet Vlag who managed the restaurant located in New York's Rand School – a small institution devoted to socialism and free thought. The restaurant attracted a number of intellectuals, and with Vlag's urging, became a locus of radical political discourse in the city. Vlag was a crusader of sorts, interested in starting a large cooperative movement in the United States based on European models with which he was familiar. He decided that a magazine might enable him to explain and publicize the cooperative idea, thereby helping others to envision worker-controlled shops and factories. By recruiting the aid of a committed socialist, and vice-president of the New York Life Insurance Company named Rufus Weeks, Vlag found the funds to print and distribute the magazine. His job at the Rand School enabled him to talk up the journal, and persuade several talented writers and artists – John Sloan, Art Young, Louis Untermeyer, and others – to contribute to the magazine. Despite an attractive set of first issues, good artwork and literature, and some inspiring editorials about the benefits of cooperative businesses, however, Vlag had trouble maintaining the magazine's circulation. The cooperative movement he had hoped to instigate did not catch on either, much to Vlag's disappointment. As the artist and cartoonist Art Young noted in his memoirs, Vlag's "cooperative stores would not coop," and so the Dutchman quit the magazine and moved to Florida.[5] Just before he left, in a desperate effort to save *The Masses*, Vlag had tried to merge it with a socialist women's magazine published in Chicago. But the artists and writers who had contributed to *The Masses* refused to go along with this scheme.

When Vlag left New York, the intellectuals who had sustained the magazine still thought it a worthy project. There were no polished, intellectual socialist magazines circulating at the time, and many artists and writers felt committed to the idea. Socialism, which for many Village residents symbolized freedom from the stodgy social norms of the period, was the critical intellectual axis around which their lives were organized. For them, socialism embodied a constellation of attitudes and campaigns – in particular, the fight against the bourgeois and the "respectable." Many of these socialists and their friends were sympathetic to causes championed by the Industrial Workers of the World (the I.W.W.), were followers of Emma Goldman or other charismatic anarchists, or simply fought convention without any type of coherent ideology or dogma. Almost all of the important members of *The Masses* crowd were able to publish their noncontroversial works elsewhere, but were more excited about distributing their experimental drawings, radical stories, and challenging editorials. Even though all of the art, poetry, and literature published in *The Masses* was donated, and none of the contributors ever made money directly from their *Masses* work, they agreed to keep working for the journal. Unfortunately, they had no editor: None of those who had contributed pieces to Vlag's project had an inclination toward editorial work, or the skills it requires.

The group (which owned the magazine cooperatively) asked Max Eastman, then a lecturer in philosophy and student of John Dewey's at Columbia University, to edit the magazine. Eastman, the son of a pair of progressive ministers from upstate New York, had come to the city just

Figure 4.1. A drawing of Piet Vlag, founder of *The Masses*, by his collab-
orator, Art Young. From *Art Young: His Life and Times*, by Art Young. Edited
by John Nicholas. Beffel, NY: Sheridan House, 1939. Used with permission from Sheridan House.

four years earlier in 1907. During his childhood, Eastman was greatly
influenced by his parents' broad-minded friends and acquaintances. As a
boy, he came into contact with a few important writers, like Mark Twain,
and found that he too wanted to be a writer and a poet. Eastman grudg-
ingly took over the bankrupt *Masses*, although it was months before he
would receive any salary for editing the magazine. From most accounts, it
seems that Eastman was persuaded to become editor for three reasons: his
attraction to the interesting group of contributors, his desire to write
forcefully about socialism, and the sheer excitement of designing a journal.
As Eastman explains in his memoirs, he was invited to a meeting of the
contributors at Charles Winter's studio, where a "mock up" of the magazine lay on the table:

[The editors] were warm and charming people, and to me impressive. They were men and women who had made a name for themselves. . . . The whole scene and situation lent itself to my effort and my then very great need to romanticize New York life and romanticize the revolution.

He continued:

The dummy of an inchoate next number lay at the end of the table with an empty chair before it. I had never even heard the word "dummy" before, and had no idea how a magazine came into being. But I soon found myself in that chair with Charles Winter above me smilingly explaining how to "paste up the dummy." No more fascinating sport has ever been invented.

Much of Eastman's time at *The Masses*, from his first issue in 1912 until the magazine closed in 1917, was spent finding contributions and writing editorials. Under his leadership, the magazine became increasingly visible and successful, although it never became financially independent. Eastman traveled often and widely, visiting sympathetic wealthy individuals who donated the funds needed to subsidize the journal. Rich patrons like Mrs. O. H. P. Belmont, the former wife of W. K. Vanderbilt, gave Eastman one or two thousand dollars after listening to his pleas, and these small sums helped to keep the magazine going. No respectable business would buy advertising in *The Masses*, due to its radical content, so Eastman and the other owners came up with creative ways to pay the printing bills and the rent for the editorial office. As Eastman's associate editor Floyd Dell recalled, the owners opened a bookshop attached to the editorial office, which sold leftist tracts, literature, poetry, and "the most enlightened books that existed upon the subject of sex."[6] In addition to book sales, *The Masses* established a Lecture Bureau. Speakers like Art Young, the orator William Noyes, and the humorist Eugene Wood would give a lecture to any organization that would pay their rail fare and purchase $10 worth of subscriptions to the magazine.[7]

Although only Eastman and Dell consistently worried about the financial problems of the magazine, all of the owners concerned themselves with its content. Monthly meetings were held, where the artistic and literary contributions of anonymous contributors were read aloud and discussed by the editorial board. Floyd Dell recalls the following people at most meetings: Horatio Winslow, Mary Heaton Vorse, William English Walling, Howard Brubaker, Art Young, John Sloan, Charles A. and Alice

Beach Winter, H. J. Turner, Maurice Becker, George Bellows, Cornelia
Barns, Stuart Davis, Glenn O. Coleman, K. R. Chamberlain, Eastman,
and himself.[8] From all accounts, these meetings were lively ones, as most
in attendance were contentious, opinionated, and argumentative. At the
meetings Dell read the literary and poetic submissions, and since he did
not reveal the name of the authors, some members of the editorial board
would get to hear vicious critiques of their own work. After hearing from
Dell, editorial board members voted on what should and should not be
published. One humorous moment from a meeting was recalled by Art
Young in his memoirs:

One evening Floyd had finished reading a poem and the vote had been taken,
when a man from a corner of the studio shouted contemptuously:
    "Bourgeois! Voting! Voting on poetry! Poetry is something from the soul. You
can't vote on poetry!" The voice was that of Hippolyte Havel, a well-known Anar-
chist. His remarks were received with silence. Some of us felt there was a good deal
of sense in his criticism.
    "But Mr. Havel," said Floyd Dell, "this is our way. Maybe you know a better one.
As assistant editor of *Mother Earth* you editors had to get together and decide on
the material for your next issue, did you not?"
    "Yes," said Mr. Havel, a little taken aback, "but we didn't abide by our decision."[9]

    The Masses enjoyed a much larger circulation than some of the other lit-
tle magazines, yet it was far less popular than *The Atlantic, Harper's,* or even
the liberal *New Republic,* which Eastman chided more than once in the
pages of his own magazine. By 1913, the magazine sold approximately
10,000 copies each year, and climbed to 17,000 by 1917.[10] Yet it is difficult
to know who read *The Masses,* since office records with subscription lists
cannot be located by historians. Perhaps *New York Journal* editor Arthur
Brisbane was partly right when he said to Art Young, "You *Masses* boys are
talking to yourselves!"[11] Was Brisbane prompted to say this in response to
Young's sardonic *Masses* cartoons about him? Or was *The Masses* really just
a newsletter for Greenwich Village bohemians? Rebecca Zurier points out
that copies of the journal were distributed through state Socialist party
organizations, though the extent of this readership is unclear. We know
that some members of the literary and political elite (e.g., Woodrow Wilson, George Santayana, John D. Rockefeller, and Clarence Darrow) knew
about and often read *The Masses* quite carefully, but there is no evidence
that large numbers of working-class men and women read it.[12]

Interestingly, despite the obvious and significant differences among the salon culture of eighteenth-century France, Bronzeville in the 1930s and 1940s, and Greenwich Village in the days before World War I, there are some strong parallels as well. Although I will take up these similarities in Chapter 6, it is useful to point to two such parallels here. In each of these bounded communities, publications were central to the communication process among residents. The salons of Paris had their newsletters, and more important, their books, plays, and poetry. *The Defender* was crucial to Bronzeville's residents' feelings of unity and cohesion. And in Greenwich Village – a society of bohemians, artists, free-thinkers, anarchists, and feminists – *The Masses* and other little magazines helped to bind together community members. Although the volumes produced by salon attendants in eighteenth-century France received wide distribution, *The Defender* and *The Masses* were organs of small enclaves – communities that had a fair amount of difficulty getting a hearing in the larger public sphere. *The Masses* editors and writers *did* write for each other, as did the editors and writers on *The Defender* staff. The fact that both of these neighborhoods developed media for expression is part of what gave them definition, and to a great extent, their purpose.

Another parallel is the centrality of salons, in the cases of eighteenth-century bourgeois Paris and early twentieth-century Greenwich Village. Mabel Dodge, the premier salonnière of the Village, had many connections to *The Masses*. She was a friend of Max Eastman's, and even edited one of the later issues when he was unable to. If *The Masses* was the political organ of the Village between 1912 and 1917, Dodge's salon was its center of social life and intrigue. At her spacious apartment on Fifth Avenue, the independently wealthy Dodge entertained a variety of luminaries: Bill Haywood of the I.W.W., Walter Lippmann (who wrote several pieces for *The Masses* as a young man), Emma Goldman, the painter Max Weber, Lincoln Steffens, Margaret Sanger, and a variety of other journalists, political activists, critics, poets, and artists. The crowd who owned *The Masses* – Dell, Eastman, and Reed in particular – were appreciative visitors to Dodge's salon, which shared a variety of characteristics with the female-operated salons of Paris. Dodge's salon, like those of Madame d'Epinay and Madame Roland, were places to "test" one's ideas before committing them to print. The salon, as Dodge had hoped, enabled people with similar interests to meet, learn of new ideas, and sometimes, become friends.[13]

THE CONTENT OF *THE MASSES*

Until Max Eastman took over the editorship at *The Masses*, its content was rather mundane. Vlag's good intentions, and his interest in the cooperative movement, set a rebellious tone for the magazine, but it lacked the radicalism and seriousness of thought Eastman would eventually bring to it. Despite its low level of sophistication under Vlag, however, the magazine was far more intellectual than previous socialist newsletters or journals.[14] In the third issue, published in March of 1911, Vlag wrote an editorial explaining and defending the high-brow tone of *The Masses*. He argued that writers should never condescend to workers, but should communicate their very best, most interesting ideas to their audience. Writers, Vlag posited, should not simplify or "sugar coat" their opinions. More than anything, authors and artists should please themselves, and if this demands sophistication in their expression, so be it.[15] Even when Eastman became editor, *The Masses* maintained this general guiding principle: Style and complexity are often part of good, original writing, and these aspects of expression would be encouraged by the magazine. In case this wasn't clear from the journal's content, Eastman and John Reed wrote the following slogan, which appeared at the front of every issue beginning in February of 1913:

A FREE MAGAZINE

This magazine is owned and published co-operatively by its editors. It has no dividends to pay, and nobody is trying to make money out of it. A revolutionary and not a reform magazine; A magazine with a sense of humor and no respect for the respectable; Frank, Arrogant, impertinent, searching for the true causes; A magazine directed against rigidity and dogma wherever it is found; printing what is too naked or true for a money-making press; A magazine whose final policy is to do as it pleases and conciliate nobody, not even its readers – there is a field for this publication in America.[16]

On the whole, *The Masses* lived up to the statement in its masthead: Its arrogance and radicalism were so offensive that the editor received a steady barrage of nasty comments and letters from readers and critics.

More serious were the libel suit filed against the magazine by the Associated Press, and its subsequent problems with federal government censors, which I discuss in this chapter.

The Masses might have been a bit too pompous and self-important had the editors not engaged in perpetual self-mockery. Not only were they ruthlessly critical of socialists and their crusades, but alongside sympathetic pictures of the American proletariat, they would on occasion gently tease the working class – the editors' raison d'être. There is Stuart Davis's cover art for the June 1913 issue, for example. In the drawing, two unattractive, badly dressed, lower-class women face each other. One says, "Gee, Mag, Think of Us Bein' on a Magazine Cover." In another, Art Young portrays two poor youngsters, standing in the midst of a slum, looking up at the stars. The caption read: "Observation DeLuxe. Young Poet: Gee, Annie, look at the stars! They're as thick as bedbugs."[17]

The very first issue of *The Masses*, published in January of 1911, was slim – only sixteen pages. It included a few drawings by Art Young, a grim description of peasant life in Russia by Leo Tolstoy, and essays on the importance of unionizing and German socialism. There was also an extensive series of advertisements for one of the few cooperatives in New York City – the American Wholesale Cooperative. The cooperative listed prices for everything, from groceries in bulk, to overalls and ladies' hats. Other early issues included book reviews, short stories, and profiles of great American socialists. An example was a long piece about Victor L. Berger of Milwaukee, the first socialist to serve in Congress.[18]

For the entire lifespan of *The Masses*, editors begged for contributions from their readers. In the course of making their pleas, they highlighted good early reactions from prominent readers. A letter from socialist leader Eugene Debs exemplifies the way that supportive mail was used as a sales tactic:

"What Eugene Debs says about us"
The first number of *The Masses* has just reached me and I congratulate you on its splendid appearance. . . . Earnestly hoping *The Masses* may meet, as I believe it will, a cordial reception wherever it finds its way and that our comrades and friends will all do their share to help it reach the masses whose cause it has come to champion.[19]

THE MASSES

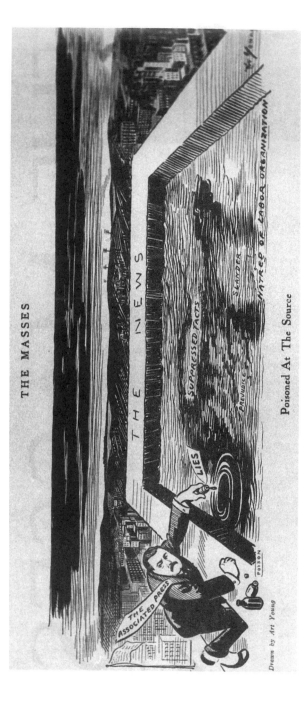

THE ASSOCIATED PRESS

THE NEWS

LIES

SUPPRESSED FACTS

SLANDER

PREJUDICE

HATRED OF LABOR ORGANIZATION

POISON

Drawn by Art Young

Poisoned At The Source

These types of letters, paired with appeals for funds, were a regular feature of the magazine, which was always struggling to stay afloat financially.

The outstanding feature of *The Masses,* and what gave it its unique tone, was its devotion to comic art and portraiture. Satiric cartoons by Art Young, John Sloan, Robert Minor, and others were highly stylized, complex, and sharply critical of American institutions. The press was one favorite target for the cartoonists, and they often portrayed newspaper magnates as tyrants, afraid of truths that might damage their empires. Although none of the cartoonists received pay for their *Masses* work, the freedom to draw whatever they wanted to was an attraction for many. The editors appreciated whatever the artists had to offer, usually without suggestions for revision. Young wrote in his memoirs: "With Vlag there was no haggling over the way in which I had interpreted an idea. It was up to me, and I felt that an audience was waiting to see what would be in the next issue. For the first time in my life I could cut loose and express my own unhampered point of view."[20]

Eastman, Young, and *The Masses* faced their first lawsuit over a cartoon, published in the July 1913 issue. The cartoon (along with editorials) accused the Associated Press of purposefully distorting reports of a West Virginia coal miners' strike by omitting certain crucial pieces of information. That the federal government had enforced martial law at the Virginia site, and that the coal company had hired its own army to fight the strikers, all went unreported in the mainstream press. A few other journals had charged the AP with distorting the labor struggle, but the news service chose to sue *The Masses.*[21] The AP eventually dropped the lawsuit, but *The Masses* editors used the suit to further their cause. While the suit was still pending, for example, they organized a mass meeting about free speech at Cooper Union to raise money. The fact that the AP sued *The Masses* and then dropped the suit signaled that the magazine had truly arrived: The journal was thought to be influential, or at least had become a contender in the world of publishing. That the suit was dropped legitimated *The Masses'* charges. Why would the AP stop legal proceedings if it felt it had covered the strike properly?

Figure 4.2. The Associated Press sued *The Masses* for libel in 1913. This cartoon by Art Young, and an Eastman editorial, both of which accused the AP of suppressing important facts about a West Virginia coal strike, were the basis for the AP's case. Published in *The Masses,* July 1913.

The art that appeared in *The Masses* achieved its satiric power by juxtaposing portraits of the working poor with amusing captions. Many of the artists drew their pictures of streetlife, or of confrontations between labor and management, and allowed the editors (Eastman or Floyd Dell) to make up captions for their work. Others, like Young, worked socialist commentary into their cartoons, so captions were unnecessary. This arrangement, between editor and artist, worked smoothly until 1916 when John Sloan and a number of younger artists held a "strike" against Eastman and Dell over the issue of captions. The artists argued that their art was being diluted or misrepresented by the captions: The work should speak for itself, without the editorial help of Eastman. The artists also objected to what they saw as a developing "policy" by *The Masses'* editors. They thought that Eastman had become too powerful in guiding the magazine and choosing its content. Although Eastman at that point was ready to leave the magazine and even tried to tender his resignation, the strike was short-lived. As it turned out, Eastman notes in his memoirs, the artists were not particularly serious in their efforts to regain control of the magazine. A few left, but most stayed and many new, talented artists were recruited.[22]

The only lasting effect of the artists' strike was a new label for the type of art one found in *The Masses* – the "Ashcan School." In an interview with *The New York Sun*, Young said that the striking artists just wanted "to run pictures of ash cans and girls hitching up their skirts in Horatio Street – regardless of ideas – and without title."[23] The art of the Ashcan School (a name the artists disliked, but couldn't seem to shake) was characterized by a gritty realism in its subject matter and its technique. The most popular subjects were the destitute, the working poor, or the decaying urban landscape of lower Manhattan. The artists drawn to *The Masses* were disturbed by the conditions in New York, and found that glossy art magazines and mainstream newspapers weren't interested in these sorts of portraits. Most were line drawings that used a combination of thick crayon and thin pen strokes. In fact, *The Masses* pioneered this drawing technique in America, as it had been used only in French newspapers prior to the publication of Eastman's journal.[24]

Though they often found it difficult to summarize the fundamental tenets of their artistic style, *The Masses'* artists emphasized the importance of artistic experimentation in the service of socialism. Young was the most bluntly socialistic in his artistic intentions. He said, "I do not care to be connected with a publication that does not try to point the way out of a sordid materialistic world."[25] Although there was some ambivalence about who they were as artists and political actors, all the members of the Ashcan School knew that they were onto something new, artistically and spiritually. As Robert Minor put it,

Just as preachers are discarding two of their three gods, as ladies are discarding cumbersome styles of corsets; as men don't wear suspenders any more, having seen that belts are sufficient to hold their trousers up . . . cartoonists are discarding affections of technique. . . . There has been a change in the newspaper field lately. Newspapers are becoming more sincere. It is but natural that cartoons would become direct, less superficial, less "stylish," more natural. . . . Of course there is more of art in the new way [of drawing] . . . partly because America is getting old enough to demand and have some art.[26]

Interestingly, although the artists usually chose the working poor as their subject, they knew that there was a great distance between themselves and the people they portrayed in *The Masses*. Most of those who served on the board of the magazine, and those who contributed, were from middle- or upper-middle-class backgrounds, and generally preferred to mingle with bohemians and socialists of their own class. This is not to say that they looked down on the working class: They simply believed that they could help the poor most by challenging the status quo through writing and art. *The Masses* intended to change the political system, and to do that, its contributors concluded, it was not necessary to befriend the proletarian. With the exception of John Reed, who really did fraternize with workers in Paterson, and in the other labor disputes he covered, many of the artists felt as John Sloan did:

As for myself, I never felt the desire to mingle with the people I painted, but observed life as a spectator rather than participant. I think this is the way of the artist who sees and interprets through sympathy. . . . I saw people living in the streets and on the rooftops of the city: and I liked their fine animal spirits. I never pitied them, or idealized them, or sought to propagandize about poverty. I felt with them but I did not think for them. . . . Sympathy with people, I am all for that, but not ideology.[27]

In this quote we detect the contradictory sentiment that led to the writers' strike – the feeling that the lives of the poor should be dramatically improved, and the distaste for ideology of any kind. Openly socialist *Masses* contributors, like Eastman, Dell, Young, Reed, and others shaped the magazine throughout its short life, although artists like Sloan felt uncomfortable with Marxian jargon or what they called "policy."

In the first volume, while Vlag was still editor of *The Masses,* the magazine's brand of socialism was rather vague. *The Masses* was "on the side of workers," but it wasn't clear how the journal's intent and ideas coincided with existing labor movements. Although the magazine strongly supported the cooperative store notion (Vlag's pet project), its ideology was not nearly as refined or coherent as it would become under Eastman. The editors of the early issues were sincerely interested in how readers conceptualized socialism, and often admitted their own confusion. In a May 1911 article entitled "The Superiority of Socialism," for example, Joseph N. Cohen wrote the following:

We must . . . pause here and tell what is meant by Socialism. That is a hard nut to crack. . . . It will suffice to say that socialism is, first of all, the movement of those who want to solve the bread and butter problem in a manner satisfactory to the great bulk of people. . . . So, whatever will make for better living among the diggers and delvers, is of prime importance to the Socialist movement and party. . . . [28]

Much of the early writing about socialism in the magazine took the form of a watered-down Marxism, centered around the alienation of workers. In an unsigned piece labeled "Do you like your work?" readers were encouraged to correspond with the magazine about their unhappy employment situations: "Out of every thousand people in the world only one works at the occupation for which he is best fitted. Millions of people are popularly charged as 'failures,' because they have never found the occupation for which they are best fitted."[29]

The incomplete and unsophisticated understanding of Marxism that characterized Vlag's editorial vision changed when Eastman took charge of *The Masses.* Far more academically inclined than Vlag had been, Eastman sought to promote socialism, but to avoid heavy-handed polemics. He wrote in his first issue as editor, in December of 1912, that "We are opposed to the dogmatic spirit which creates and sustains [factional] disputes [within the Socialist party]. Our appeal will be to the masses, both Socialist and non-Socialist, with entertainment, education, and the livelier kinds of propaganda."[30] Eastman's greatest accomplishment was the development of a new form of socialist writing – one that backed revolutionary action, but never took itself too seriously. The magazine was so flip and so ironic that uncontrolled polemics and dogmatic Marxism simply had no place. Although some socialists of the period believed the magazine was useless in furthering the Socialist party, an intelligent, critical form of socialism was the only type that Eastman, his writers, and his artists, could promote. The magazine maintained its mix of ideology, self-reflexivity, and humor until it shut down in 1917.

THE MASSES AND PREWAR AMERICAN CULTURE

Through editorials, graphic art, poetry, letters to the editor, and book reviews, *The Masses* addressed almost all of the important economic, political, and social issues facing America from 1911 through 1917. Yet there were particular issues and debates that remained central to the magazine. Among these issues were the status of American laborers, feminism, birth control, the socialization of children, lynching of blacks in the south, psychoanalysis, the role of the church in America, and foreign policy. In this section and the next, I'll describe how the magazine approached some of these controversial topics.

One of the first crusades of the early *Masses*, besides the cooperative movement, was its attack on the Boy Scouts, founded just a few years earlier. The Boy Scout movement was a starting point for *The Masses'* editors to elaborate their ideas about pacifism – a theme that would resurface in a much stronger and more cultivated style during the war. In the days before both world wars, before the rise of the Nazis, and the Vietnam War, *The Masses* was one of the earliest and most compelling voices of pacifism. When there was an opportunity to speak to pacifism, in any context, the magazine took it. An assault on a youth organization might seem a bit trivial from a contemporary vantage point, but the editors believed the Boy Scouts to be a quintessential American institution. Because the Scouts defined the mainstream, and also embodied American manhood at its best, it was a fine target for the early *Masses*: With such assaults, the magazine began to develop its rhetorical approach – critical, ironic, and concerned with peace. In the second issue of *The Masses*, one writer outlined the case against the Scouts:

The Boy Scout movement is an organized, craftily subsidized effort for creating the kill-lust in boys, the love of arms, the desire for military life, and the brainlessly automatic obedience of soldiers. . . . The pretense – of course there is some fine pretense – is that "the boys are to be physically developed." . . . While the boys are to be physically developed they are to have their intellects ossified and their sociability suffocated. A boy scout is an incipient assassin, a budding jingo, a germinating butcher of men – a boy, innocent and excellent fruit of love, being transformed into a blood-lusting fool and tool to serve in the great class struggle as an iron fist for the employer class against the working class.[31]

Here the author attacks the Scouts from several angles, while questioning the value of nationalism, war, and violence. This and other articles about the Boy Scouts were quite well reasoned, although they were sprinkled with hyperbole about class struggle from time to time. Why couldn't working-class boys join the Scouts, we wonder? It's as if in attacking a mainstream institution, the author felt the need to tie back the assault to the socialist roots of the magazine, regardless of the relevance of class.

As the magazine grew and developed, its opposition to militarism, and indeed to masculinity as conventionally defined, became even more strident. As we shall soon see, femininity – which embodied the values of equality, peace, and freedom – was often celebrated through editorializing, fiction, and graphic art. In direct response to the Boy Scouts, though, the editors decided to start a boy's movement of their own – the Socialist Boy Scouts. In ironic ads on the back cover of the magazine, boys were encouraged to sell $10 of subscriptions to *The Masses*. For their efforts they would receive either (a) five copies of "*War – What For?*" by George R. Kirkpatrick; (b) a five-piece Socialist Boy Scout Suit; or (c) the Kirkpatrick book plus two others – *The Spy* by Maxim Gorky and *Socialism and Success* by W. J. Ghent.[32]

The anti-Scout campaign was short-lived, as the magazine started to sharpen its focus on labor issues. In April of 1911 W. J. Ghent wrote about the need for good workman's compensation laws. He argued that although many foreign nations had such laws, the United States was far behind them. Ghent called for all socialists to campaign for compensation legislation, so that American laborers might be afforded some protection from their employers by the government. By 1913, *The Masses* had greatly expanded its coverage of labor issues. By then, articles, short fiction, and letters to the editor were devoted to publicizing horrific working conditions in a variety of industries. The generalized cause of the working person, and the goals of men like Bill Haywood of the I.W.W. became pivotal themes of the magazine. Even poetry about child labor, such as this nursery rhyme spoof by "M.F.," found its way into the magazine:

Mother Gooselet

Little Tommy Tucker works for his supper,
His breakfast and his dinner,
And his clothes and shoes and such.
Little Tommy's wage is
Small because his age is.
A little eight year older
Ain't entitled to earn much.

Graphic art and cartoons about labor were omnipresent. They were used to punctuate stories about labor disputes and issues, or were published on their own. Most emphasized the mistreatment of laborers by management or portrayed the dreary everyday lives of workers (see Figure 4.3, for example). Often Eastman or Dell wrote captions for the drawings in ethnic dialect, to underscore the fact that so many immigrants constituted the American working class.

Perhaps the best, most dramatic writings on labor ever published by *The Masses* were John Reed's articles on the Paterson, New Jersey labor strike. Reed had arrived in New York in the spring of 1911, and after a while, became a regular contributor. In 1913 Reed visited Mabel Dodge's salon, heard I.W.W. leader Bill Haywood describe the silk workers strike in Paterson, and became obsessed with the struggle. He began to make regular trips to New Jersey, to see for himself the confrontations between striking workers and the police. During one trip in April of 1913, he spoke to striking workers on the porch of one of the workers' homes, and was arrested along with the other men. He spent four days in jail, during which he learned more about the reasons for the strike – low pay, maltreatment by management, and the like.[33] For *The Masses*, he wrote compelling articles describing the scene in Paterson, where police beat and arrested strikers without provocation. By June of 1913, Reed had become a labor

Drawn by Arthur Young.

"I, GORRY, I'M TIRED!"

"THERE YOU GO! YOU'RE TIRED! HERE I BE A-STANDIN' OVER A HOT STOVE ALL DAY, AN' YOU WURKIN' IN A NICE COOL SEWER!"

organizer, speaking to large crowds of striking workers, leading them in song, and organizing a play in Madison Square Garden that described and celebrated their struggle.[34] More than that, he had become friends with many of the largely Italian workers, and had grown to respect the strike's courageous leaders. Reed wrote in the romantic, personal style that he would use in his subsequent chronicle of the Russian Revolution, *Ten Days That Shook the World*:

We saw a young woman with an umbrella, who had been picketing, suddenly confronted by a big policeman.

"What the hell are *you* doing here?" he roared. "God damn you, you go home!" and he jammed his club against her mouth. "I *no* go home!" she shrilled passionately, with blazing eyes. "You bigga stiff!"[35]

Labor was not the only downtrodden group whose cause *The Masses* took up. The magazine devoted considerable space to civil rights for women and African-Americans. The writing on black lynching in the south, and the plight of black workers was powerful at times – so strong that it shares characteristics with radical black rhetoric of the civil rights movement. After well-publicized lynchings, *The Masses* would react quickly and vigorously. Here, in an unsigned article entitled, "Niggers and Nightriders," *The Masses* had advice for blacks forced to migrate north:

White men of Northern Georgia have banded together in a conspiracy to drive out the negroes. They slink out at night and paste threats of death on the doors of black families – death if they aren't out of the country in twenty-four hours. . . . We believe there will be less innocent blood and misery spread over the history of the next century, if the black citizens arise and demand respect in the name of power. . . . If the Negroes were to drive the white men out of Northern Georgia, or some other section of the country, it would go far nearer to a solving of the race problem than this homeless and destitute migration of good citizens from one unwelcome to another.[36]

Yet the editors of *The Masses*, despite what were probably good intentions, were ambivalent about blacks. They seemed to move back and forth between two positions – righteous indignation about the treatment of African-Americans (especially in the south), and the worst sort of racist stereotyping. The cartoonists and artists on several occasions portrayed

Figure 4.3. This cartoon, by Art Young, was typical of *The Masses*, which regularly portrayed working-class troubles in a humorous light. Published in *The Masses*, May 1913.

Drawn by John Sloan.

RACE   SUPERIORITY

Figure 4.4. This cartoon by John Sloan captures the ambivalent attitudes of some *Masses* artists, who often spoke out against racism, but found it difficult to abandon their own racist stereotypes. Published in *The Masses*, June 1913. Courtesy of the Beinecke Library, Yale University.

blacks as noble savages or primitives. In one particularly confused drawing by John Sloan, white southerners are portrayed as pathetic drones headed for the factory. As they pass, a black boy sits unperturbed on a fence, enjoying a watermelon (see Figure 4.4). Why would Sloan depict the child in such a manner, given the grim economic and political status of southern blacks? It is likely that Sloan hadn't given much thought to the fact that stereotypes, despite good intentions, reinforce racism on a very fundamental level. *The Masses*' written word about blacks was oriented around emancipation, but pictorially, the magazine was slow in understanding racial discrimination.

When it came to the role of women, *The Masses'* editors, writers, and artists were far more sophisticated and humane. The women's suffrage movement was already well under way by the time the magazine appeared, and many women served the magazine as owners, writers, and poets. In general, the magazine glorified women and femininity, often linking the advancement of women to the advancement of socialism and the achievement of enlightenment. Women, as a class, could do no wrong in the eyes of *The Masses'* editors, writers, and graphic artists. In his analysis of the magazine, Leslie Fishbein argues that both Eastman and Dell idolized their own mothers, and that their admiration affected how the magazine viewed women. Although these sorts of links between one's socialization and his or her work are always difficult to prove, the argument seems plausible. Eastman's mother was an extremely strong-willed woman, who raised several children after her husband died. Although she loved her children, Eastman's mother always yearned "to *be something*."[37] She eventually became a minister – a rare job for a woman in Elmira, New York during the late nineteenth century. So from early childhood, Eastman realized just how capable, intelligent, and ambitious women could be. Dell had much the same kind of admiration for his own mother: He lovingly describes her interest in his intellectual development in his memoir, *Homecoming*.[38]

The Masses fought hard for women's suffrage, at times tying it to socialism, and at other times speaking to the issue in a more conventional manner. Many editorials and letters argued that women should not be treated as if they were the property of men: Women could and should speak for themselves.[39] Giving women the vote was the first step toward granting them equal political and economic citizenship. Some of the most fiery writing reinforced the relationship of socialism and feminism, as this 1911 editorial by Josephine Kaneko exemplifies:

There are two significant movements in the world to-day – that of the working class for economic freedom, and that of the woman for political freedom. . . . That the slavery of the workingman, and the double slavery of women, has been essential in the upbuilding of the present social forms, seems evident. . . . When the woman of the working class . . . has learned the necessity of economic freedom as well as of political freedom, then shall we see the beginning of the end of human slavery.[40]

The Masses did not privilege the women's suffrage issue over socialism, but viewed the two as inextricably intertwined aspects of social reform. Men connected to the magazine seemed to believe that the fight for women's liberties would benefit them as well. Eighty years before the American "men's movement," the men who wrote for *The Masses* realized that they too were victims of oppressive sex roles: If women were free to pursue their own desires, men would be free to abandon the traditional confines of masculinity, and explore alternative lifestyles.

All proper "rules of polite behavior" for women were dismissed as bourgeois nonsense by the magazine. Political and economic freedom were central causes championed by the magazine from its earliest issues, but social and sexual freedom were thought to be equally critical. In what must be one of the earliest American discussions of sexual harassment in the workplace, for example, *The Masses* published a drawing of a heavy, cigar-smoking businessman leering at his attractive, young secretary. Underneath the picture was the following caption:

The Brainy Business Man enjoys a bargain in women. Considering the over supply of women who are looking for jobs a bargain in this commodity is not hard to find. A great deal of rot is talked about the divorce evil and the social evil and the sweating of women workers and similar topics. If women were made economically independent these things would settle themselves automatically, and many a Brainy Business Man without any Back to his Head would settle down into his proper sphere – whatever that is.[41]

That women were trapped, socially and sexually, was obvious to *The Masses* crowd. Articles and editorials about reproductive rights appeared often in the pages of the magazine. For years *The Masses* included pieces celebrating the efforts of Emma Goldman and Margaret Sanger to educate people about birth control, and to distribute birth control devices. In the typical issue, there were a variety of advertisements for books and periodicals about sex and birth control: *Problems of Sex*, written by two college professors, *The Brownsville Birth Control Clinic*, by a social worker affiliated with Margaret Sanger, and Margaret Sanger's two books, *What Every Woman Should Know* and *What Every Girl Should Know*. One could find many of these publications at the Masses Book Shop on West 14th Street. One book, *The Sexual Crisis* by Grete Meisel-Hess, claimed to be "A social and psychologic study that solves many apparently baffling problems of sexual radicalism. . . . It is the Magna Carta of the *new* woman's movement."[42] *The Masses'* editors, taking their lead from Goldman and Sanger, argued that birth control was critical for three reasons: It enabled women to pursue careers outside the home, it made recreational sex possible and thereby allowed women to engage in it more often, and it gave women a sense of control over their own destinies. *The Masses* was one of the few magazines of the period brave enough to publicize Sanger's controversial crusade. The editors helped her raise money, educate the public, and sell books.

Birth control was not the only sexual subject that *The Masses* focused upon. The magazine was a pioneer in the popularization of Freudian theory, since very few Americans were familiar with notions from psychoanalysis in the days before the war. Whether *The Masses'* writers and editors understood Freud's ideas is unclear. They seemed to have a very confused and superficial interpretation of many parts of the theory, and it is not evident that any of the writers studied Freud very rigorously at all. How the theory fit with other ideas promoted in the magazine – socialism, women's liberation, and so forth – went largely unaddressed.[43] Yet their rudimentary (and often faulty) understanding of Freud didn't stop *The Masses'* writers from using the language of psychoanalysis liberally in the pages of the magazine. Eastman, in his memoirs, is so taken by Freudian analysis that he often seems to divide history into two periods – before Freud and after Freud.[44]

In general, the editors of *The Masses* fought all that they considered "bourgeois" – from mindless religiosity (they were antichurch, but pro-Christianity) to gender roles. Eastman and his colleagues responded to government policies and to current events, while at the same time, they played a proactive role in furthering socialist ideas. The rebelliousness of the text and graphics was vehement, despite the lack of coherence in some of the editors' positions. The most serious crusade *The Masses* undertook during its short life was a rejection of the war effort. This was the magazine's most impassioned battle, and the one that eventually destroyed it.

WORLD WAR I AND THE DEMISE
OF *THE MASSES*

The Masses had always been a pacifist journal. Since its earliest crusade – against the paramilitaristic Boy Scouts – the editors maintained a vague antiwar sensibility. With the outbreak of war in Europe in 1914, and the declaration of war by the United States in 1917, *The Masses* began a tireless campaign against American involvement in the conflict. Through December of 1917, when *The Masses* was forced to close, Eastman, Reed, Young, and other contributors used every argument they could think of to demean the war effort. Though the editors were simply exercising their right to free speech, prowar sentiment was so fierce, and patriotism ran so high, that *The Masses* became a central target in the government's censorship effort.

Beyond their general pacifism, there were several reasons why the editors believed America should stay out of what they believed was a European conflict. For one, the writers could discern no justification for entering the war, because even an American victory would be meaningless. Eastman, in a June 1917 editorial titled, "Advertising Democracy," argued that the war effort was akin to a public relations campaign. He feared that we would not democratize European nations, and in the heat of the war, would turn America into a jingoistic police state – complete with censorship:

It is not a war for democracy. It did not originate in a dispute about democracy, and it is unlikely to terminate in a democratic settlement. There is a bare possibility that a victory of the Allies will hasten the fall of the autocracies in Central Europe, but there is a practical certainty that in trimming for such a victory the Allies will throw out most of the essence of their own democracy. We will Prussianize ourselves, and we will probably not democratize Prussia.[45]

The Masses staff hypothesized that intelligent, thoughtful people shared their beliefs about the lack of justification to enter the war. They often appealed to the nebulous entity of "public opinion" to legitimate their arguments: *The Masses* spoke for the masses, who were largely pacifists like the editors themselves.

Some of these arguments about the war took the form of attacks on *The New Republic*, which supported the war effort. Eastman accused *The New Republic* of mindless imperialism, despite its "proper" stands on radical issues like birth control and labor strikes. *The New Republic*'s editors, Eastman wrote, "seem to have been seized with a highly intellectualized lust for bloody combat."[46] In June of 1917, Eastman stepped up his critique of the liberal magazine by demonstrating how little its editors understood about economics. *The New Republic*, Eastman wrote, gave intellectual and moral justification to a war that was, very simply, in the best economic interest of the ruling elite. Eastman craftily employed some data that *The New Republic* used to attract advertisers in order to make his point: Among the magazine's subscribers were directors of 1,214 "important" New York companies and one-third of the members of the New York Social Register. Furthermore, a quarter of *New Republic* subscribers owned a car worth at least $2,500. The "intellectual class" who subscribe to *The New Republic* might support the war, Eastman posited, but that "'intellectuality' (for most people) costs money."[47]

John Reed was as fervently against the war as Eastman was, and wrote several editorials on the subject. In "Whose War?" Reed argued that the war was intended to benefit the wealthy, not the average workingman. He believed that the war would be a financial boon to capitalists, pointing out how far the stock market climbed with the American declaration of war. Reed especially feared the patriotic zeal breaking out in New York, and worried about censorship. He wrote,

War means an ugly mob-madness, crucifying the truth-tellers, choking the artists, side-tracking reforms, revolutions, and the working of social forces. Already in America those citizens who opposed the entrance of their country into the European melée are called "traitors," and those who protest against the curtailing of our meagre rights of free speech are spoken of as "dangerous lunatics." . . . The press is howling for war. The church is howling for war. Lawyers, politicians, stock-brokers, social leaders are all howling for war.[48]

The Masses repeatedly underscored the notion that strong supporters of the war were not members of the working class, but either capitalists or intellectuals who had been co-opted by the "money men." Editors at the magazine worried about the number of casualities that the United States would suffer, since soldiers were putting their lives in danger for upper-class interests and not for their own.

The magazine's editors saw patriotism as a religion of sorts, believing that people during this period were looking for something to believe in – something on which they could focus their passion and their energy. *The Masses* had always criticized organized religion, so the writers were able to draw parallels between what they saw as the absurdity of religion and the absurdity of war. Eastman wrote a long editorial on the subject in July of

1917, making much of the support for the war among Christian ministers: "They have repressed so much more personal spleen, as a matter of professional necessity, than the rest of us, that they let go all the more violently into the national spout."[49] Support for the war, Eastman believed, was part of a constellation of bourgeois attitudes – righteousness among them. From his perspective, people seemed unable to reason about the justification for war thoughtfully or rationally, and automatically rallied around the president. That the war was a fight for democracy seemed to *The Masses* editor a sham: The United States was acting like an imperial power, intent on controlling foreign events more than spreading the ideals of equality and freedom.

Eventually, the impassioned antiwar sentiment of *The Masses* became too much for the government to withstand. Federal officials singled out the August 1917 issue to make its case against the magazine. Among the items in the journal that month were an editorial about peace by Floyd Dell, a tribute to Emma Goldman by Josephine Bell, a cartoon by Young mocking the war effort (see Figure 4.5), a collection of letters written by British conscientious objectors, and a petition for the repeal of the conscription law. The petition, which readers were encouraged to clip and send to the president, contained statistics about antiwar sentiment: straw votes and referenda from Wisconsin, Massachusetts, and Minnesota demonstrating that the large majority of Americans objected to the war. The petition stated that *the people* never endorsed the war, so why should they go? These magazine items, along with some sarcastic tidbits about the ridiculous nature of the war effort (American flags made of diamonds, rubies, and sapphires were on sale at a Fifth Avenue jeweler), were not atypical for *The Masses*. Yet during 1917, the federal government and local officials had become very concerned with internal dissent about the war effort.

The editors brought the August issue to the post office for mailing in early July. But the solicitor of the Post Office and the attorney general, who had seen an advance copy, deemed the magazine a violation of the Espionage Act. At issue were eight items from the magazine – four drawings and four written pieces. A lawyer for *The Masses* argued before Judge Learned Hand that this sort of censorship was illegal. Hand agreed, writing that the magazine fell "within the scope of that right to criticise, either by temperate reasoning or by immoderate and indecent invective."[50]

Figure 4.5. This cartoon, by Art Young, was part of the federal government's case against *The Masses*. Published in *The Masses*, September 1917.

Hand's decision was then overturned by the Court of Appeals for the Second Circuit. The September, October, and December issues could not be mailed according to government regulations, claimed the postmaster, since the absence of an August issue meant that *The Masses* was no longer a monthly magazine. Because sales on newsstands could not sustain the magazine, the December issue was its last.

In April 1918, the government accused five *Masses* contributors of conspiring to block military enlistment. There was a jury trial, which gave Dell and Eastman the opportunity to publicize their cause. They made speeches for the judge and jury, but their real audience was the public. Although all the defendants faced serious prison terms, they were undeterred, and put an enormous amount of energy and emotion into the trial. Their views on the war, on pacifism and conscription, but also on the class struggle, all received considerable attention in the press. Floyd Dell joked in 1918 that,

I had always secretly felt that my opinions were of a certain importance. It appeared that the government agreed with me. And a government does not do things by halves: It had provided a spacious room, and a special and carefully selected audience of twelve men, who were under sworn obligation to sit and listen to me. Under such circumstances it was naturally a pleasure to tell the government what I thought about war, militarism, conscientious objectors and other related subjects.[51]

The humor that had always characterized the text of *The Masses* found its way into the courtroom as well. Art Young, who had a tendency to fall asleep during the trial, was called upon to defend his cartoon, "Having Their Fling" (Figure 4.5). When asked why he drew a devil conducting the orchestra, Young responded, "Well, since General Sherman described war as Hell, it seemed to me appropriate that the Devil should lead the band."[52] During the trial, which was long and held in a hot stuffy room, Young passed the time by drawing caricatures of all the defendants, attorneys, and jurors. Though ten jurors voted to convict *The Masses* group, two disagreed, and the defendants were set free.

A second trial, also for conspiracy, was held in October 1918, but again resulted in a divided jury and dismissal of the case. Judge Hand had never believed *The Masses* was seditious, and some members of the public (including several stubborn jurors) felt the same way. A few historians have speculated that the magazine's contributors were saved by their good educational backgrounds and their ethnicity. Perhaps things might have gone differently if *The Masses* defendants hadn't been so well spoken and well mannered: Many people did serve prison terms for sedition during this period. As a staffer in the District Attorney's office said about the defendants after one of the trials, "You are Americans. You *looked* like Americans. . . . You can't convict an American for sedition before a New York judge."[53]

After *The Masses* closed down, Max Eastman and his sister started up another magazine called *The Liberator*. Many of *The Masses* crowd contributed fiction, editorials, and artwork to the new magazine. *The Liberator* published reports of events in the Soviet Union, and eventually merged with the *Workers Monthly* out of financial necessity. Despite the desire of some artists and writers to resuscitate the old *Masses*, they were unsuccessful in their attempts at reorganization.[54] Another magazine with a similar title, *The New Masses*, was published from 1926 through 1948. Although the editors of *The New Masses* claimed that it was a continuation of *The Masses*, this is far from the truth: *The New Masses* was a polemical magazine, in thrall to the Communist Party.[55]

THE MASSES, COMMUNITY, AND PUBLIC EXPRESSION

The central theme of this book concerns the creation of alternative public space – arenas for political discourse and action that lie parallel to mainstream public life. In previous chapters, I explored the ways that bourgeois women of the eighteenth century and black Chicagoans created their own political spheres, since their ideas and their grievances were rarely acknowledged by those in power. In the case of *The Masses*, the cast of characters is different: Those who wrote for the magazine were largely from "proper" middle-class families and tended to be well educated. Yet their ideas, which hardly seem radical to us almost eighty years later, branded them as political outcasts. Their marginality began with the publication of *The Masses*, but was concretized and dramatized by the sedition trials of 1917 and 1918. Not only did these men and women hold nonnormative social and political ideals, but they were also labeled as traitors by their own government.

Greenwich Village itself was the parallel public sphere in which Eastman, Dell, Young, Reed, and the other *Masses* writers and illustrators developed their ideas and talents. The Village was a place to which social-

Figure 4.6. Max Eastman (third from left) and colleagues outside of the New York court-house where they were indicted under the Espionage Act. Left to right: Crystal Eastman, Art Young, Eastman, Morris Hillquit, Merrill Rogers, and Floyd Dell. The photo was taken in May of 1918. Courtesy of the National Archives.

ists, anarchists, and bohemians of all sorts gravitated in the early years of the twentieth century. Rents were cheap, and one could find a unique forum for free expression there. Floyd Dell, who came to New York from Chicago, found community in the Village. His memories of the area, although somewhat romantic, are corroborated by many of *The Masses'* writers:

My friends and I often talked about what the Village meant. It was more than a place where there were cheap rents; more than a place where struggling artists and writers lived. It was more, and less, than a place where people were free to "be themselves." It was, among other things, very conspicuously to an insider, a place where people came to solve some of their life problems. . . . People who found in themselves inadequate emotional motives for sticking to their jobs or their marriages in the outside world, and were cracking under the strain, dropped everything and came here, found peace and tolerance, and a chance to discover what they were like and could do.[56]

The Village wasn't paradise, as Dell and others have noted. Many of the same problems Villagers had fled, plagued them in lower Manhattan as well – broken love affairs, alienating work, depression, and the like. Yet there is no doubt that the Village was a place for those who were different, and those who liked to experiment. Eastman and his circle spoke often and loudly about "living life to its fullest" and ignoring nonsensical social and political conventions. These feelings – that life was short, and mainstream life oppressive – were shared by the men and women who devoted an extraordinary amount of time to *The Masses.*

Interestingly, Dodge's salon – so similar in character to the more liberal eighteenth-century salons – was at the center of Village intellectual life during the days before the war. At Mabel Dodge's apartment, artists, Wobblies, poets, anarchists, birth control advocates, and others met to discuss what meant the most to them: love, work, and politics. It was partly through the salon that Villagers figured out who they were as a group, and discussed the character of life out of the mainstream. *The Masses,* which was already two years old before Dodge opened her salon, was already defining a new sort of public space for political expression. Dodge's salon accelerated these community-building efforts, even though it closed years before *The Masses* sedition trials forced the magazine out of business. Good salons become a place for creative expression, heated discussion, and the exchange of new ideas. They are also places that build intellectual and political community, and that is exactly what Dodge's New York salon encouraged.

How did *The Masses'* editors resonate with and nurture the community of "outsiders" already in the Village? There were several ways: through its advertisements, text, and its editorial practices.

To my knowledge, most literary critics, historians, and others who have evaluated *The Masses* have failed to scrutinize the fascinating advertisements that appeared at the back of most issues. Interspersed between ads for books and political groups are an enormous number of announcements for parties and activities for radicals, socialists, and bohemians. One such ad in the July 1911 issue attempted to recruit people for a boat trip on the Hudson, with refreshments, costumes, and entertainment. The text read,

"Excursion to be pulled off in the Light of the Moon by the Socialist Writers and Artists. And we want you to come. We want you to come even if you live in California or Manila, P.I. And if you live anywhere near New York you've got to come."[57] Another ad from 1917 asked the reader, "Are you a Radical? Whether or not, come to the Greenwich Village Carnival."[58] These and many other ads and announcements emphasized the cohesive nature of Village social life, and underscored the connections between social and political activity among residents. The Rand School Restaurant at 19th street, where Vlag had worked, advertised frequently with illustrations of people dining and talking. A 1911 advertisement for the restaurant read: "This socialist den offers an excellent opportunity for socialist workers to introduce their shopmates during luncheon into socialist circles."[59]

Many of the ads were for products, those one could buy at the cooperative stores, or those one could purchase through the mail. The ads tended to reflect the irony and humor of *The Masses* itself, and at the same time stressed the need for socialists and radicals to stick together – socially, politically, and through what they consumed. The Commonwealth Co-Operative Association of Reading, Pennsylvania advertised their Karl Marx Cigar: "Sumatra wrapper and seed and Havana filler. Made by the SOCIALIST CO-OPERATORS OF READING. All profits used for the Socialist propaganda. Box of 50 by mail $2.00."[60] One could raise a child to be a socialist by buying socialist, as this Brooklyn entrepreneur pointed out to *Masses* readers:

"How To Feed Young Socialists"

Feed them on H. C. Will's Zwieback. The finest food for children. Used in most of the large hospitals. Made by a socialist. Take no other, and demand of your grocer that he will supply you with H. C. Will's Zwieback.[61]

These advertisements implied that the socialist world of the Village, and the broader world of *Masses* readers, were in fact one world. The magazine made it seem as though the socialist world had everything one could want – political discourse, social life, and commerce.

As I mentioned earlier, Vlag and then Eastman both made concerted efforts to reach out to their readers. The editors consistently asked readers how they felt about the magazine, and about the issues of the day. Both men gave the impression that they were open to correspondence and advice, and both did publish a large number of letters, poems, editorials, and jokes sent in by the larger socialist community outside of the Village. Although the locus of intellectual American socialism was in the Village (from the editors' point of view), they were always trying to extend the borders of the community as far as they could. Just as the editors of *The Chicago Defender* tried to make Bronzeville bigger than the south side of the city by appealing to the national black community, *The Masses'* editors attempted to extend the scope of their own socialist "neighborhood."

The manner in which the editorial board ran *The Masses* served as a parable for how they saw the entire socialist movement: There was internal disagreement, but a strong sense of community and purpose. At editorial meetings, Eastman would usually paste up the next issue, while the contributors hung around, eating or talking. There was so much chatter about current affairs, and so little work being done, that visitors to the meetings wondered how the magazine ever got published. The fiction writer Mary Heaton Vorse noted in a letter, "I don't know how their 'Masses' happens every month. It makes one believe in the stories of the little gnomes that come and do your work for you while you are in a trance."[62] The truth is that Eastman and Dell always did most of the work for the magazine, and gave it direction, although they did not entirely dictate its content. The editorial meetings were rituals in the sense that they were regular, rule-governed, and had a great degree of significance for the writers and artists.[63] From their memoirs, it seems, all took pride in what they were doing, despite the fact that they worked for free and often worked inefficiently. Eastman said, for example, that "[John] Sloan loved *The Masses* and would waste time on it in the same childish way I would."[64]

It is clear that *The Masses* served as an important medium of communication for socialists, anarchists, artists, and intellectuals in the Village. There were many other media – Dodge's salon, local restaurants, union meetings, parties, and even other publications. But Eastman's journal was unique in that it consistently published some of the most controversial art and writing of the period. *The Masses* provided an opportunity for alternative expression, since much of the work that appeared in the magazine was rejected or could not even be submitted to a mainstream artistic and literary magazine. John Sloan said, "The strange thing was that if I got a good idea I gave it to *The Masses*. If I got a second-rate one I might sell it to Harper's. . . . [65]

THE MASSES AND PUBLIC OPINION

The young intellectuals of the Village were clearly out of step with American public opinion: They were radicals, many of whom believed in free love, in the coming proletariat revolution, and in the rejection of organized religion. Because the mainstream press was not interested in their more controversial ideas, writers used *The Masses* as their vehicle for opinion expression. At first, the authors and artists worked to entertain and support each other. Yet by the time war broke out in Europe, the contributors were writing as if their audience were America – its policy makers, leaders, and citizens. Whether or not the magazine had an effect on influential leaders like Woodrow Wilson is impossible to determine, but many powerful men in Washington, New York, and Chicago *knew* of *The Masses*. In that respect the magazine was a backchannel of sorts: It wasn't the type of publication cited by the mainstream press or by public speakers. Yet those of a certain intellectual class were at least acquainted with the "little magazines" produced in Greenwich Village. The magazine had a clublike readership, making it somewhat private, but it was publicly advertised and distributed.

Like the editors of *The Chicago Defender*, *The Masses'* editors were guided by two principles simultaneously. They worked to build a community, but also to send a message to America at large. Not surprisingly, *The Masses* made its most significant statements while being sued or prosecuted by powerful institutions. When the Associated Press sued the editors for libel, *The Masses* was suddenly a focus of attention. This concern was brief, though, in comparison to the attention the editors received during the sedition proceedings. When on trial, Eastman and the others used the forum to elaborate their ideas for the public. Although the progress of the war in Europe dominated the headlines in 1918, newspapers like *The New York Times* covered the trial consistently. Among ads for Liberty Bonds, and consumer goods made for the patriotic, were articles about the details of the trial and its progress.

The *Times* reported on the trial in a fairly unbiased manner, presenting the government's case and giving an extraordinary amount of space to the defendants' statements and reactions. On November 7, 1917, when newsdealers refused to sell *The Masses* because of the espionage charges, the newspaper quoted the magazine's business manager (Merrill Rogers) at length. The article closes with Rogers's comment that the postmaster and others were interpreting the Espionage Act to mean that Congress can ban speech it doesn't like: "Congress can prohibit and make unlawful the utterance of any sentiment it chooses. The guarantee of free speech in the Constitution, under this, amounts to practically nothing."[66] When the indictment from the federal grand jury came down twelve days later, the *Times* reported it and described the defendants. The descriptions highlighted the social status and talents of the men, noting that Dell was a literary editor from Chicago, that Rogers had recently graduated from Harvard, and that Young was a cartoonist whose drawings had "appeared in several prominent magazines."[67]

In its coverage of the trial in April of 1918, the *Times* published an article about the difficulty of selecting a jury. One of the defendants' lawyers, Morris Hillquit, used four of his preemptory challenges to dismiss jurors biased against socialists. Dialogue between Hillquit, various jurors, and Judge Hand was published verbatim, and seemed to confirm Hillquit's concerns about finding an unbiased jury. Upon questioning by Judge Hand about whether he could come to a verdict based on the evidence in the case, one juror said, "If the evidence was balanced I think my mind would lean toward conviction because of [the defendants'] faith."[68] In another report on the trial, the newspaper noted that President Wilson and Max Eastman had corresponded during the war. This article seemed to legitimate Eastman as a member of the president's communication and social networks. In a friendly tone, Wilson had written to Eastman,

I wish I could agree with those parts of your letter which concern the other matters we were discussing when you were down here. I think a time of war must be regarded as wholly exceptional and that it is legitimate to regard things which would in ordinary circumstances be innocent as very dangerous to the public welfare. But the line is manifestly exceedingly hard to draw, and I cannot say that I have any confidence that I know how to draw it. I can only say that a line must be drawn, and that we are trying – it may be clumsily, but genuinely – to draw it without fear or favor or prejudice.[69]

Such sympathetic coverage by the *Times* finally enabled Eastman and his colleagues to voice their concerns about the war to the very large and influential readership of the newspaper.[70] Ironically, *The Masses* made its most significant impact when it was already defunct. The magazine had been out of print for four months by the time Eastman and the others were tried.

Beyond the postmaster and the federal government, though, *The Masses* had always had its critics. Right-wing, moderate, and liberal leaders, journalists, and citizens deplored the radical ideas in the magazine. Even some sympathetic liberals like Walter Lippmann turned against the magazine at times. Lippmann, who went through a variety of political metamorphoses in his life, had been a friend of John Reed's at Harvard but thought that his friend had strayed too far left. He wrote in *The New Republic* that Reed

Assumed that all capitalists were fat, bald and unctuous, that reformers were cowardly or scheming, that all newspapers are corrupt. ... He made an effort to believe that the working class is not composed of miners, plumbers, and workingmen generally, but is a fine statuesque giant who stands on a high hill facing the sun.[71]

Although Reed and his crowd accused Lippmann and *The New Republic* of being in thrall to the conservative, Wall Street-backed, "reformers," there is a grain of truth in Lippmann's comments. *The Masses* contributors – Art Young in particular – saw the capitalists as an undifferentiated mass of greedy dangerous individuals. The mainstream press, which was far more ideological and careless in the early years of the twentieth century than it is today, deserved much of the criticism *The Masses* doled out. But the magazine's editors and contributors thought it nearly impossible to find material worth citing from American newspapers. *The Masses* would occasionally engage in silly boasting about its mission, or unsophisticated polemical attacks on the institutions it most despised – the church, the press, and big business. Now and then, despite their humanitarian intentions, *The Masses* would use the very racist or sexist stereotypes they should have rejected.

These criticisms, though, don't detract from the importance of *The Masses'* struggles as important chapters in the history of American public expression. Literary critics, social historians, and art historians have long recognized the significance of the publication for their disciplines, but political scientists and those who study political expression have failed to acknowledge or study the magazine's history and its goals. Not only did *The Masses* help to create a parallel space for radical discourse in Greenwich Village: It opened a channel for alternative political discourse more generally, and served as a model for numerous subsequent publications. How often this or other alternative channels are used depends on the tenor of the times. In America, socialism, anarchy, free love, and the other movements *The Masses* trumpeted are absent during some periods (e.g., the 1950s), but seem to spring up again decades later (e.g., the 1960s and 1970s). This case study, and the others in this book, have purposely focused on *how* these channels are created, what becomes of these media, and what these forums mean to those who erect them.

The next chapter is a contemporary case study in the construction of parallel public space. It concentrates on a state branch of the American Libertarian party, a third party founded in the early 1970s to respond to increasing government intervention in a variety of political and economic domains. Long after I had completed my study of *The Masses*, I began to do some preliminary interviews with Libertarians about their lives and their work. Oddly, in my first interview, a longtime Libertarian compared her political group with the socialists of Greenwich Village. That this informant could make such a comparison on her own, without knowing that I was also studying *The Masses* crowd, confirmed my hunch that the two groups have much in common.[72] It is to the Libertarians – a vibrant, although greatly misunderstood social movement – that I now turn.

5

Contemporary Outsiders:
The Libertarians

Third parties have appeared regularly on the American political land-scape. From the early Know-Nothings and the Free-Soil movements of the nineteenth century, to the New Alliance party of today, a variety of groups have attempted to challenge the mainstream political parties. At times these third parties have gained widespread support: The Progressive party of Theodore Roosevelt, for example, garnered 27 percent of the popular vote in the 1912 presidential election. With Robert LaFollette as their candidate, the Progressives received almost 17 percent of the national vote in 1924. And in 1992, Independent presidential candidate H. Ross Perot made a very strong showing, receiving almost 19 percent of the popular vote.[1] Yet, despite these occasional successes, no third party has been able to survive for very long. Due in part to the hegemony and the flexibility of the larger parties, smaller ones find it difficult to raise money, field candidates for elective office, or receive attention from the mass media. Recent charismatic third-party candidates for the U.S. pres-idency, such as George Wallace, John Anderson, and Ross Perot, attracted large constituencies early in their campaigns, but were unable to establish cohesive parties from this temporary public support.

This chapter describes the ideas, activities, and goals of a small but very active third party in the United States. The Libertarian[2] party is only twenty years old, but its members have worked to create a solid infrastruc-ture for action and communication. For instance, many Libertarian state organizations and foundations publish books and newsletters, establish local clubs, hold annual conventions, and organize petition drives, among other things. All of these activities serve to facilitate contact among mem-bers of the party, and to educate the public at large about the aims of the libertarian movement. The Libertarians are interesting for our purposes, because their marginalization is rooted in uninformed prejudice: Most journalists, policy makers, and citizens do not know what "libertarianism" means, and seem unwilling to find out. For example, not long ago, the conservative newspaper columnist George Will wrote a scathing editorial about the Libertarians, arguing that they weren't a legitimate third party. Although he did not explain why the party was "illegitimate," he called the 1992 Libertarian presidential candidate, Andre Marrou, a "fanatic," and his ideas "frivolous."[3] The Libertarians have even greater recognition and legitimacy problems with the general public. One large scale, systematic study of public attitudes toward the Libertarian party found that only 8 percent of respondents knew what the party stood for. Only 11 percent of those surveyed had a favorable opinion of the party, whereas 74 percent didn't know enough about libertarianism to answer either positively or negatively to the query.[4]

Unfortunately, even though the activities of Libertarians and other third parties are very interesting, academic literature about their behavior is scanty. There are some historical accounts of third parties, documenting the platforms and ideas of groups like the Native American party, or the Progressives.[5] In addition, there are a few empirical studies of historical third parties that correlate census data with voting records in order to discern the demographic nature of third-party support.[6] We also know, from one systematic analysis, that people vote for third-party candidates when they are dissatisfied with the major parties.[7] A recent example is the 1992 candidacy of Ross Perot, who was able to draw upon the disgust of an alienated electorate, and achieve temporary high standing in opinion polls. Despite enormous popular support early on, and plentiful campaign funds, however, Perot was ultimately unsuccessful.

The political science literature sheds some light on why third parties succeed or fail, but rarely addresses the activities and infrastructures these parties build.[8] There is some research on mainstream political activism and social movements, however, that can be applied to the case of third-party activists. For example, Samuel Eldersveld has conducted survey research with mainstream party activists in Detroit, but has also collated studies of political activists undertaken by other social scientists.[9] From his research, Eldersveld concluded that a party "consists of party operatives and campaign workers who are involved in party work for a multiplicity of motives, holding to a variety of role perceptions."[10] In terms of why people become activists, Eldersveld reviewed various studies and concluded that

Only a small group [of activists], in the last analysis, are consistent, bona fide amateurs adhering stubbornly to a set of idealistic and ideological orientations toward politics and working only for such goals. . . . Ideology binds [activists] together into a group of like-minded individuals; but the diversity in views about policy is too great, and ideology is too negligible as a primary motivation to be a strong unifying force.[11]

Eldersveld notes that major party activists get involved because they are socialized into the party by family members (40 percent), are self-starters who became interested in politics as adults (35 percent), or became involved almost by accident (25 percent). As one gets increasingly involved in party work, he argues, ideology becomes less important, and other factors – fun, social networking, and business connections – sustain individuals' involvement.

This work by Eldersveld and other political scientists does not describe the Libertarians very well at all. Almost without exception, they tend to be *highly* ideological, and are mostly "self-starters." As I shall explain, many Libertarians find the party through their extensive reading, and are not recruited in the ways that major party activists are usually drafted.[12] Also, although Libertarians try to get their candidates for the U.S. presidency, the Senate, and other offices on all state ballots, they see themselves as ideological crusaders and educators. Unlike major party activists who try to teach the public about a narrow range of current *issues*, Libertarians have developed an ideological *system* that they broadcast whenever they have an attentive audience. Finally, Libertarians are far less interested in the kinds of professional rewards and patronage benefits that one receives through service to the major parties. Most Libertarians are involved in politics because of their ideological disdain for the two major parties. They believe that libertarianism offers the most logical and humane political philosophy.

In this chapter, I report on a series of in-depth interviews that I conducted with Libertarian activists. With the help of a longtime activist, a research assistant and I were able to recruit twenty members of the Libertarian party of Illinois (LPI), each of whom spoke with us at length in response to a structured set of open-ended queries.[13] Through these interviews, I was able to probe the activists about their work in the party, their motivations, and the communication infrastructures they have created.[14] Here I describe my results, and discuss them in light of this book's themes: how marginal groups create parallel public space, community-building efforts among political outsiders, and the establishment of communication backchannels and environments.

LIBERTARIAN BELIEFS AND ACTIVISM

Currently there are over 10,000 dues-paying members on national Libertarian mailing lists, although many more Americans probably hold particular beliefs, or sets of beliefs, that are libertarian in nature.[15] The national Libertarian party (LP) was founded in 1971 by David Nolan, who was disturbed by a perceived erosion of civil liberties under the Nixon administration. The next year, the LP held its first national convention, and attracted 800 members. In the 1972 election, the LP nominated its first slate of candidates, who appeared on the Colorado and Washington state ballots that November. The ticket, with John Hospers for U.S. president and Tonnie Nathan for vice-president, received 5,000 votes. In the 1976 presidential race, the LP garnered 173,011 votes for its ticket, 921,299 in 1980, 228,314 in 1984, 432,000 in 1988, and 281,805 in 1992.[16] That the party has often gained the necessary number of petition signatures needed to get its candidates on the ballot in different states speaks strongly to the party's commitment, since this is a difficult and time-consuming task. Many states require a very large number of signatures from third parties: 761,714 in California, 73,629 in Maryland, and 58,552 in Oklahoma, for example. Policy makers who support such balloting requirements do so to keep trivial candidates out of serious elections, although such frivolous candidates have not been a problem in states with easy ballot access rules.[17]

It is difficult to generalize about libertarian belief systems, since there is a fair amount of variance within the party. Some Libertarians hold anarchistic ideals, believing in no government at all, whereas others believe that some degree of government intervention is necessary and useful. Many of the Libertarians I spoke with think that government-run court systems and police forces are important, and that the state needs to maintain a minimal armed forces infrastructure for defensive purposes only. Despite disagreement among Libertarians about particular issues, however, there is an enormous amount of consensus – far more than one finds within either the Democratic or Republican parties. In fact, the coherence of libertarian ideology is one of its most notable characteristics. In this way (and in this way only) it is similar to orthodox Marxism and other well-elaborated ideological systems.

Not all libertarians belong to the LP. In fact, members of both major parties hold views similar to the Libertarians on a variety of subjects. For example, the Democratic party upholds abortion rights, and so do the Libertarians, who oppose parental consent laws, waiting periods, and other such abortion restrictions. Similarly, many Republicans and Democrats undoubtedly share the sentiments behind the antitax sections of the Libertarian party platform.

In 1972, John Hospers drafted a Statement of Principles, which effectively captures the group's ideals. It reads:

We hold that all individuals have the right to exercise sole dominion over their own lives, and have the right to live in whatever manner they choose, so long as they do not forcibly interfere with the equal right of others to live in whatever manner they choose. Governments throughout history have regularly operated on the opposite principle, that the State has the right to dispose of the lives of individuals and the fruits of their labor. . . . Where governments exist, they must not violate the rights of any individual: namely, (1) the right to life–accordingly we support prohibition of the initiation of physical force against others; (2) the right to liberty of speech and action–accordingly we oppose all attempts by government to abridge the freedom of speech and press, as well as government censorship in any form; and (3) the right to property–accordingly we oppose all government interference with private property, such as confiscation, nationalization, and eminent domain . . . [18]

A centerpiece of libertarian ideology is the notion of voluntary cooperation in economics and in politics. Libertarians argue that free markets, where they are allowed to flourish, work very well, and that capitalism should be our guiding metaphor when it comes to systems of governance: Globally, hundreds of millions of people cooperate with each other daily to produce goods and services in the name of profit. Libertarians believe that such voluntary networks are evidence that large numbers of citizens can organize themselves – and achieve personal goals – without a centralized authority.

There is no need, Libertarians argue, for government regulation of the marketplace since this sort of intervention and compulsion can lead to more inequity than results under laissez-faire models. Libertarians often point to the subsidization of the tobacco industry in the United States as a case in point. Why should that industry, or any other, receive special treatment from states or the federal government? Tobacco price supports are also contradictory from the standpoint of public health, Libertarians argue: The government tries to educate people not to smoke, via public service announcements and warning labels, while at the same time, supporting tobacco growers financially.

Economic freedom, in the tradition of Milton Friedman, is only one part of the libertarian ideological edifice. Members of the party spend considerable time thinking about and discussing individual rights of many sorts. The Libertarian platform holds, for example, that so-called victimless crimes should not be considered crimes at all, because people have the right to choose the kind of life they want to lead: Drug use, prostitution, suicide, and gambling should all be legal activities. Furthermore, Libertarians argue that laws restricting alcohol sales, the distribution of sexually explicit publications, and homosexual activity should all be repealed immediately. In the realm of judicial practice, they believe strongly in all-volunteer juries, the repeal of gag orders for journalists covering court cases, and also support stringent safeguards for those accused of criminal activity. Libertarians are opposed to all restrictions on gun sales, citing the "right to bear arms" in the Constitution. Finally, the LP is firmly against conscription of any sort, believing in the "abolition of the still-functioning elements of the Selective Service System." A full discussion of these and other beliefs is impossible here, but this is a fair sampling of libertarian stands, drawn from party literature.[19]

Although much Libertarian writing is devoted to contemporary issues, the party frequently notes the parallels between its ideas and the intentions of the Founding Fathers. LP publications highlight Jeffersonian principles whenever possible, and cite the "natural rights" philosophy of John Locke. Reference to the Founding Fathers, the Bill of Rights, and the American Revolution is rhetorically powerful for the Libertarians on several levels. First, citing the framers of the Constitution automatically gives the party a long, proud history. Even though the LP was founded in 1971, arguing that John Locke and Jefferson were libertarian in their beliefs makes the party seem much older. In this way, the LP becomes *traditional*, in the sense that its ideas have been part of American politics and culture for a long time. Beyond history, reference to the Founding Fathers gives a certain air of legitimacy to the party. And finally, this sort of rhetoric pre-empts attacks on libertarianism as somehow "un-American." If the Founding Fathers were, in fact, Libertarians, then the LP should hardly be a threat to Americans or their value system.

David Bergland, Libertarian presidential candidate in the 1984 election, points out that there are several "obstacles to clear thinking" that prevent people from understanding libertarianism.[20] First, he posits, there is the "reification fallacy": As a people we tend to forget that government is an aggregation of people, not an all-powerful, faceless body that decides our fate. If we think of the government as an institution made up of people, we can think more critically about its actions, and feel less intimidated by it, Bergland argues. Another fallacy is something Bergland calls "PANG" – the "People Are No Good" assumption. He explains,

The unstated premise [of the PANG fallacy] is that people are weak, stupid, help-less, incompetent, dishonest, and dangerous to themselves and others. . . . Social Security programs are necessary because people would not otherwise provide for their own future, . . . drug laws are necessary because without them we would be a nation of stoned-out people incapable of doing anything, . . . [and] compulsory school attendance laws are necessary because parents wouldn't bother to educate their children. . . . If the PANG premise were valid, then government personnel making the rules for the rest of us and exercising power over us would necessarily have to do so in a weak, stupid, helpless, incompetent and dangerous manner. If the PANG premise were valid, the last thing anyone would want is a large, powerful government being managed by such people. As one wag put it: "If people are basi-cally good, you don't need a government; if people are basically bad, you don't dare have one."[21]

Another "fallacy," Bergland argues, is that "laws work." He posits that people often do what they want anyway, so many laws are simply ineffec-tual. To make his point, he uses the Prohibition illustration, a popular example among Libertarians. In the 1920s and 1930s, when alcohol pro-duction and consumption were banned, drinking declined only slightly and crime rates soared. Prohibition was eventually repealed, since its ben-efits were minimal. Similarly, millions of Americans currently smoke mar-ijuana, despite antidrug laws meant to deter this behavior.

A final "fallacy" cited by Bergland, which comes up repeatedly in conversations with Libertarians, is what he calls the "free lunch fallacy." Libertarians do not believe that citizens have a right to low cost (or free) health care, or even a free education. From the libertarian perspective, someone always pays for someone else's services. Whether or not one has children in public school, uses the local park or recreation facilities, or receives unemployment compensation, he or she must pay for these services in the forms of property and income taxes. The Libertarians firmly believe that "nothing is free," nor should it be.

Libertarians are political outsiders. Very few Americans understand their ideological system, and only in 1980 did their presidential candidate win over 1 percent of the popular vote (Ed Clark received 1.1 percent in the 1980 election). Systematic, empirical evidence about *why* Libertarians are marginalized is difficult to come by, because most people haven't even heard of the party. I believe that there are several reasons why the LP is a marginal force in American politics. First, Bergland is probably correct about our generalized trust and reliance on government.[22] Despite some declines of trust in government as measured by social surveys, it is very difficult for most citizens to imagine *dismantling* the regulations, tax structure, and social programs we've created. In their 1992 election platforms, both major parties emphasized the critical role of government in our lives, although the Democrats tend to be more explicit about the expansion of social programs.

A second reason why Libertarians are marginal is that a variety of demagogic and disreputable public figures have loudly and repeatedly claimed that they are Libertarians. As a result, people tend to associate such individuals with the party. One of these men is Lyndon LaRouche – a charismatic figure who was convicted on fraud and conspiracy charges in 1988.[23] When I began studying the Libertarians years ago, friends and colleagues, upon hearing about my work, would immediately name LaRouche as an LP figure. This association of the party with such a man is aggravating to the Libertarians, who argue that LaRouche does not hold (and never has) libertarian positions. In fact, LaRouche followers often run as Democrats.

Other reasons why the Libertarians are marginal include their lack of funds for extensive political advertising, and their absence from election coverage in the news media. Although in some local areas smaller newspapers will interview local Libertarians for articles, the television networks and large, metropolitan dailies tend to ignore Libertarian candidates and positions.[24] Finally, many people think that Libertarians are simply Republican party extremists: Right-wing Republicans are often associated with the fight for lower taxes, and with decreased government regulation of various industries. Yet the Libertarians are far from the Republicans on many other issues – abortion, prayer in schools (generally, Libertarians are against it, and do not believe in government-supported public schools anyway), and drug legalization, among other things.

The marginal position of the Libertarians, relative to the dual party mainstream, is ironic because so many Libertarian activists tend to be well-educated professionals. In their survey of 100 contributors to the Libertarian National Committee, for example, John Green and James Guth found that 36 percent of those surveyed had graduated from college, and another 48 percent had completed at least some graduate work.[25] Many held jobs in computer-related fields, were managers, or owned small businesses oriented around "new technology."[26] For the interviews in this chapter, I deliberately chose a diverse group of Libertarians – some had multiple graduate degrees, whereas several had only a few college courses. There are no systematic, national surveys of Libertarians at this point in time, and very little interpretive research in political science on third parties, because they normally do not win high elective office.

THE STUDY

In order to understand how it is that political activists, marginalized because of their ideology, create alternative space for political discourse, build community, and use communication backchannels, a research assistant and I conducted in-depth interviews with twenty libertarian activists. All were members of the Libertarian party of Illinois (LPI), a state organization that holds its own annual conferences, publishes a newsletter, engages in petition drives for ballot access, and plans parades, parties, and other events. The LPI has about 300 dues-paying members, who live across the state, although much activity centers around Chicago, its suburbs, and surrounding counties. Associated with the LPI are seven local clubs, representing DuPage county, north and northwest Cook county,

Springfield, Will county, Illinois Valley, and the Bellebille area. These local clubs meet monthly at restaurants, homes, and schools, at times drawing large crowds of fifty or more, and other times attracting only four or five people. Some of the clubs are more active than others, depending on the number of LPI members in the area. Members find these meetings enjoyable since the gatherings give them a chance to talk, organize events, and hear from speakers of various sorts.

The group of Libertarians we interviewed for this study was diverse. Their ages ranged from twenty-two to over sixty, with many in their thirties and forties. Educational background also varied greatly. Some informants had not completed high school or college, but others had graduate degrees – MBAs, MAs, and CPAs. These men and women held a variety of occupations. Among them were the chief financial officer of a manufacturing company, a farmer, a locksmith, a systems analyst, a homemaker, a commodities trader, a psychotherapist, a receiver on a loading dock, an artist, an owner of a men's clothing store, a manager/owner of a temporary employment agency, and a loan originator. Almost all of the participants in the study were very well informed about current events, keeping abreast of the news through major metropolitan dailies or local newspapers. Many of the Libertarians we talked with had written letters to newspaper editors, expressing their views on abortion, taxes, and property rights, among other things.

We asked all of our informants about their parents' political ideologies, and also about whether they grew up in highly politicized households, in order to explore why people become Libertarians.[27] As I suspected, Libertarians' families had mixed political affiliations – some had parents who were Democrats, others' parents were Republicans, and many families were apolitical. Not many grew up in households where politics was a central topic of conversation. There were a few Libertarians who were raised by intensely political individuals, as in the case of one forty-nine-year-old computer analyst, but even in these families, political *ideology* was not key:

[When I was growing up] we lived politics. My father was an elected public official during some of my youth and was very active in the Republican party, so I grew up loving to watch conventions on television and being aware of who was who as far as elected public officials. But to sit down and talk – I don't know. I guess we did, without even thinking about it being anything different than normal conversation on the weather, or anything else. Not philosophical, we didn't talk.

All of the people we interviewed described themselves as Libertarians. Before they found the party, though, most had considered themselves Republicans or Democrats. All were dissatisfied with the two major parties, and through various means, discovered libertarianism. Several found out about libertarian ideology by reading works by Milton Friedman (who does not call himself a Libertarian), Ayn Rand, or other writers with libertarian ideas. One man, who ran for state political office on the Libertarian ticket in the 1992 election, recalled the way he got involved:

When I grew up in heavily Republican [Chicago suburb], in my high school years, one of my neighbors who I was very close with, we'd go over to their house and I'd find a lot of talk centered around politics there, and at that time I thought Jimmy Carter was the greatest thing in the world. And the economy. . . . We went into a tailspin during the later part of his term and things weren't going the greatest, and it was the first time I ever heard Jewish people ever put down a Democratic leader. And so it really started changing my thinking in a different direction. . . . And I think the most major turning point, when it comes to politics, is when I took home a book called *Free to Choose* by Milton Friedman. I read that book and it just made total sense. . . .

A fifty-two-year old man, who is a vice-president at a manufacturing firm, said

I guess I was kind of disgusted generally with what politicians were saying and was looking for something different, and I don't know why, [but] I read Friedman. First what I read was *Capitalism and Freedom*, *Tyranny of the Status Quo*, and *Free to Choose*. . . . [I read] some Ayn Rand, although she's kind of far out in some ways. . . . I'm more of a classical liberal, again influenced mostly by Friedman.

His wife, who works in the home, and is a busy local activist, was encouraged by her husband to read books by Friedman and Rand. She had been raised by two Democrats on a tobacco farm in Ohio, and was a college activist for Goldwater before she found the Libertarian party.

The youngest member of the group we interviewed was a college senior, who organizes a variety of Libertarian events on his campus in central Illinois. He explained

I guess I was kind of Republican when I came into the university, and I thought George Bush was such an idiot. . . . I read a little bit about the Libertarians, and it was somewhat appealing to me, and I started reading more, and it became really appealing to me. . . . [I read] *Reason* magazine . . . and I guess I started paying attention when somewhat libertarian-leaning people would write in the paper, like Milton Friedman . . .

Another man, who owns a small business, found out about libertarianism "by accident." He had taken a college course on political cynicism, and realized that he needed to think more constructively about his own ideological framework. While at a library book sale he bought a libertarian tract for a quarter:

I thought, "We'll, I've heard of these Libertarian characters. They're kind of radical goofballs or something." It sounded interesting, so I picked [the book up] for yucks. And I started reading the book, and I got about fifteen or twenty pages in, and I thought, "This is really weird. Everything this guy says makes sense. . . . These people really have all the answers. As soon as everybody hears about this, everybody's going to be a Libertarian."

Not all Libertarians got involved in the party through their reading, however. Most also harbored a distaste for both of the major parties' positions, or found themselves resenting the power wielded by the state and federal governments. When asked if there was a particular incident that made him join the party, one forty-three-year-old man said

I can't think of one thing. It's just my experience with the government. They've done things I don't like. They drafted me. They arrested me for smoking pot once. They acted like they were right, and I didn't think so then or now.

None of the Libertarians in this group considered themselves anarchists. They expressed the need for some, minimal amount of government intervention in our lives. One self-employed man, who writes a tremendous number of letters to local newspapers on libertarian themes, gave a typical response to my question about state regulation:

I think we need a court system and police and some kind of defense establishment. I don't personally feel like going out and fixing the pothole in front of my building right now . . . Going to [Lake Michigan] to fetch my own water doesn't really grab me [either].

Informants argued that members of any given community would – under a libertarian system – organize themselves, *voluntarily*, to establish local utilities, parks, and events. One Libertarian explained that the party would like to start phasing out government intervention in every sphere, and evaluate the results on a case-by-case basis. By erasing government control slowly and incrementally, he noted, we can simply stop the deregulation process when we have achieved maximum efficiency in each sector.

ON CREATING ALTERNATIVE PUBLIC SPACE

Most activists, driven by ideological concerns, envision a different kind of world – populated by people with their values and goals. The Libertarians interviewed here know that such a place exists only in their imagination, but orient their activities around creating alternative space for discourse and action. Through their meetings, writing, recruiting, and public speaking, Libertarians have already created parallel public space. Yet their difficulties breaking into the mainstream frustrate them, because many have such vivid personal visions of a libertarian world. As one very active woman, who has held several positions in the state party, put it

If there was a place that I could go, my family would leave. I would leave if I could find a place that had more of a Libertarian life – I'd split. I think most of my friends would, too, that are true Libertarians. We've talked about it. Why don't we make a city?

Another woman, also in her forties, echoed these thoughts,

I guess I just enjoy the fact that the [libertarian] ideas are just beautiful. There is no utopia, but I feel like if people lived more libertarian lives, it would be a much more beautiful world. And I'm thinking so oftentimes of people voluntarily doing things. People just being motivated without being pressured. That appeals to me a great deal.

Several of the activists spoke in these terms, mentioning the goal of creating a "Libertarian society" based on free will, voluntarism, and individuality. Almost all of the informants were realistic about building such a society, though, and often emphasized that their plans were to be realized over the long term: Most claimed they were "in it for the long haul," hoping that their children would someday live in a changed world. One prominent activist in his early forties, who helped to run a Libertarian presidential campaign, put it this way:

They say the country's been evolving the way it's been for 30, 40, 50, 60 years. It's clearly moving in a more socialistic direction. Certainly during the New Deal, but for 20 years before that, as well. And I'm a believer that there is not going to be a strike of lightning, and everything getting better either through the electoral process or the legislative process. I do believe that unwinding the mess, that I perceive we're in, is going to take a substantial period of time. So one of the goals I have is small, measurable, successful, incremental steps in the right direction.

The Libertarians I spoke with were not particularly religious, but talked about politics with a sort of fervor one associates with the organized religions. It is the strength of their beliefs that keeps Libertarians motivated, despite their regular defeats in mainstream politics. One man in his forties, who holds a divinity degree, said

[I stay involved] because it is very connected and very harmonious with my religious faith, which is that of nonviolence. Thou shalt not kill, thou shalt not steal, thou shalt not send thy congressman to do either for you.

The libertarian public sphere is oriented around a new ideological continuum. Libertarians stress over and over again that the traditional left/ right political spectrum is intellectually bankrupt. Moreover, the two major political parties have trouble maintaining consistently left-wing or right-wing positions because the left/right continuum makes so little logical sense. One Libertarian publication reads:

The traditional left–right spectrum is a misleading myth. It doesn't measure anything. It's useless. The purpose of political labels is to be able to make predictions about a person's positions on the issues. Labels like Democrat, Republican, liberal and conservative do that job poorly.[28]

In the political world of Libertarianism, there are two important continua – the degree of personal freedom you support, and the degree of economic freedom you advocate. People who don't value either, Libertarians believe, are socialists or populists. People who value personal freedom but not economic freedom are liberals, whereas those who advocate economic autonomy but not personal liberties are conservatives. Those who value both personal and economic freedom are Libertarians, who most often liken themselves to "classical liberals." That the Libertarians have created an entirely different political geography, in which they can place the major parties and themselves, underlines the rigorous nature of their alternative worldview. They hope to recast American politics *in its entirety*, by redefining the ideological map.

I have already mentioned that most people have no idea what libertarianism stands for, and that activists find this fact aggravating. Part of the problem is that non-Libertarians have used the Libertarian label to describe themselves, and make the ideology seem (to the public) intellectually dubious and inconsistent. As a result, the Libertarians have set up some mechanisms for policing the public sphere and their own public space – making sure that those who claim to be Libertarians really are professing libertarian notions. The goal of the Judicial Committee of the LPI, for example, is to make sure that the parallel political arena created by Libertarians is kept "clean." One of my informants, a property manager with a background in building construction, explains:

> The primary purpose of the judicial committee is it's kind of like internal policing, internal enforcement of the pledge [an agreement to uphold libertarian ideals that new members sign]. . . . Say a professed Libertarian candidate started advocating some program that would involve the use of coercion or fraud, or something, or that we would perceive that. The judicial committee is the mechanism by which that person could be removed from the party. [The committee allows us to], like, separate ourselves from them.

Although this informant said that the judicial committee acted only once during his tenure, throwing someone out of the party, the existence of the body is interesting nonetheless. It underscores how seriously the Libertarians take their label, and highlights their desire to keep their ideology pristine: There is a *purity* to libertarian ideology, a sort of logical consistency that attracts many to the party. As a result, keeping the party free from "contamination" is vital. This notion, that the ideology of the party must remain consistent and nonnegotiable, distinguishes their organization from the two major political parties. The Democrats and Republicans, over the past several decades, have emphasized the "big tent" idea – the fact that the parties are large enough to provide a home for a wide variety of worldviews. The Libertarian "tent," on the other hand, is actually quite small: It welcomes members of all demographic sorts – ethnic minorities, the poor, and the wealthy – but does not encourage ideological revisionism or diversity.

Building alternative public space demands the creation of an extensive communications infrastructure. The Libertarians have done well in this regard, given that the party is only twenty years old. Yet they still have far to go. One very active Libertarian, who has a graduate degree in management and considerable business experience, spoke at length about the challenge of organizing party activities:

When I first came into the party [around 1980], I think it would be fair to say that there were a lot of very bright people who were an organized rabble. Very bright, good philosophical ideas, but by and large, few, if any, of the skills required to organize or grow anything. . . . I think, to some extent, what I've been able to offer, and trying to bring in other people who could offer, is a set of general management skills. Bookkeeping, just little things. Simple things that ideologues are not tuned into. . . . The chair of the party currently has an M.B.A. from Harvard. . . . We're building up some organizational structure and decision making. Until about a year and a half ago, maybe two years ago, we had no executive committee. . . . There was relatively little opportunity for the members of the national committee to percolate, to get ideas together and improve on them before we implemented them. We spun our wheels a lot. I was instrumental in setting up a structure with an executive committee which meets on the phone every second week. . . . I'm not sure we're implementing them any better, but I think we're making better decisions. And at least we aren't stagnating, waiting three months to make one.

The membership of the LPI has grown over the last few years, although not as quickly as the Libertarians would like. Also, the Libertarian presidential ticket, which garnered almost one million votes in 1980, has not had nearly as much success in recent elections. Yet the Libertarians keep building their organization because of their long-term goals: Temporary setbacks (e.g., not getting enough petition signatures to achieve ballot access) are disappointing, but rarely cause people to leave the party once they've become involved.

Beyond the multiple newsletters, meetings, seminars, and books that enable Libertarians to keep in touch with each other, the activists make extensive use of telecommunications technology. The telephone is vital for spreading the word about upcoming events, or the appearance of Libertarians in the media. As one of the informants mentioned earlier, the Executive Committee of the party regularly uses teleconferencing to plan national campaigns, discuss media strategy, and manage the financial affairs of the party. The Libertarians have also established a computer bulletin board, called "Libernet." One activist even speculated, after conducting a survey over Libernet, that there is a strong relationship between libertarian tendencies and what he calls "Computer Science IQ." Commenting on the results of his survey, he sent the following message over Libernet. It reveals the sort of sophisticated dialogue one finds among many groups of Libertarian activists:

From my observation, libertarians tend to think that all political questions can be answered with an almost mathematical certitude. There is no such thing as "a friendly disagreement" in mathematics. If two mathematicians disagree, then one is mistaken. Similarly, if two libertarians disagree, each asserts that the other is either operating from a false assumption or has a flaw in his logic. I think nonlibertarians are really turned off by this, particularly because it comes across as obnoxious and egotistical. But libertarians seem to thrive on it. The community has a kind of intellectual-warrior ethos.

Although only a small segment of Libertarians participate regularly in bulletin board conversation, the establishment of such a channel for the exchange of ideas does seem appropriate for the party. Libertarians tend to be fairly cerebral, and delight in collecting information, photocopying articles for each other, and recommending books.

Though Libertarians often console themselves by focusing on long-term goals and not short-term success or failure, they also take comfort in the idea that there are millions of "hidden" Libertarians – people who are Libertarians but just don't know it yet. Several activists told me about certain individuals – public figures and private citizens – who are Libertarians but don't realize it. Here is an example from one of my informants, a forty-two-year-old accountant:

Probably 80 to 90 percent of the people that are out there are Libertarians. The only problem is they don't know it yet. They don't have to change their philosophy; they don't have to change their thought, what they want, what they like. All they have to do is open their minds up enough to listen and hear what the Libertarian philosophy is all about, and what the Libertarian Party is all about.

The Libertarian who learned about the party by accident at a library book sale said:

Milton Friedman is a kind of a small "L" libertarian. He won't come out and say he's a Libertarian, because everybody would stop listening to him. But he's stated so far this year [1992], that neither of the major parties have anything approaching an economic plan that would actually work or make sense, and that the only party that did is the Libertarians, but they're not really a contender.

These sorts of statements are reminiscent of two other cases of marginality in this book – the blacks of Bronzeville and the socialists of *The Masses*. Both of these groups also thought that their communities were *much larger than they appeared*. The boundaries of Bronzeville seemed to expand indefinitely, as the mayoral contest gained popularity. Similarly, *The Masses'* writers believed there were many "closet socialists" dispersed throughout America, regardless of whether or not they belonged to socialist organizations.[29]

BUILDING AND MAINTAINING COMMUNITY

The libertarian activists studied here were linked to each other on a variety of levels – ideological, intellectual, and social. They spoke of their meetings as opportunities to gather with other like-minded people. In general, Libertarians feel politically "homeless," and value their ideological solidarity. One of the female activists said, "Most people do not quite think the same way as we do. It's kind of like being a Star Trek person, which I'm one of those, too, so it's that feeling." Another man from southern Illinois, where the Libertarian organization is weak, said:

There's so few [Libertarians] in our area. It's good to talk to another Libertarian . . . as opposed to just someone else who's maybe interested in politics or likes a good argument like I do. You don't have to start over from step one all the time . . . You can already assume they agree up to a certain level, and you can kind of take off from there so you get a chance to kind of shoot the breeze on a higher plane. . . . It's kind of a morale builder.

When asked what he would miss most if he left the party, one man, who reads a lot of libertarian economic philosophy, said

The people. They are very independent thinkers. They're challenging. They think for themselves, and that's very refreshing. . . . I had visions that the average income [of party members] would be higher than average, and it's not. I was surprised [at what a mixed group the Libertarians are]. We've got grocery clerks, and many people that are unemployed now. Bartenders, you know, there's . . . [a] cross-section of people. It's fascinating. And to have the same political philosophy, and to be real thinkers and readers. . . .

Beyond this comfort in finding compatriots in ideology, though, is a real desire for intellectual stimulation. Libertarians need the party for this function, as one member explains

I like the exchange of ideas and the debate amongst people. Maybe, if nothing else, I find it intellectually refreshing. I mean, I don't go to college anymore. You lose a lot of that. I mean, I used to teach at [a local] Community College part-time. . . . I find the people to be pretty much open and willing to listen.

The Libertarians I spoke with were a fairly social group, and were linked to each other through friendship, as well as ideology and intellectual compatibility. Like the socialists of Greenwich Village, the Libertarian activists often organized parties around political events – after parades or meetings, for example. Many mentioned that they met close friends through the party, or recruited their own friends into the party. Although she doesn't go to many Libertarian meetings these days, one woman from Rockford said that she had gone to many Libertarian picnics, and even went on a vacation to Mexico with other Libertarians. She explained that

Some of the Libertarians who I used to have regular meetings with are very good friends of ours, so I visit them socially. But I didn't know them before I became a Libertarian. . . . Plus there are some Libertarians in the Chicagoland area that we became very good friends with, and we send Christmas cards to each other, and it's not political. It's just because we have become very good friends.

Another longtime Libertarian said that

[We have parties] after petition drives, after protests. But sometimes we just plain have parties. There's a group of us that take at least one if not two canoe trips a year. . . . There's a group of Objectivists that go to the [skeet] shooting range. I do that [also] . . . I've met a lot of people through the party – a lot of people that I still feel that I can call them up and talk to them if I want to. . . . So yes, I have a really good network of people that I know quite well.

Although political scientists tend not to emphasize it, the social aspect of activism is critical to the maintenance of any political community. Activists told me that their contact with others inspires them, and keeps them involved. I spoke to a few people whose spouses or significant others had also become interested in libertarianism, and joined the party. One fifty-year-old woman said:

My boyfriend and I went out together [to collect petition signatures], and so we kind of talked it over afterwards, and laughed about some of the obnoxious people we saw. . . . So there's a kind of a camaraderie there, a reinforcing thing, and I think a lot of people do that. They go out in groups and kind of support each other.

Social and ideological links tend to be mutually reinforcing, and many Libertarians did not distinguish clearly between their social, political, and intellectual lives and friends.

Although the Libertarians would like to increase the number of people involved in the local and national parties, they tend not to proselytize in order to expand the size of their community. Almost without exception, the Libertarians in this study said that they tried to persuade people by using a gentle form of the Socratic method, instead of arguing with them about the superiority of libertarian ideology. One Libertarian explains her method of recruiting:

For me personally, I've essentially abandoned persuasion. . . . No arguments. Persuasion, for me, now has become, I don't know, maybe kind of Quakerish. I just say things quietly and gently and come back to it, but I don't hammer. Early on, it's like any convert to any religion or any movement. In the beginning, everybody hammers on everybody, on the contacts. I used to do that. It doesn't work. It just turns people off.

Another activist agrees that arguing doesn't work for her:

I think arguing is always ineffective. I think you have to be very positive in what you say. I think you have to be very low key in what you say, because if you get into an argument with the person, you never change their mind. . . .

One of the most popular techniques Libertarians use to recruit new members, and to educate people about their ideas is the "Fritz quiz" or the "World's Smallest Political Quiz" (see Figure 5.1). This short questionnaire, developed by Libertarian Marshall Fritz, is printed on small cards that many activists carry around with them. The goal of the quiz is to probe people about a variety of issues, and then let respondents use their answers to place themselves on the "Self-Government Chart."

Many Libertarians use the chart as a starting point for conversation, hoping that it will spark some interest on the part of the quiz-taker. One

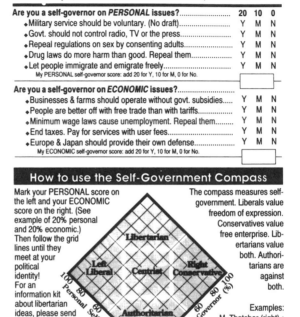

World's Smallest Political Quiz

Take the **WORLD'S SMALLEST POLITICAL QUIZ**. Then use the Self-Government Compass to find your political identity. Circle **Y** when you agree with a statement, circle **M** for Maybe, Sometimes, or Need-More-Information, or circle **N** for No.

Are you a self-governor on *PERSONAL* issues?	20	10	0
♦Military service should be voluntary. (No draft)	Y	M	N
♦Govt. should not control radio, TV or the press	Y	M	N
♦Repeal regulations on sex by consenting adults	Y	M	N
♦Drug laws do more harm than good. Repeal them	Y	M	N
♦Let people immigrate and emigrate freely	Y	M	N

My PERSONAL self-governor score: add 20 for Y, 10 for M, 0 for No.

Are you a self-governor on *ECONOMIC* issues?			
♦Businesses & farms should operate without govt. subsidies	Y	M	N
♦People are better off with free trade than with tariffs	Y	M	N
♦Minimum wage laws cause unemployment. Repeal them	Y	M	N
♦End taxes. Pay for services with user fees	Y	M	N
♦Europe & Japan should provide their own defense	Y	M	N

My ECONOMIC self-governor score: add 20 for Y, 10 for M, 0 for No.

How to use the Self-Government Compass

Mark your PERSONAL score on the left and your ECONOMIC score on the right. (See example of 20% personal and 20% economic.) Then follow the grid lines until they meet at your political identity! For an information kit about libertarian ideas, please send $8.00 to Advocates for Self-Government, 3955 Pleasantdale Road #106 A, Atlanta, GA 30340. Telephone: 404-417-1304.

The compass measures self-government. Liberals value freedom of expression. Conservatives value free enterprise. Libertarians value both. Authoritarians are against both.

Examples:
M. Thatcher (right) •
F.D. Roosevelt (left) •
Henry David Thoreau and
Thomas Jefferson (top) •
Stalin and Hitler (bottom) •

Bonus Insight: Take this quiz for any politician.

Figure 5.1. The World's Smallest Political Quiz. Some Libertarians use this quiz, printed on the front and back of a small card, to educate people about their ideology, or to recruit new members. Courtesy of Advocates for Self-Government, Inc.

Libertarian said he passed out five or ten cards a month, "just dropping them places and handing them to people." In Libertarian booths, at street fairs, conventions, or festivals, activists will set up a large version of the quiz on an easel, and work through the questions with passersby.

The quiz is interesting on several levels. First, it is a device that encourages self-confrontation and dissonance: It forces people to think about the consistency (or lack of consistency) in their own ideological frameworks. Most people are accustomed to the ideological labels they've chosen for themselves, and the quiz often puts them into a new category. The quiz is manipulative, in that its questions are carefully worded, and the issues carefully chosen. Libertarians find that, because of the nature of the questions, the large majority of quiz-takers fall into the Libertarian quadrant. In many ways, the "Fritz quiz" is an intellectuals' recruiting device, since it forces self-reflection and introspection, fitting well with the cerebral nature of libertarian activism.

Along these lines, the quiz is also interesting because of what it *does not* do. It does not capitalize on the quiz-takers' emotions, their guilt, or their fears. In fact, because Libertarians pride themselves on being logical and rational, emotional appeals are usually absent in their recruiting techniques and literature. This is not to say that Libertarians don't care about poverty, suffering, homelessness, and other public issues that tend to elicit strong feelings. Libertarians grant that such problems exist, and, like many liberal and leftist political activists, believe them to be serious and compelling. They also believe, however, that their particular economic and political reform proposals provide the only reasonable solutions.

In general, party activists feel as though the best recruits are those who have come to believe in libertarianism on their own: It is a waste of time, they believe, to try to actively "convert" a hardcore liberal or conservative to libertarianism. Since the Libertarians feel strongly about this approach to recruiting, they often focus on people within their social circle. Although Libertarians set up booths at street fairs and festivals, hoping to enlist new members, they tend to concentrate on recruiting individuals they meet at parties, work, or in their local communities. One businessman said that he brings petitions to work, and also tries to educate people in his office about libertarianism:

Because I'm a Libertarian, I don't want to coerce anybody, so I'm reluctant to do it [recruit]. I do it for people at my same level – like my own boss [who is] the president of the company. He and I have a great time arguing. He's actually about 95 percent on the Nolan chart [the political quiz in Figure 5.1], but he's afraid to vote that way. . . . He's against [then Democratic presidential candidate Bill] Clinton, but I said, "Well, there's not much difference between Clinton and [President]

Bush, so. . . . But, so then, just people that I know well and I feel that I'm not coerc-
ing, I'll have them sign the petition [for ballot access] first. Everybody knows I'm
a Libertarian.

One Libertarian has persuaded some of his twelve children to become
Libertarians, and said that he also recruited three of his children's friends
to join the party.

  Besides talking about politics with people they know, many Libertarian
activists strike up conversations with strangers in public places. One
thirty-two-year old farmer, who occasionally visits Chicago, explained:

Any time I'm in a crowd, even like on an [elevated] train in Chicago, and hear
someone make what I'd interpret to be a blatantly libertarian remark, I'll jump right
in. And I tell them what they said, and how it relates to the political scene.

When I asked him whether this was effective, he said

No one seems to be offended. Usually that person, whoever makes a really loud and
definitive political statement, is looking for a response anyway, and I've never had
anyone respond negatively. But I can't say that I've – as far as I know – none of them
has ever actually joined. But maybe they'll vote Libertarian next time. I don't know.
Certainly they'd have to think about it when they see it on the ballot.

Another Libertarian seeks the same kind of contact with strangers, and
told us:

A few weeks ago, I was standing at the train station in Elgin, and overheard a group
of three gentlemen next to me discussing Ross Perot. And I just kind of eased my
way into the conversation. They were talking about how they were kind of thinking
about Perot – a lot because he was an alternative. And so I went, "Oh. Did you
realize there is another alternative?" And in this particular case, it didn't work out
very well: They were for Ross Perot, although they didn't seem to have any idea
what Perot really stood for.

Libertarians tend to look for openings and opportunities where they can
put the Socratic method to work. Through their "soft" recruiting tactics,
they try to enlarge their community and make people aware of the party.

RITUALS AMONG THE LIBERTARIANS

In the previous case studies, I underlined ritual action, because these regular patterns of behavior often encapsulate important aspects of political marginality. Libertarians, like the activists of *The Masses*, have regular club meetings and gatherings. They use these meetings to organize petition drives and other events, but also enjoy them as moments of solidarity. Since there are so few self-proclaimed Libertarians, members find great comfort in the meetings.

Libertarians have a large repertoire of symbols, phrases, and slogans that they invoke in conversation and in their publications. Their favorite symbol is the Statue of Liberty, which appears often in stationery letterhead, and on other official documents. Many members of the party, who hold official positions, have business cards with the statue on them. One can also find the Liberty Bell and the likenesses of the Founding Fathers on many Libertarian newsletters, pamphlets, and flyers. As I mentioned earlier, these conventionally American symbols make the party seem mainstream and traditional, despite its youth. Because the two major political parties in the United States have symbols (the donkey and the elephant), Libertarians feel obliged to have their own icon. Interestingly, books and their authors are also invoked ritually by Libertarians. Writers like Milton Friedman and Ayn Rand are held up as central libertarian figures, and their works have a sort of sacred position in the libertarian pantheon.

Of all of the activities Libertarians engage in, petitioning for ballot access is the most time-consuming. This particular activity is thought to be critical by most of the individuals I spoke with, although there is a heated debate within the party about how much effort should go into ballot access, since Libertarians often fail to gather the necessary number of signatures. In many ways, petitioning is a ritual for the Libertarians, who stand outside of stores and on street corners before every election, trying to get the requisite number of signatures. Labeling the petitioning process a ritual is not to demean it, because it does have a clear instrumental function. But beyond achieving ballot access, petitioning breeds feelings of solidarity: It is a kind of hard, labor-intensive work that most of the activists have done, so they can sympathize with each other about the process.

For some activists, being on the ballot symbolizes their legitimacy as a third party. One Libertarian said that ballot access "adds credibility," and several others echoed that notion. Yet many others wondered whether the petition drives were really worth the effort, given how often they fail. One member, who has been active since 1985, said that petitioning was almost like "a habit" among Libertarians. Still others thought of petitioning as an educational tool, more than as a way to get access and votes. Chris Barker, chairman of the Libertarian Club of Springfield, wrote in a party newsletter:

At this stage in our development, the electoral process can only be used for one thing by us. And that is education. Yes, EDUCATION! We get our best bang for the buck on the national and statewide ballots. As Steve Nelson [a longtime Libertarian] said, "Let's not underestimate the value of having every voter see the word Libertarian on the ballot on election day."[30]

Although the ostensible purpose of petitioning, then, is to achieve ballot access, this prospect is often so dim that Libertarians focus on other aspects of petitioning: the educative function, and its symbolic meaning. Discussions with Libertarians revealed that the petitioning process was akin to a rite of passage for becoming a libertarian activist. Almost all of the Libertarians I spoke with had engaged in petitioning, and some have been doing it intensely for years.

ON BEING POLITICALLY MARGINAL

Libertarians are well aware of their marginality with respect to the mainstream parties, and the political system as a whole. As with other politically marginal groups studied here (e.g., the black writers on *The Defender* staff, and *The Masses'* writers and artists), Libertarians poke fun at themselves and their practices. Libertarian newsletters are replete with humorous anecdotes and cartoons, many of which refer to their marginality and their policy preferences. One Libertarian gave me a "But-Are-You-A-Real-Libertarian Survey," which had the following question on it:

When someone says they are from the government and they are there to help you, you————.
  a)   Breath a sigh of relief.
  b)   Say "But there are so many more worthy of help than me."

c) Wonder at the benevolence and efficiency of government.
d) Move and change your name.
e) Reach for your .45.
f) Reach for the Vaseline.

Political work, especially as a third-party activist, can often be frustrating and depressing. Many of the Libertarians in this study seemed to think that laughter, and a good deal of self-mockery, made their work enjoyable despite its challenges.

Libertarians list several reasons why they are marginalized, and often name the parties responsible for their legitimacy problems. One culprit is the media, which tend either to ignore the Libertarians, or portray them in a freakish light. One Libertarian, referring to the coverage his party receives for its drug legalization stands, complained:

I think the general image of a Libertarian [is] as either kind of a wild-eyed druggie, who just basically doesn't want the government in his stash anymore, or the "Luft-menschen," – the "air people" – people that are just kind of flaky.

The activists think that the media either distort Libertarian positions, or just ignore the party altogether. One member gave this example of distortion:

I heard on Crossfire [a CNN political program], I think it was, one of the guys on there saying, "And you know, then we've got these Libertarians, that want to take the stop signs down and stuff." And I'm going, "Huh?" I don't think I ever heard anybody propose that. I looked at the platform and I don't find it anywhere. But a lot of people think we're for no government at all and no rules. Just everybody do whatever you want, whenever you want.

More often, Libertarian ideas and candidates are simply ignored by the media. As one prominent activist explained:

I think the media is ideologically liberal and Libertarians are perceived, although not correctly perceived, as conservative. Yes, I think some of it is an ideological bias. My experience dealing with the media in campaigns is basically media people are no different from anybody else. They're lazy. They'd rather do less work than more if they could. And dealing with a third party is more work.

He went on to give an example of an experience he had with the media during the 1992 presidential campaign:

We held a – I don't know what you'd call it – a meeting last Friday at the National Press Club in Washington, and its subject was our [presidential] campaign and our ballot status. . . . And we went through, state by state, and we spent a lot of time briefing the media on the silly nuances of each state's ballot access law. And it was very well attended, and not a single thing went out from it. Not a single thing, so far as we can determine, went into print, went on a newswire, went on anything.

Another activist, who lives in Rockford, said that her newspaper doesn't even report vote totals received by Libertarian candidates in elections: "They act like, 'out of sight, out of mind.'"

Some of the Libertarians think that their message may be too complex for the media to handle, in this age of broadcast news and short sound-bites. One activist said that the libertarian system "can't be explained in two minutes. I think, like on the Today Show, the average interview is 2 minutes and a half." One woman put it this way:

Certain positions have been taken out of context [by the media], and those posi-tions in the past seemed very unpopular and very radical, such as decriminalizing marijuana or legalizing prostitution, or even some of the positions on the military. . . . So I think the average person just getting a soundbite would be turned off by things.

Another man said, "When you stand there and say the Libertarians favor reduced government control, and increased personal liberty, to the aver-age person, he doesn't understand that."

The media are only part of the problem for Libertarians. They also believe that elected officials and policy makers either distort or ignore the libertarian viewpoint. Politicians make ballot access very difficult for third parties in many states, because, Libertarians think, such alternative par-ties threaten office holders. As far as why public officials make ballot access difficult, one Libertarian explained that it wasn't an ideological threat but a matter of job security:

We're trying to crush their little thing that they have going – their little cosa nostra. A lot of them would find themselves without a job, at least without a cushy public sector job, and I think that contributes to it. Or they just wouldn't have the power and status if Libertarian ideas are taken more seriously.

One Libertarian even wrote himself in as a candidate on the ballot during one election to see whether or not local officials would count his vote.

They did not include his vote in the official election results, and when confronted, they told him, "Well, you did it [the write-in vote] right," and "My, I can't afford to have them go recount it."

One need not conduct a systematic content analysis of the major news media, during the typical campaign season, to see that Libertarians are largely absent. Journalists might defend themselves by pointing to the small number of people who actually vote the Libertarian ticket, and justify the lack of coverage this way. Libertarian activists believe, however, that the sheer number of signatures they gather to get a presidential candidate on the ballot in all fifty states justifies more coverage than they currently receive. None of the Libertarians I spoke with believed that the 1992 Libertarian presidential candidate [Andre Marrou] should be included in the debates between the major party candidates, or that their ideas should be highlighted nightly by the news media. Yet they do feel that they receive less than a fair hearing from journalists, given that they are an established, and well-organized third party.

SHAPING THE COMMUNICATION ENVIRONMENT

Unlike the salonnières of Chapter 2 or the mayors of Bronzeville, Libertarians do not believe in backchannels. They think that their best chance to change the status quo is not through behind-the-scenes activity. Instead, they hope to educate the public about libertarian philosophy, and expand the scope of political discourse to include libertarian ideas. They very much want their point of view included in debates about welfare, tax reform, defense spending, crime, and other major issues. Although the Libertarians have already effectively created a parallel space for themselves, where they can engage in the kind of political dialogue they deem worthwhile, they have far to go in terms of influencing or shaping debate in the larger public sphere.

Many of the Libertarians pointed out that they have had some recent success in getting recognized by mainstream publications. Some major newspapers print their letters, or carry columns by writers who have strong libertarian tendencies. One man told me that he sees the Libertarians mentioned more and more frequently in the conservative journal, *The*

National Review. Several pointed to local radio and television talk shows, which will often invite Libertarians to speak.[31] One longtime activist, and a co-chair of the libertarian-inspired "Free Market Feminist" club, said:

> The talk shows are better and more open, I think, than like the [Chicago] *Tribune* [which] never mentions Libertarians. The TV, when we do have candidates running, the local shows sometimes have them on. When Steve Givot ran for U.S. Senate, he was on a lot of the local TV interviews. Downstate [Illinois] is much more open for TV and radio and for newspapers . . .

Unlike television news broadcasts, which use short soundbites, talk shows do allow for more discussion and sustained argument, so Libertarians find them attractive. The longer format gives them time to explain their positions in greater depth, than does traditional political programming. Talk shows are becoming increasingly central to American politics, but whether Libertarians can get access to this programming is a function of their perceived legitimacy. Many of the activists were frustrated by the "chicken and egg" problem: They can't get media coverage unless they build their constituency, but they have trouble attracting members because they don't get publicity.

Several Libertarians were excited about the way that some libertarian ideas have become part of the mainstream political dialogue. They point to such things as school choice systems (educational vouchers), the capital gains tax cut, diminishing our defense commitments in Western Europe, and other such ideas as notions that Libertarians introduced. One activist told me that

> "Enterprise zone" – that came from libertarianism. That wasn't anybody else's language. So when I hear or read things [in the mainstream media] that I know that I read [about] twelve years ago [in libertarian documents] . . . , it makes me feel good, even though it's not . . . attributed to Libertarians. So that's success, a small success.

Although libertarian "think tanks"[32] are often quite effective in providing statistics and terminology for public issue debates, the Libertarians have yet to educate many citizens about their philosophical system. Libertarians like to hear their ideas discussed, but think that their ideas are decontextualized: They want people to understand their *philosophy,* not just their issue positions.

The fact that the media and mainstream politicians occasionally pick up libertarian jargon or ideas inspires some of the activists. Others related stories of personal victory to me – moments when they felt they were heard by local media, citizens, and public officials. One man, who came within a few hundred votes of getting elected to his suburban Chicago school board, by emphasizing school choice, said:

[During my campaign] I had no problem having people listen to me. And many people understood objectively what it was that I was talking about. . . . I made the front page of the *Daily Herald* out here several times. . . . I made a friend in the reporter that covers the school district. She told me, "You're right on the money." So she kept getting me on the front page. And the other three people [candidates] kept complaining to her, she told me. . . . She said, "He's the only one that says anything."

Despite their radically different ideas, contemporary Libertarians and the socialists of the prewar period are very similar. Like *The Masses* activists, Libertarians have created an extensive infrastructure for public expression: Their parallel public sphere is characterized by heated debate, passionate feeling, symbolic communication, and ritual action. In addition, both generations of activists were, to some extent, purists. Libertarians, like the socialists of Greenwich Village, seek to change the way we think about politics. They desire revolution more than reform, although the Libertarians are practical enough to support major party initiatives that have a libertarian bent (e.g., school vouchers, or civil rights legislation). Just as the activists writing and drawing for *The Masses* used irony, and self-deprecating wit, the Libertarians try to maintain a sense of humor, which comes through in conversation and in their publications. Libertarians, like many political activists, also engage in a fair amount of soul-searching, wondering if their persuasive strategies work, or if certain events are worth the trouble.

Libertarians are not uncertain about the value of their ideas, however, and the fervor with which they hold their views has some negative effects. Although they stand firmly against proselytizing of any sort, and prefer the company of other Libertarians, they do reveal a sort of intellectual arrogance reminiscent of the haughty *Masses* crowd. A few of the Libertarians I interviewed worried about the purist, uncompromising nature of the party, and wondered if the party should become more "practical." In

other words, should Libertarians try to sell their ideas to local, state, and
national politicians by becoming more of a pressure group and less of an
independent party? Throughout history, other marginal groups have often
found backchannel communication – which is what interest groups use to
achieve their goals – very useful. Yet the behind-the-scenes communication that backchannels demand is characterized by compromise, which
makes some Libertarians uncomfortable. A few activists I spoke with
understand these problems well. The man who often talks about politics
at his office explained:

> [My boss] says we [Libertarians] really can't make a difference because of some of
> [our] extreme positions, or until we get somebody [a national candidate] who is not
> so philosophical. . . . [We won't succeed] unless we would modify, or change, or
> become, I guess, better salespersons. . . . There's a tendency in the party to be very
> much of a purist philosophically and politically, and not be very practical [in order
> to become more popular with the public]. . . .

In both cases of intentional political marginality studied here – the Libertarians and *The Masses* socialists – activists maintain their marginality
through extremism and an unwillingness to compromise. As the man just
quoted notes, the Libertarians' marginality problem is a multifaceted one:
They are outsiders because of their intellectual purity, their radicalism,
and their rhetorical strategies or presentational tactics.

The marginalization of the Libertarians, and the frustration they feel
concerning their outsider status, challenges many of the assumptions students of politics tend to make. Most of the scholarly literature in American
politics either ignores or dismisses third parties, usually with rather superficial commentary. Since Libertarians, and other *established* third parties,
don't receive many votes in the typical election, political scientists tend to
discount them as uninteresting.[33] It seems as though scholars analyze
third-party "threats" to the two-party system only when some charismatic
candidate appears on the national scene (e.g., Wallace, Anderson, or
Perot).[34] This approach – studying individual third party candidates, who
temporarily seize public attention – does not help us understand the
deeper problems of political marginality, however. If we are to comprehend
organized political dissent we must study third parties *regardless of whether
they field a successful presidential candidate.* From the case of the Libertarians, for example, we can learn much about political outsiders – their inter-

actions with the mass media and elected officials, how they maintain their organizations, and why they do what they do.

Beyond learning about marginality from cases of political radicalism, studying activists enables us to ask and answer broader questions about political participation in America. In these days of political cynicism and alienation, the Libertarians are truly an anomaly: They keep up their struggle despite some serious electoral and "public relations" setbacks (e.g., the Lyndon LaRouche problem). Libertarians believe in the free market, and the protection of civil liberties, with an intensity and consistency we rarely see in American politics today. By comparison, the two major parties are so large, and so opportunistic, that their ideologies seem to become less and less coherent over time: Many citizens fail to see the differences between the two major parties, except in the most general terms – that one party is conservative and the other liberal. This inability to see the clash between party *ideologies*, plus a growing distrust of politicians, breeds a general unhappiness with "politics as usual" among many Americans. Libertarians, in contrast, are undaunted by the kind of political alienation that is pervasive in American politics today. If students of politics are truly interested in the fundamental bases of political participation, they would do best to study ideal-typical activists – those who do political work regardless of short-term failure.

6

Conclusion

Political marginality leads to the creation of innovative forms of public expression. Groups who are excluded from mainstream political activity, because of their race, gender, or political ideology, realize a unique kind of communicative freedom, since conventional rules of discourse and behavior do not apply to them. Political outsiders, as we've seen in the preceding case studies, construct their own communication infrastructures, rituals, and media, in an attempt to build community, and to influence mainstream social discourse. In this chapter, I look across the case studies with an eye toward enhancing theory about political communication and political marginality. When we look at the cases as a group, what are the points of intersection and the areas of difference? And what have we learned about the character of outsider political expression from these diverse cases? Finally, where should students of political marginality focus, in order to discover common ground? If we are to strengthen our understanding of fringe groups – who are either unable or unwilling to participate in mainstream politics – we must build coherent, interdisciplinary approaches to the subject. Although this chapter raises more questions than it answers, my hope is that it can serve as a starting point for scholarly research on marginality in political communication – by mapping out some new directions for research. I also hope that this chapter highlights how communication concepts and approaches can enhance theory about marginality in other fields – sociology, history, and Cultural Studies, in particular.

PARALLEL PUBLIC SPHERES

In Chapter 1, I discussed the notion of alternative or parallel public space. A few feminist scholars have written that the ideal Habermasian public sphere — a place where people gather for rational, critical, political discourse — is an inadequate theoretical framework for understanding the experience of political outsiders. The case studies in this book illustrate just how important this revision of Habermas's theory really is: All four groups evaluated here were (or currently are) unable to "break into" mainstream political dialogue because of their demographic characteristics or their ideas. When we look closely at the institutions, publications, and forums they created, it becomes clear that these groups did more than simply react to mainstream discourse. They used the conventional public sphere as a starting point or a foil, in order to build a political world in which they could express themselves without constraint.

When one reads *The Masses* and *The Defender*, or speaks with contemporary Libertarians, one finds a fair amount of utopianism. One of the Libertarians, a forty-three-year-old property manager, made a statement that could have been made by any of his fellow activists, or — with a few words changed — by any other member of the marginalized groups studied here:

I guess I have a deeper faith that over the long haul, that there will come a time when our society will recognize the folly of their ways. I think eventually they will have to. I really believe that the present course we're on is self-destructive to our society, and there will be a major change in our society. And when that time comes, I think the field will be more fertile for the Libertarian idea than it is right now.

It isn't that the groups analyzed here were inordinately idealistic, since they each had a very sophisticated understanding of where they stood relative to the mainstream. Most of the writers of *The Masses* knew that revolution was either impossible or improbable, and black editors of *The Defender* in the 1930s certainly didn't expect any dramatic changes in their status. Yet having a vision about some alternative political universe was still critical: These visions provided the foundations upon which marginal groups built their own political infrastructures and institutions. In a way, this cognitive process on the part of marginal actors comes close to the Marxian notion of "projective consciousness." Marx believed that what distinguishes humans from animals is their ability to imagine a structure, and their attempts to build that structure in reality.[1] Although the marginal groups discussed here had some success (e.g., the ways Mesdames d'Epinay or Lespinasse influenced the philosophes), their creative *attempts* to build alternative worlds are most interesting. In some cases, these parallel public spheres imitate the mainstream (e.g., the elections for a Bronzeville mayor), whereas in others, individuals create altogether new formats for expressing their ideas (e.g., the artwork of *The Masses*, or the Libertarian political quiz).

In all cases where parallel public space develops, there are central characters who express a group's vision, and begin to map out the means to realize it. One cannot write a book on marginality without at least underlining, however briefly, the courage of particular individuals. People like Madame Roland, Robert Abbott, Max Eastman, and some contemporary libertarian activists all have a fearless quality that pervades their writings, their artwork, and their public speeches. A celebration of this courage is best left to biographers. For our purposes here, it is important simply to note that particular individuals tend to "carve out" alternative public space and give it purpose. This space changes dramatically, as more individuals find comfort in alternative political realms, adding their own talents and expressing their own views. In fact, these parallel public spheres undergo constant redefinition as participants, goals, and political conditions change. In the case of *The Masses*, for example, artwork gradually became critical to the journal. It was as important, and many times, more compelling than the editorials and reports. Similarly, Libertarians are always innovating, as the party grows in size. Two Libertarian women recently created a feminist group inside the party, hoping to show women in the traditional parties why libertarian philosophy best suits female needs and goals.

Communication is central to the creation and maintenance of alternative public space, just as it was central to the eighteenth-century mainstream public sphere Habermas described so well. An independent press, in the seventeenth and eighteenth centuries, enabled people of higher social classes to express their discontent or agreement with government. The press was a forum that allowed dissent, and made some men realize that their interests were not always shared by the crown. A free press is also critical in our own time, and is highlighted as the centerpiece of American democracy. Interestingly, publications are also a vital part of parallel political space. Examples from the preceding case studies abound: the newsletters and correspondence associated with the salons, *The Defender, The Masses,* and the large number of Libertarian magazines and pamphlets. All of these writings serve to bind together members of marginal groups, and give them direction. Radicals looked to *The Masses* for ideas, just as modern-day Libertarians wait for *Reason* magazine and other publications. These publications were not documents created by leaders to dictate opinions to constituents, but they simply served as starting points for conversation. Max Eastman, for example, despite his strong socialist leanings, never felt as though he could dictate ideology to the radicals who read his journal – they were far too sophisticated for undiluted polemics. Similarly, the newsletters of the salons helped to establish a world of political conversation apart from the court, a place where criticism of the state was lauded.

The notion that publications are critical to community building was one focus of Robert Park and the Chicago School of sociologists, who studied urban areas in the early decades of the twentieth century. These social scientists found that newspapers were important to immigrants, who needed to feel "connected" to each other in rather alienating, foreign cities. In much the same way, mass media bring together members of marginal groups, even though they don't always share a common neighborhood.

Interpersonal communication, in all the cases studied here, did tend to solidify parallel public space once established. Conversation was key to the maintenance of the salon, whereas the Bronzeville races often included campaign-related debates and gatherings. Likewise, from the memoirs of *The Masses* editors, it seems that editorial board meetings were as important to members as was the publication itself. Since Libertarians are scattered across the nation, they keep in touch by telephone, computer bulletin boards, state and national conventions, as well as smaller meetings. Conversation is as critical to the formation of alternative public space as it was to the initial establishment of the bourgeois public sphere Habermas described. Because marginal communities are diminutive in comparison to the national public spheres Habermas wrote about, interpersonal discussion is even more important and more valued: *Unmediated* conversation helps to sustain groups closed out of mainstream political dialogue. In the instances of parallel public space analyzed here, communication infrastructure is characterized by written and oral expression, and both forms are mutually reinforcing and vital to dialogue.

The groups studied here – from the citizens of Bronzeville to the Libertarians – spoke primarily to each other, occasionally trying to influence the public at large. With the exception of the salons, mainstream political actors rarely tried to contribute to the dialogue among outsiders. The mayors of Chicago may have talked to the mayors of Bronzeville, for example, but they did not try to augment (in any serious, sustained way) the discourse created by *The Defender*. Similarly, contemporary mainstream political leaders and candidates rarely, if ever, appeal to Libertarians by writing to their publications, or by trying to win their votes. Libertarians, like many third parties before them, are viewed as outsiders by elected officials, who have no practical reason to seek them out, unless an upcoming election looks very close. Although marginal political actors try to influence the mainstream, through their publications and speeches, political insiders do not often return the favor.

In this book, I speak of alternative public space metaphorically: It is not a physical place as much as a forum for the exchange of ideas. Yet in each of the four cases described here, geographical location mattered very much, although the relationships between place and public space varied greatly. In the cases of Enlightenment Paris, Bronzeville, and Greenwich Village, place and public space overlapped – although not perfectly. The fact that Mesdames d'Epinay and Geoffrin could entertain once or twice a week, and invite many of the same people, gave their salons continuity. Their salons developed, in part, because they were sustained by men and women who lived in Paris, and rarely left the city for very long. On the other hand, however, foreign visitors to the salons were also critical, since they added fresh perspectives. The Abbé Galiani is a case in point, as many salon attendants were upset or disappointed upon his return to Italy. The salons had permeable boundaries, but they were always held at the same houses, at appointed times of day.

Bronzeville, as I noted, had very nebulous borders as the black population in Chicago grew. New migrations from the south meant an expanded neighborhood, and a higher circulation for *The Defender*. *The Defender*'s editors wanted Bronzeville – the place *and* the idea – to be powerful and exciting. Bronzeville was located on Chicago's South Side in the beginning, but grew because its primary news organ also expanded. In this case, mass media extended the borders of a geographical community, creating a very large, national arena for dialogue about black concerns. Similarly, *The Masses* was born in Greenwich Village, but eventually expanded, and appealed to a much larger socialist constituency. The bases from which these publications sprang – Bronzeville and Greenwich Village – remained important, but became increasingly less so over time, as a new sort of public arena developed. This new public space was a linguistic place, established for a variety of reasons: It was a place for public expression, for critical perspectives on mainstream politics, and in some cases, a tool for changing the world.

The Libertarians care the least about geographical place. They are trying to expand what is already a national party, so they tend to think more globally than the other marginal groups studied here. New communication technologies – telephones, computer modems, and fax machines – have enabled them to broaden their network. The Libertarians I spoke with saw themselves as part of a large community, and often developed friendships with people in different states. After I began studying the Libertarians in Illinois several years ago, activists from a variety of places wrote to me, asking about the study and offering their assistance. Some of these men and women had heard about my research directly from people I interviewed, and others got news of the study through the Libertarian communication network. Along with political information and ideological commentary, rumors, gossip, and other sorts of talk have a place in the libertarian public sphere.

Humor, parody, and satire often characterize marginal public space. Irony and wit were greatly valued in the salons, of course, and the salonnières contributed humorous comments when they could. This sort of humor was playful, though, and was not crucial to the sustained critique of the state/court. Among Libertarians, the writers on *The Defender* staff, and contributors to *The Masses*, on the other hand, comedy was central. All three groups felt the need to poke fun at themselves and their efforts, even though their crusades for a variety of causes were very serious. No matter how often mainstream institutions and political leaders threatened *The Masses'* existence, for example, Art Young continued to draw his sarcastic cartoons. *The Defender's* editors had a fine time injecting humor into the Bronzeville campaign reports, hoping that their jokes would get people excited about the contest. And Libertarians, as I pointed out in the previous chapter, are constantly engaged in humorous exchanges and self-mockery – very close in tone to the self-reflexive humor of *The Masses*. Humor and irony, as so many have pointed out, enable people to cope with the trials of everyday life, and are particularly important in the case of political outsiders. Marginal political actors come to realize that they cannot take themselves too seriously, and conviviality makes an alternative public sphere attractive to its constituents. *The Masses* was not an interesting or successful publication under Piet Vlag, in part because of its serious tone. When Eastman, Dell, and Young turned the magazine into a witty socialist journal, *The Masses* began to receive respect from socialists and nonsocialists alike.

One last observation about parallel public space concerns its fate. In all of the cases discussed here, different groups established their own arenas for discourse, *because* they were marginal. Since participation in mainstream electoral politics or discourse was difficult (as in Bronzeville) or impossible (in the case of salonnières), outsiders had no other real options for public expression. In two cases – *The Masses* and the Parisian salons – forums for expression were destroyed by governments. *The Masses* was effectively undermined by the postmaster and the federal government, whereas the revolutionary government of France made it impossible for salonnières like Madame Roland to continue their efforts. The case of *The Masses* is particularly disturbing to us over seventy years later, since the editorials and drawings in the magazine don't seem very seditious at all. In 1917, however, the war, and a less sophisticated understanding of the value of free speech, made *The Masses* a perfect target for nervous bureaucrats and politicians.

In the case of Bronzeville, the mayoral elections faded away because they became unnecessary, not because they were squashed by government officials. African-Americans were beginning to play a more prominent role in mainstream Chicago politics. Also, the civil rights movement made the elections seem almost trivial: Why elect a mayor of one's own community, when one could focus upon more important types of power – places on the city council, state assembly seats, and the like? We can't evaluate the fate of the Libertarian party yet, because it is fairly young, and is still growing. It is most likely that the party will gain influence through the sorts of debates it generates, among mainstream politicians and among citizens. An example is the drug legalization debate of the late 1980s, in which Libertarians played a significant role. It is far less likely that we will see the rise of Libertarian members of Congress or presidents, since at this point, much of libertarian philosophy is rather difficult for Americans to embrace.

Parallel public space is just that – it exists side by side with mainstream politics, and even shares some of its characteristics. It is difficult to generalize about its nature, because the form it takes depends on the marginal population in question, and the historical era in which it thrives. I have found, however, several traits that are common to all the case studies: the importance of a visionary individual who sees a need for an alternative forum, a rich communication infrastructure to link people to a network, and a kind of playful self-awareness. Shared geography becomes increasingly less important in the late twentieth century, although there are a variety of communities that seem very much like Greenwich Village or Bronzeville of years past – the "Castro" in San Francisco or Hasidic neighborhoods in Brooklyn, for example. All of these places have their media of communication (papers, newsletters, and meeting places), as well as a neighborhood that truly "belongs" to them. Despite this, communication technology has obliterated traditional notions of gemeinschaft, where "community" implied a shared neighborhood.

RITUAL AND COMMUNITY BUILDING

Ritual plays a role in all of our lives. We use the term to discuss a broad range of things we do – drinking our "ritual" cup of morning coffee or taking children on "ritual" weekend outings. In this book, I've been a bit more strict in my definition of ritual, preferring to think of it as patterned behavior that has special meaning to participants.[2] In all four cases evaluated here, ritual was vital. Salonnières, for example, took great care organizing their gatherings. And in some of the more formal salons, conversation, meals, and exits were handled with an extraordinary amount of planning. Bronzeville provides the "cleanest" case of ritual, because the manipulation of symbols and the degree of ceremonial action was so great. *The Masses* engaged in ritualized criticism of certain American institutions – the press, in particular – whereas the Libertarians have their petitioning rituals every election year.

That ritualized behavior can be found among marginal groups is obvious, but exactly what function does it play? I believe that ritual is an axis, around which people build their communities. It emerges gradually, as the community develops, and then becomes a sort of organizing principle for that community. Bronzeville and *The Defender* both existed before the mayoral contests began, but the elections became a rallying point for the paper and for many of its citizens. It enabled them to celebrate their community: The mayor made a loose network seem like a more coherent form of social organization – a tiny kingdom with its own monarch. Similarly, there were scores of feminists, socialists, anarchists, and artists living in Greenwich Village before Piet Vlag founded *The Masses*. But within a few short years, the publication became a vital axis around which socialist life revolved. The writers working on *The Masses* would look forward to their ritual editorial meetings each month, where they spent more time discussing current events than planning the next issue. I found some good-natured jokes about the editorial meetings in memoirs of those who attended, but did not find any board members who wanted to eliminate them. The meetings were a crucial metaphor for the entire undertaking, because they exemplified cooperation and indeed, socialism. The board owned *The Masses*, and no matter how much work was done by Eastman and Dell, it was a socialist operation in all respects. Rituals draw together members of a community, and help them to elaborate their common purpose. Ritual action develops as marginal groups try to "send messages" to the mainstream – either through their own elections, their publications, or their petitioning.

In the four cases discussed here, relationships among members of marginal groups were multifaceted. People shared intellectual bonds, friendship, and even romance. In many cases, they depended upon each other for inspiration or spiritual sustenance. The socialists of Greenwich Village had tough battles to fight, and were arrested or harassed by the authorities. They often came to each other's aid, and correspondence between Eastman and Dell indicates just how close their friendships were.[3] The point is that social networks among political outsiders are very dense, with many links among members of the groups. The links serve multiple functions for network members, who are at times so marginal that they depend on their communities for survival. One need only think about the espionage trials of *The Masses* staff. As they faced long jail terms, they relied on each other for intellectual support and comic relief, in a situation that was far from humorous.

What about the definition of community from Chapter 1, that "community" implies boundaries? Clearly, a community cannot exist unless some people belong to it and others don't. In certain cases, like the salons, boundaries were permeable but the gatherings were still very exclusive. Women were on the "inside" of communities they themselves created – communities established because of their marginal political status. An inability to vote, participate freely in mainstream French politics, or even receive a formal education had forced them to develop the salon and to define its culture. In this respect, the salons are much like the outsider community of Bronzeville, which developed in response to racial discrimination in Chicago. The editors of *The Defender*, unlike the salonnièrcs, however, did not think of their community in terms of exclusion. Inclusion was their operating principle, since they were always trying to expand the boundaries of their community – first to the suburbs of Chicago, then to the nation.

In the two cases of intentional political marginality – *The Masses* and the Libertarians – community members played a much stronger role in defining the borders of their communities. Women in France and blacks in Chicago were forced into communities, whether they liked it or not, and they made the best of their conditions. Socialists and Libertarians, on the other hand, purposefully withdrew from mainstream politics. The socialists of Greenwich Village used a very firm "we/they" dichotomy in their anti-status-quo rhetoric. They declared themselves as "different," and beckoned others to join them in their separate, alternative public sphere. The Libertarians also engage in a rhetoric of difference, by claiming that their philosophy defies the conventional left/right ideological continuum. This quarrel is very serious, because the left/right scale has been the centerpiece of American ideological identification for some time now. Some Libertarians do not worry about creating very severe boundaries between themselves and other political parties. There are, in fact, "purists" in the party – those who prefer absolutely no compromise of libertarian views. However, other Libertarians point out that such purists are far too rigid: They should spend far less time on "we/they" divisions, and far more time trying to accomplish manageable goals.

One common theme, touched upon in some way by each of the case studies, is the importance of *imagination* in the formation of communities and nations.[4] A community is, to some extent, empirical: Real people develop real relationships in real settings. Yet there is also a shared *idea* among members of a marginal community, which helps them to distinguish themselves from other groups, and from the dominant culture. A community is empirical, but it is also a "state of mind." Even the salonnières, the least "organized" and self-aware among the groups studied here, were conscious of the alternative community they imagined and constructed. Suzanne Necker, wife of the finance minster Jacques Necker, and one of the most admired salonnières, spoke of a "government of conversation [that] very much resembles that of a State."[5] That she could compare the conversational arena developed by herself and other women as a *nation* reveals that she had imagined a parallel world of sorts. How well this world was realized by the salonnières will always be a matter of some controversy among Enlightenment historians, but there is substantial evidence that a small group of women did accomplish their intellectual goals through the salon culture.

That the editors of *The Defender* imagined a different world than the racist one they were born into is obvious. Along with businessmen, social activists, ministers, and others, men like Robert Abbott and John Sengstacke probably let themselves imagine more cohesiveness in Bronzeville than was actually present. We know, from sociological studies, that the South Side of Chicago was populated mainly by African-Americans, but that there were some serious class divisions within that community.[6] Very wealthy men, who made their money in consumer goods or the funeral business, lived just blocks from desperately poor blacks, only recently arrived from the south. Although the mayoral races in Bronzeville clearly had popular appeal, those who came to the celebratory ball were mostly middle- and upper-class African-Americans. Yet the matter of race did override, at some moments, class differences. All African-Americans living in Chicago before the beginning of the civil rights movement knew that no matter how much money they made, they were still black, and therefore, still marginal. It wasn't hard to imagine a black nation of sorts, given that assimilation seemed unlikely and unattractive in many ways.

The two cases of ideological marginality – *The Masses* and the Libertarians – best illustrate Benedict Anderson's point about imagined communities. In both of these alternative public spheres, a variety of publications and cultural artifacts point to the idea of *nation*. The Libertarians see themselves as a nation within a nation: They are connected through a complex infrastructure of written and oral communication. Much of the time, they describe their philosophy as the only one that truly realizes the Founding Fathers' ideals of democratic life. Libertarians find it ironic that they are so marginal, given that they are the carriers of the real American message – that of minimal government and maximum individual freedom. The socialists of *The Masses* knew that they were far from the ideals of the Founding Fathers, and avoided invoking such figures. These artists and writers looked to another nation – Russia – to imagine their own. The American socialists also saw themselves as a nation within a nation, complete with ideology and infrastructure. And like the Libertarians, they were often depressed and frustrated with their lack of progress.

These ideas about communities and "nations" of discourse are in many ways related to debates about communitarianism and democracy in political theory. Most of the theorists engaged in this debate are attempting to build grand, normative theory about the kinds of participation that are possible, and indeed necessary, in mass democracies. Although it is difficult to apply much of this theory to cases of outsider communities, since they are not usually described by their members as "working democracies," one connection is clear: Individuals do realize an informal type of *citizenship* in these imagined nations through communication. With the exception of the salonnières, who did not organize a community amongst themselves, the outsiders studied here often acted (or act) like the ideal citizens described by theorist Benjamin Barber: They had shared goals and a profound sense of what was right for their communities. In describing the ideal "strong democracy," Barber argues:

The individual members are transformed, through their participation in common seeing and common work, into citizens. Citizens are autonomous persons whom participation endows with a capacity for common vision. A community of citizens owes the character of its existence to what its constituent members have in common and therefore cannot be treated as a mere aggregation of individuals.[7]

The point here is that men and women became citizens of Bronzeville, of the Greenwich Village socialist scene, and the Libertarian party through their discursive participation. In all three cases, members of these communities engaged in protests and marches, but it was talk – interpersonal and mediated – that bound them together with a shared sense of purpose. If there are imagined communities and nations, then there is also meaningful, imagined citizenship.

MARGINALITY AND PUBLIC
OPINION RESEARCH

As I mentioned in Chapter 1, public opinion researchers have not paid much attention to marginality, leaving this sort of work to anthropologists and sociologists. Yet, marginal opinions themselves, and the fact that marginal groups can shape the environment for mass opinion formation, are interesting and important. Studying political outsiders can enhance the field of public opinion in several ways.

First, the backchannels created by marginal groups reveal that there are alternative means for expressing public opinion, which can never be located through methods like survey research. Although all of us create these routes for informal communication, such paths are often the only channels available to marginal groups who want to influence leaders. Historians who study prerevolutionary France, for example, have realized that the salons are critical in understanding public opinion formation during the Old Regime. One can look at the public speeches of famous men, and the books, pamphlets, and newspapers of the period. But the dialogue of the salons, and the correspondence between salonnières and the philosophes greatly enrich our understanding of political discourse of that time. Consensus about the nature of the state, the role of religion, and the place of the monarchy was often reached in the salons. This is why the king felt the need to send "spies" to the salons, who reported back to him the content of these conversations. Accounts of the salons help us to put much of the political literature of the day in its proper context, demonstrating which ideas were "in the air" at the salons, and which were arrived at independently by writers working alone.

Beyond the fact that the salons influenced mass opinion formation, and generated some of the most important political tracts of the period, studying the salons enables us to achieve some, albeit limited, understanding of female opinion. Given that most French women were illiterate, or uneducated, and that their voices were suppressed in the decades before the revolution, accounts of the salons are vital records. Along with the few books written by women (many of whom were salonnières), these accounts of conversation document where women stood in relation to issues of the day – education, religion, and economics. In order to find the opinions of political outsiders, one must often look for unusual types of evidence.

Public opinion researchers interested in the contemporary political scene would undoubtedly benefit from close analyses of marginal groups as well. Libertarians have considerable trouble answering most political questionnaires because they don't believe in the left–right ideological continuum. Many have told me that the wording of poll questions "misses" their opinions, and many have had frustrating interactions with interviewers as a result. One of my students conducted a mail survey of Libertarians, and was bombarded with phone calls: Several of the respondents wanted to debate the meaning and choice of questions, and said they would send her extended answers, instead of simply checking off answers to the closed-ended questions. This incident was particularly interesting, because most of the questions on the survey were standard ones, drawn from Gallup, Roper, and the like.[8]

One might argue that the Libertarians are such a small group that their ideas really don't matter very much. If a survey distorts their opinions, no real crime is committed. Yet this sort of rationalization is intellectually problematic. There are, undoubtedly, many groups that have problems with pollsters' questions, but aren't quite as articulate as most libertarian activists. As Pierre Bourdieu has argued so eloquently, opinion researchers and citizens don't always speak the same language. Questions that represent a litmus test on an issue in pollsters' eyes, for example, may not be seen that way at all by respondents. Many people, answering a survey, may not view the questions in the same light that pollsters or their clients do – perhaps not even recognizing some of the questions as *political* ones.[9] Simply because people answer survey questions doesn't necessarily mean that the queries are accurate or complete measures of political attitudes.

Students of public opinion can shed unique light on the problems of outsiders. Political communication researchers should attend to discourse, to backchannels, and to the shape of political dialogue (public and private) among the marginal. Noticing and studying these things might enhance survey research, but will most certainly lead to the development of new, more textured techniques for understanding public opinion. As I argued early in this book, public opinion is not simply an aggregation of individual opinions, since people live in groups and communities: Opinions are not formed in a vacuum. They are arrived at through discussion, in a rich social context. If we want to grasp the complex nature of public opinion, ignoring social context and the dialogues of communities (marginal or not) is to fool ourselves. Although the study of Libertarians here is small and exploratory, for example, I found some evidence that they do influence mainstream politics in local communities. Researching how Libertarians, or other political outsiders, use backchannels and shape communication environments is difficult and labor-intensive, but worth the effort.

Along these lines, public opinion researchers have not been interested in studying the sort of dialogue or conversation that occurs within *natural* communities. Several philosophers and sociologists, from Gabriel Tarde to Jürgen Habermas, have emphasized the critical role of conversation in opinion formation, but their ideas have fallen on deaf ears in the field of opinion research.[10] Conversation is difficult to study, as so many interpersonal communication researchers have discovered. Yet conversation is clearly a centerpiece of democratic theory: Participation in politics entails talk, and talk leads to action or inaction. The only way to understand the relationship between conversation, action, and the larger political discourse is to rejuvenate the case study. How can we track the spread of an idea, and its development, unless we look carefully at the way people discuss that idea? The media do not form our opinions for us: They pick up on conversation, develop it, and stimulate more discussion. Communication researchers, interested in opinion formation and change, have developed a few rather narrow ideas, but they have in many ways reached a theoretical dead end. Agenda-setting research, for example, which measures opinions of isolated individuals and correlates these data with the salience of issues in the media, will never capture the essence of conversation and dialogue. If public opinion researchers ignore conversation by simply focusing on opinions expressed to pollsters, they are neglecting one of the most vital aspects of life in a democracy.

One last point about public opinion research concerns the communication of symbols. Although work on the subject by sociologists like Durkheim has been acknowledged by students of American politics, we engage in more lip service than empirical study.[11] In fact, the political science literature is full of unsupported statements about the importance of political symbols. Public opinion researchers are well aware of the fact that symbols matter – whether they are symbols of presidential authority, symbols used by protest groups, or symbols related to a presidential candidate's character. Symbols are important when studying any social movement or political party, but they are particularly meaningful in the analysis of marginal group communication. With the exception of the salonnières, who were unable to protest their status openly, each group evaluated in this book introduced and used symbols. The editors of *The Defender* established a symbolic mayor of their community, and one mayor even wanted to build an alternative city hall for Bronzeville. The radicals of Greenwich Village, writing in *The Masses*, used socialism, its jargon, and its iconography to great effect, just as the Libertarians make extensive use of symbols of liberty. The ways that each of these groups used their chosen symbols tells us much about their intentions and their perspectives. If we are to understand what goes on "inside people's heads," a goal of so much social analysis, symbols provide a way to do this: They highlight what is central to a group's ideology, and reveal something about their discursive style and approach.

ON STUDYING THE POLITICALLY MARGINAL

Studies of marginal groups – both superficial analyses and more in-depth case studies – abound in the academic literature. At this point, however, it is difficult to discern any commonalities across theoretical frameworks or methodological approaches. Literary critics might closely analyze a marginal "text," but ignore sociological issues (e.g., real power or actual group activity), whereas more sociological approaches tend to neglect the discourse and texts produced by marginal groups. The goal of this book is to demonstrate how a few, fairly simple concepts can help us link the disparate studies of marginality across disciplines. Among these concepts were the notions of communication backchannels, discursive environments, and ritual. Yet the most important is the idea of parallel public space – the fact that marginal groups create worlds of discourse and action beside the mainstream public sphere.

There are a few reasons why the idea of alternative public space is useful to those studying marginal public opinion, and why we should orient

our work around the concept. First, if we think about political outsiders
building their own public spheres, as arenas for talk and action, we are
alerted to their new forms of media and unique styles of communication.
When we think of one Habermasian-type public sphere, instead of thinking about multiple ones, we tend to concentrate on how marginal groups
are left out of political discourse – how the mainstream news media
ignores a group's ideas or demands. If we think about a multiplicity of
alternative public spheres, however, we will be forced to recognize (and
study) the complex communication infrastructures they build. These
infrastructures, as we've seen, include mass media as well as interpersonal
channels for public expression. The case of Bronzeville illustrates this
point very well. If we studied that thriving community by focusing on the
ways blacks were ignored by white Chicago media and institutions, something that many scholars have already done, we might not see the other
side of the phenomenon – the ways that *The Defender*'s editors worked to
create a symbolic nation out of a small South Side community. Bronzeville
wasn't simply a nickname for an African-American neighborhood. It had
great meaning for many men and women, who lived and worked in the face
of degrading and unrelenting prejudice.

Another reason why the idea of parallel public space is worthwhile concerns community building. If we think about alternative arenas for public
discourse and political conversation, we expand – and even reinvent – the
concept of community itself. Community is not necessarily a physical place,
or a geographic location, but a constellation of people and ideas, as well as
the media individuals create to communicate with each other. The preceding case studies provide ample evidence that feelings of community and
belonging are enhanced by the construction of alternative public spheres.
For example, the Libertarian computer network enables such activists –
regardless of how geographically isolated they might be – to feel as though
they are part of a community. In this case, advances in communication technology – the sheer ability to move information across space – make it possible for those with similar ideas to find each other.[12] These sorts of
technologies are especially important to those outside of mainstream politics, since the mass media do tend to ignore or trivialize their concerns.

Although we have come a long way since *The Masses* staff was tried under
the Espionage Act, political outsiders still face considerable barriers

to free speech and political participation. African-Americans and women – the first two groups discussed in this book – are obviously not yet central players in mainstream American politics. Women and blacks are underrepresented in the Congress, on the federal bench, and in the upper echelons of major corporations and television networks. And third parties, as the case of the Libertarians demonstrates, struggle constantly against a political system that seems closed to anyone who isn't a Republican or a Democrat. How political outsiders express themselves, and the problems they face, should be of interest to students of political communication as well as to citizens and policy makers. Perhaps the growing emphasis on multiculturalism, in our schools and in the commercial world, will make studying marginal politics and opinions more natural, and more engaging.

Notes

INTRODUCTION

1. Two good examples are Abdul JanMohamed and David Lloyd's *The Nature and Context of Minority Discourse* (New York: Oxford University Press, 1990), and Russell Ferguson, Martha Gever, Trinh Minh-ha, and Cornel West's *Out There: Marginalization and Contemporary Cultures* (Cambridge, MA: MIT Press, 1990).

2. To be fair, experienced survey researchers and pollsters break out their opinion data into demographic *categories*. Journalists, interest groups, and politicians are the ones who then try to transform these categories into *groups*, through their rhetoric.

3. Although the number of works across these fields is tremendously large, I am referring to ethnographic studies like John Lofland's classic, *Doomsday Cult: A Study of Conversion, Proselytization, and Maintenance of Faith* (Englewood Cliffs, NJ: Prentice-Hall, 1966), and to more recent text-based studies like those in Andrew Parker et al., *Nationalisms and Sexualities* (New York: Routledge, 1992).

4. An interesting example of this sort of history is Lillian Faderman's *Odd Girls and Twilight Lovers: A History of Lesbian Life in Twentieth-Century America* (New York: Columbia University Press, 1991).

5. The idea of a "repertoire" for public expression is Charles Tilly's. See his article, "Speaking Your Mind Without Elections, Surveys, or Social Movements," *Public Opinion Quarterly* 47 (1983): 461–78.

6. Nancy Fraser has used the phrase, "parallel discursive arenas," to describe a similar phenomenon. See her essay, "Rethinking the Public Sphere: A Contribution to the Critique of Actually Existing Democracy," in *Habermas and the Public Sphere*, ed. Craig Calhoun (Cambridge, MA: MIT Press, 1992), pp. 110–42.

1. POLITICS, EXPRESSION, AND MARGINALITY

1. On audience segmentation, mass society theory, and the expansion of the mass media, see W. Russell Neuman, *The Future of the Mass Audience* (New York: Cambridge University Press, 1991). Some scholars, like Robert Entman, find that despite the growing number of media outlets, there is very little diversity of content in political news. See his *Democracy Without Citizens: Media and the Decay of American Politics* (New York: Oxford University Press, 1989).

2. On the efforts of small, poor interest groups who labor to gain the attention of local media, see Edie Goldenberg's interesting book, *Making the Papers: The Access of Resource-Poor Groups to the Metropolitan Press* (Lexington, MA: Lexington Books, 1975).

3. An illustration of my point is Craig Calhoun's excellent collection of essays, *Habermas and the Public Sphere* (Cambridge, MA: MIT Press, 1992). Among the contributors (and cited authors) are sociologists, historians, and literary critics. Yet I count only one contributor who is associated with a department of government or political science. My point is not that *all* political scientists have ignored Habermas's work. Many political theorists do write about his ideas, but they are usually ghettoized: I have yet to see many political scientists, who study American politics, apply Habermasian perspectives. An exception is Dan Hallin's use of Habermas's ideas to shed light on trends in journalism. See his piece, "The American News Media: A Critical Theory Perspective," *Mass Communication Yearbook: Volume 6* (Newbury Park: Sage, 1987), pp. 293–318.

4. Max Horkheimer and Theodor Adorno, *Dialectic of Enlightenment,* trans. John Cumming (New York: 1987), p. 123. Weberian themes of rationalization are omnipresent in Adorno and Horkheimer's early work, and in Habermas's writing. See Max Weber, *Economy and Society: An Outline of Interpretive Sociology,* ed. Guenther Roth and Claus Wittich (Berkeley: University of California Press, 1978). Also see Rogers Brubaker, *The Limits of Rationality: An Essay on the Social and Moral Thought of Max Weber* (London: George Allen & Unwin, 1984).

5. Jürgen Habermas, *The Structural Transformation of the Public Sphere: An Inquiry into a Category of Bourgeois Society,* trans. Thomas Burger (Cambridge, MA: MIT Press, 1989), pp. 33–4.

6. The notion that the media are far less critical of the government than they could be is shared by a variety of media critics. See, for example, Entman's *Democracy Without Citizens.*

7. Habermas, "The Public Sphere: An Encyclopedia Article," *New German Critique* 1 (Fall 1974): 49.

8. For a more lengthy discussion of "technologies" of public expression, see my *Numbered Voices: How Opinion Polling Has Shaped American Politics* (Chicago: University of Chicago Press, 1993).

9. In communications, Dan Hallin and Paolo Mancini have done some interesting cross-cultural research, comparing the contemporary public spheres in the United States and Italy. See their article, "Speaking of the President: Political Structure and Representational Form in U.S. and Italian Television News," *Theory and Society* 13 (1984): 829–50. In terms of historical work using the public sphere notion, see the review by Benjamin Nathans, "Habermas's 'Public Sphere' in the Era of the French Revolution," *French Historical Studies* 16 (Spring 1990): 620–44.

10. Nancy Fraser, "Rethinking the Public Sphere: A Contribution to the Critique of Actually Existing Democracy," in *Habermas and the Public Sphere*, ed. Craig Calhoun (Cambridge, MA: MIT Press), p. 123. Also on subaltern publics, see Gayatri Spivak, "Can the Subaltern Speak," in *Marxism and the Interpretation of Culture*, eds. Cary Nelson and Lawrence Grossberg (Urbana: University of Illinois Press, 1988), pp. 271–312.

    Interestingly, some political scientists – despite their field's emphasis on national, aggregate statistics – are reviving the Columbia School's emphasis on multiple, subnational publics. The best recent example is Robert Huckfeldt and John Sprague's *Citizens, Politics, and Social Communication: Information and Influence in an Election Campaign* (New York: Cambridge University Press, in press).

11. Ibid., p. 126.

12. Rita Felski, *Beyond Feminist Aesthetics: Feminist Literature and Social Change* (Cambridge, MA: Harvard University Press, 1989).

13. The "social movements" literature in sociology is large, and scholars working in this area have recently become more interested in communication issues – the use of media and symbolic ritual in everyday life, for example. Among the most interesting works in this area is *Frontiers in Social Movement Theory*, eds. Aldon Morris and Carol McClurg Mueller (New Haven, CT: Yale University Press, 1992). Although the literature in social movements has been very useful to me, I tend to use the interdisciplinary language of communication research. There are a variety of connections between the case studies in this book and case studies in the social movement literature. See, for example, Verta Taylor and Nancy Whittier's fascinating essay in the Morris and Mueller book entitled, "Collective Identity in Social Movement Communities: Lesbian Feminist Mobilization."

14. Quoted in Lawrence Grossberg, Cary Nelson, and Paula Treichler, *Cultural Studies* (New York: Routledge, 1992), p. 3.

15. Ibid.

16. Russell Ferguson, "Introduction," in *Out There: Marginalization and Contemporary Cultures,* eds. Russell Ferguson, Martha Gever, Trinh Minh-ha, and Cornel West (Cambridge, MA: MIT Press, 1990), p. 10.

17. Cornel West, "The New Cultural Politics of Difference," in *Out There,* p. 35.

18. On fiction and marginality, see Gilles Deleuze and Félix Guattari's interesting essay, "What is a Minor Literature," in *Out There,* pp. 59–69.

19. See Dan Hallin, *The "Uncensored War": The Media and Vietnam* (New York: Oxford University Press, 1986).

20. See Douglas Kellner, *The Persian Gulf TV War* (Boulder, CO: Westview Press, 1992).

21. See Benjamin Ginsberg, *The Captive Public: How Mass Opinion Promotes State Power* (New York: Basic, 1986).

22. See Pierre Bourdieu, "Public Opinion Does Not Exist," in *Communication and Class Struggle,* eds. A. Mattelart and S. Siegelaub (New York: International General, 1979); and Walter Lippmann's *The Phantom Public* (New York: Harcourt, Brace, 1925) or *Public Opinion* (New York: The Free Press, 1965). For another view of polls, see the *Public Opinion Quarterly,* a journal of theory and methodology published by the American Association for Public Opinion Research. Also see Benjamin Page and Robert Shapiro's *The Rational Public: Fifty Years of Trends in Americans' Policy Preferences* (Chicago: University of Chicago Press, 1991).

23. Arthur Bentley, *The Process of Government* (Cambridge, MA: Harvard University Press, 1967), pp. 236–37.

24. Herbert Blumer, "Public Opinion and Public Opinion Polling," *American Sociological Review* 13 (1948): 544.

25. On opinion infrastructures, see Susan Herbst and James R. Beniger, "The Changing Infrastructure of Public Opinion," in *Audiencemaking,* eds. D. Charles Whitney and James Ettema (Newbury Park, CA: Sage, 1994).

26. An example of what I mean by contemporary community studies is Anthony Cohen's collection of essays, *Belonging: Identity and Social Organisation in British Rural Cultures* (Manchester: Manchester University Press, 1982). This book contains eleven studies of communities across the United Kingdom – from Whalsay, Shetland in the north to Elmdon, Essex in the south. As far as theoretical work, Joseph Gusfield's *Community: A Critical Response* (New York: Harper & Row, 1975) is very comprehensive and interesting: It summarizes many of the essential arguments about community in sociology. C. J. Calhoun's provocative essay, "Community: Toward a Variable Conceptualization for Comparative Research," discusses the concept of community as it relates to historical analysis (*Social History* 5, January 1980, pp. 105–29).

27. Ferdinand Tönnies, *Community and Association*, trans. C. Loomis (London: Routledge & Kegan Paul, 1955).

28. Emile Durkheim, *The Division of Labor in Society*, trans. George Simpson (New York: The Free Press, 1947).

29. G. A. Hillery, "Definitions of Community: Areas of Agreement," *Rural Sociology* 20 (1955): 117.

30. Robert Bellah et al., *Habits of the Heart: Individualism and Commitment in American Life* (New York: Harper & Row, 1985), p. 333.

31. I recognize that the inside/outside distinction is somewhat problematic. Some communities have extremely permeable or shifting boundaries, whereas others do not. In the former, one can theoretically go from inside to outside (and vice-versa) without much effort or commitment, or simply stay close to the fringes. Although we can describe community membership as a sort of continuum where individuals are central participants or occasional ones who aren't truly "inside" in any consistent way, it is difficult (and probably not very useful) to stray too far from the idea of borders – no matter how permeable or weakly drawn.

32. A. P. Cohen, *The Symbolic Construction of Community* (London: Tavistock Publications, 1985), p. 12. Also see Cohen's excellent critique of Robert Park and the Chicago School of Sociology on pages 28–38 of his book. Park's work, however flawed, was and still is an important contribution to the literature on urban communities. See Park et al., *The City* (Chicago: University of Chicago Press, 1925). A very useful, comprehensive book on community is Colin Bell and Howard Newby's *Community Studies: An Introduction to the Sociology of the Local Community* (New York: Praeger, 1972).

33. See Andrew Rosenthal, "Quayle Says Riots Sprang from Lack of Family Values," *The New York Times*, May 20, 1992: A1.

34. Calhoun, *Habermas and the Public Sphere*, p. 117.

35. Benedict Anderson, *Imagined Communities: Reflections on the Origin and Spread of Nationalism* (London: Verso, 1991), p. 6.

36. Steven Lukes, "Political Ritual and Social Integration," *Sociology* 9 (May 1975): 291.

37. It is especially unlikely the salonnières, discussed in the next chapter, were conscious of the fact that they had created rituals. For them, the salons were fun, educational, and enabled them to exert some intellectual influence. Other individuals described in this book – the editors of *The Defender* and *The Masses*, and the Libertarian activists – may have been more conscious of ritual, although only in a vague sense.

38. The previously cited book, *Out There: Marginalization and Contemporary Cul-*

tures, contains numerous examples of autobiographical essays, artwork, and polemical tracts created by contemporary marginal groups. I highly recommend it as an example of the sort of creative expression one finds when studying political outsiders.

39. See Roderick Bell, David Edwards, and R. Harrison Wagnes, *Political Power: A Reader in Theory and Research* (New York: Free Press, 1969).

40. See, in particular, Michel Foucault, *Power/Knowledge: Selected Interviews and Other Writings 1972–1977,* ed. Colin Gordon (New York: Pantheon, 1976). Also, see Steven Lukes's collection of essays on power by Habermas, Parsons, Arendt, Weber, and others, entitled *Power* (New York: New York University Press, 1986).

41. Foucault, *The History of Sexuality,* vol. 1, trans. R. Hurley (New York: Vintage, 1990), p. 92. There is an enormous amount of literature – across disciplines – about Foucauldian views of power. Among the helpful explications are Barry Smart, *Foucault, Marxism, and Critique* (London: Routledge & Kegan Paul, 1985), and Hubert Dreyfus and Paul Rabinow, *Michael Foucault: Beyond Structuralism and Hermeneutics* (Chicago: University of Chicago Press, 1983).

42. Foucault, *History of Sexuality,* pp. 95–6.

43. See Lukes, *Power: A Radical View* (London: Macmillan, 1974).

44. Ibid., p. 23.

45. On the general topic of news and its ability to shape citizens' agendas see Lance Bennett, *News: The Politics of Illusion* (New York: Longman, 1988) or David Swanson and Dan Nimmo's encyclopedic, *New Directions in Political Communication: A Resource Book* (Newbury Park, CA: Sage, 1990).

46. An excellent example of this framing process was *Time* magazine's cover story on April 20, 1992. The title of the story was, "Why Voters Don't Trust Clinton" (pp. 38–44).

47. This point was made by Elihu Katz. See his article, "Communications Research Since Lazarsfeld," *Public Opinion Quarterly* 51 (Winter, 1987): S25–S45.

48. The literature on how media shape public discourse is tremendously large. There are good case studies, such as Todd Gitlin's *The Whole World Is Watching* (Berkeley: University of California Press 1980), as well as theoretically informed essays like Murray Edelman's *The Symbolic Uses of Politics* (Urbana: University of Illinois Press, 1985).

49. Interestingly, during the 1992 presidential election campaign, Governor Bill Clinton's wife, Hillary, received some positive and negative media coverage for her comments about backchannels. Hillary Clinton claimed that she would (and should) have influence over some of her husband's decisions as president, simply because she had been married to him for so long. In other

words, her backchannel was so important, and so well-established, that she would feel compelled to use it.

50. Anthony Downs, *Inside Bureaucracy* (Boston: Little, Brown & Company, 1967), chap. 10. Also see Everett Rogers and Rekha Agarwala-Rogers, *Communication in Organizations* (New York: Free Press, 1976).

51. I have, in the past, had considerable difficulty recruiting left-wing political groups to study. These groups tend to be wary of people who want to observe them, because many have been persecuted by the FBI or other governmental representatives. One cooperative group was CISPES (the Committee in Solidarity with the People of El Salvador), whose members spoke with me despite some rather disturbing confrontations with the federal government. The focus of this study was on conceptions of public opinion among political activists. See my "Mass Media and Public Opinion: Citizens' Constructions of Political Reality," *Media, Culture and Society* 15 (1993): 437–54.

52. Dena Goodman's work on the Enlightenment salons is particularly good, because she singles them out for attention. Other historians have had a tendency to gloss over the existence of the salons as a trivial historical detail, while they focused on other aspects of the Old Regime – the writings of the philosophes, the politics of the court, or the economy of prerevolutionary France. Goodman's research, as well as the work of other contemporary social historians, is cited in Chapter 2.

53. The most widely cited studies of political activists have been those conducted by Samuel Eldersveld. See his *Political Parties in American Society* (New York: Basic, 1982).

2. BACKCHANNELS OF COMMUNICATION

1. The number of books and articles devoted to feminist theory and women's history published over the last two decades is enormous. For a good, general introduction to women's history, see Sara M. Evans, *Born for Liberty: A History of Women in America* (New York: Free Press, 1989) or Mary Ryan's smaller study *Women in Public* (Baltimore: Johns Hopkins University Press, 1990). For a review of continental and American feminist theory, see Toril Moi's comprehensive *Sexual/Textual Politics: Feminist Literary Theory* (London: Methuen, 1986). Another influential book on feminist theory building is Nancy Chodorow's *The Reproduction of Mothering: Psychoanalysis and the Sociology of Gender* (Berkeley: University of California Press, 1978). Also see Nancy Fraser, *Unruly Practices: Power, Discourse, and Gender in Contemporary Social Theory* (Minneapolis: University of Minnesota Press, 1989).

2. Much historical work in recent years has uncovered the ways that women affected the course of social, political, and economic events in their nations. See, for example, Carol R. Berkin and Clara M. Lovett, eds., *Women, War, and Revolution* (New York: Holmes & Meier, 1980) or Renate Bridenthal and Claudia Koonz, eds., *Becoming Visible: Women in European History* (Boston: Houghton Mifflin, 1977).

3. There were two very important exceptions in the case of Enlightenment and revolutionary France. The first is the role of women in the court – female members of the royal family and mistresses of the men. As Joan Landes has pointed out, women of the court were often thought of as influential "power-brokers": "Through sexual intrigue or marriage, women achieved a jealously guarded intimacy with the monarch or his personal representatives. They often served as conduits or mediators for aspiring courtiers and socially ambitious gentlemen" (p. 20). See Landes, *Women and the Public Sphere in the Age of the French Revolution* (Ithaca, NY: Cornell University Press, 1988).

   Another exception was the role of women in grain riots during the revolution. Working-class women initiated these collective uprisings, and the riots were political in the sense that they threatened those in power. As Olwen Hufton put it, "A bread riot without women is an inherent contradiction." See his article, "Women in Revolution 1789–1796," *Past and Present* 53 (1971): 90–108.

4. See Ruth Graham, "Loaves and Liberty: Women in the French Revolution," in *Women, War and Revolution*; Steven Hause and Anne Kenny, *Women's Suffrage and Social Politics in the French Third Republic* (Princeton, NJ: Princeton University Press, 1984); and Darline Gay Levy, Harriet Branson Applewhite, and Mary Durham Johnson, eds., *Women in Revolutionary Paris, 1789–1795, Selected Documents* (Urbana: University of Illinois Press, 1979).

5. Nina Rattner Gelbart, "Introduction" in Fontenelle's *Conversations on the Plurality of Worlds*, trans. H. A. Hargreaves (Berkeley: University of California Press, 1990), p. xxvi.

6. Although this chapter concentrates on the salons of eighteenth-century Paris (often believed to be the most active period for these sorts of meetings), salons have existed during a variety of eras in Eastern and Western history. On German salons, see Deborah Hertz, "Salonières and Literary Women in Late Eighteenth-Century Berlin," *New German Critique* 14 (1978): 97–108. On British salons, and the relationship between these and French salons, see Evelyn Gordon Bodek, "Salonières and Bluestockings: Educated Obsolescence and Germinating Feminism," *Feminist Studies* 3 (1976): 185–99. Interestingly, the American progressive magazine, *The Utne Reader*, recently established a program to encourage the formation of salons across the United

States. If readers are interested in joining a salon, they simply contact the magazine and are told about existing salons in their areas. See Stephanie Mills, "Salons and Beyond: Changing the World One Evening at a Time," *The Utne Reader* 44 (March/April 1991): 68–78.

7. Denis Diderot, *Dialogues*, trans. Francis Birrell (London: Routledge, 1927), p. 196.

8. Jürgen Habermas has argued that the salons of prerevolutionary Paris represent the emergence of a "public sphere" – a place where people gather to assess critically the nature of their institutions. See his discussion of salons in *The Structural Transformation of the Public Sphere* (Cambridge, MA: MIT Press, 1989).

9. See Helen Clergue, *The Salon: A Study of French Society and Personalities in the Eighteenth Century* (New York: Burt Franklin, 1971). More comprehensive work on the early salons was done by Carolyn Lougee. See her *Le Paradis des Femmes: Women, Salons, and Social Stratification in Seventeenth-Century France* (Princeton, NJ: Princeton University Press, 1976).

10. Lougee, *Le Paradis des Femmes*, p. 136.

11. Bodek, "Salonières and Bluestockings," p. 186

12. Quoted in Lougee, *Le Patadis des Femmes*, p. 84.

13. Chauncey Brewster Tinker, *The Salon and English Letters* (New York: Mac-Millan, 1915), p. 23.

14. Although nobility was not a requirement, it didn't seem to hurt one's chances of being invited to join the salon culture. As Lougee points out, almost half of the salon attendants of the seventeenth century were of noble background.

15. Tinker, *The Salon and English Letters*, p. 27

16. Anny Latour, *Uncrowned Queens*, trans. A. A. Dent (London: J. M. Dent, 1970), p.60.

17. Catherine Charlotte (Lady Jackson), *The Old Régime: Court, Salons, and Theatres* (London: Richard Bentley, 1880), p. 72.

18. See, for example, S. G. Tallentyre (pseudonym for Evelyn Beatrice Hall), *The Women of the Salons and Other French Portraits* (London: Longman, Green, and Co., 1901), pp. 40–41.

19. Helen Clergue, *The Salon: A Study of French Society and Personalities in the Eighteenth Century* (New York: Burt Franklin, 1971), p. 278.

20. In one oft repeated anecdote, Monsieur Geoffrin allegedly tried to read the *Encyclopedia*. Each page had two columns, but M. Geoffrin tried to read across the columns instead of reading the first before the second. He supposedly concluded that the "book seemed very fair, but a trifle obscure" (Tallentyre, *The Women of the Salons*, p. 42). Tallentyre also recounts several other stories: "[M. Geoffrin] would read the first volume of a history or book

of travels, written in several volumes, over and over again, and then wonder that the author should so much repeat himself." In another tale: A visitor to the salon noticed the absence of an old man who usually sat at the table. When asked about this, Madame Geoffrin supposedly said, "Cétait mon mari; il est mort [It was my husband; he is dead]" (Ibid., pp. 42–3. See also Clergue, *The Salon*, p. 282 and Charlotte, *The Old Régine*, p.77).

21. Dena Goodman, "Filial Rebellion in the Salon: Madame Geoffrin and Her Daughter," *French Historical Studies* 16 (1989): 31. Geoffrin and her daughter did not get along with each other particularly well. Often, according to Goodman, mentors and their adopted daughters established closer relationships than did mothers and daughters.

22. Madame Tencin led a rather wild life. She left a convent where she was training to be a nun, and gave birth to d'Alembert, whom she then abandoned. See Tinker, *The Salon and English Letters*, p. 43.

23. See Shirley Jones, "Madame de Tencin: An Eighteenth-Century Woman Novelist," in *Woman and Society in Eighteenth-Century France: Essays in Honour of John Stephenson Spink*, eds. Eva Jacobs, W. H. Barber, Jean H. Bloch, F. W. Leakey, and Eileen Le Breton (London: Athlone, 1979).

24. Dena Goodman, "Enlightenment Salons: The Convergence of Female and Philosophic Ambitions," *Eighteenth-Century Studies* 22 (1989): 337.

25. De Lespinasse, who lived with her mentor Du Deffand, began her own salon in Du Deffand's house while her mentor slept in the late afternoon. Upon Du Deffand's discovery of this competing salon operating in her own house, the Du Deffand/Lespinasse friendship ended. See Tallentyre, *The Women of the Salons*, pp. 27–8.

26. See Clergue, *The Salon*, pp. 123–32.

27. Tallentyre, *The Women of the Salons*, p. 83.

28. Madame d'Epinay, *Memoirs and Correspondence of Madame D'Epinay*, trans. E. G. Allingham (London: George Routledge, 1930), pp. 56–7.

29. Jean-Jacques Rousseau, *The Confessions of Jean-Jacques Rousseau*, trans. J. M. Cohen (New York: Penguin, 1985), pp. 383–4.

30. This correspondence is described in Francis Steegmuller, *A Woman, a Man, and Two Kingdoms: The Story of Madame d'Epinay and the Abbé Galiani* (New York: Alfred A. Knopf, 1991).

31. Steven Laurence Kaplan, *La Bagarre: Galiani's "Lost" Parody* (Netherlands: Martinus Nijhoff, 1979), p. 17.

32. See the excellent study of Holbach and his salon by Alan Kors, *D'Holbach's Coterie: An Enlightenment in Paris* (Princeton, NJ: Princeton University Press, 1976). The meetings at Holbach's house are often recounted in books about female-dominated salons, since the same men often attended both sorts of

gatherings. Kingsley Martin argues that Holbach's gatherings were less intellectually stifling that those of his female contemporaries: "Best of all, from the point of view of the philosophe, however, were Holbach's dinner-parties. It was there that Diderot, unkempt, indecorous, pouring out a stream of exuberant and blasphemous eloquence, was really at home. At Holbach's too, one might meet others who seldom frequented the Paris drawing rooms: Turgot and the young Condorcet, and foreign celebrities like Hume, Wilkes, Shelburne, Garrick, Franklin and Priestley all from time to time enjoyed the hospitality of the "Maître d'Hôtel of Philosophy" in the house that was nick-named the 'Café de l'Europe.'" See Kingsley Martin, *The Rise of French Liberal Thought: A Study of Political Ideas From Bayle to Condorcet* (New York: New York University Press, 1954), p. 108.

33. See Kaplan, *La Bagarre*, p. 63. An even more extensive discussion of d'Epinay's relationship with Galiani can be found in Ruth Plaut Weinreb's *Eagle in a Gauze Cage: Louise D'Epinay Femme de Lettres* (New York: AMS Press, 1993).

34. Steegmuller, *A Woman, a Man, and Two Kingdoms*, p. 229.

35. Quoted in ibid., p. 6.

36. Ibid., p. 31.

37. *Memoirs of Madame D'Epinay*, p. 16.

38. See Weinreb, *Eagle in a Gauze Cage*, pp. 99–158.

39. Most of the scholarly work about salons was done in the early decades of the twentieth century or within the last ten years. Many of the books about salons from the early twentieth century were written by women and emphasize the role of women. These authors were probably inspired, in part, by the suffrage movement in the United States. Contemporary work on salons is the result of a relatively new interest in social history and women's history on the part of academics. Dena Goodman, a historian of Enlightenment France, has written most eloquently and rigorously about the Parisian salons. Parts of this chapter owe a great deal to her archival research and her analysis.

40. *Memoirs of Madame D'Epinay*, pp. 136–8.

41. Tinker, *The Salon and English Letters*, p. 37.

42. Dena Goodman, "Governing the Republic of Letters: The Politics of Culture in the French Enlightenment," *History of European Ideas* 13 (1991): 193.

43. Ibid., p. 184.

44. Martin, *The Rise of French Liberal Thought*, p.104.

45. Goodman, "Governing the Republic of Letters," p. 194.

46. David Hume, *Essays, Moral, Political, and Literary* (Indianapolis, IN: Liberty Classics, 1987), p. 536.

47. Quoted in Goodman, "Governing the Republic of Letters," p. 194.

48. Quoted in Edmond and Jules de Goncourt, *The Woman of the Eighteenth Century: Her Life, From Birth to Death, Her Love and Her Philosophy in the Worlds of Salon, Shop and Street* (Freeport, NY: Books for Libraries Press, 1972), p. 259.

49. Judy Cornelia Pearson, *Gender and Communication* (Dubuque, IA: William C. Brown, 1985), p. 319.

50. Tallentyre, *The Women of the Salons*, p. 45.

51. Quoted in Goodman, "Governing the Republic of Letters," p. 185.

52. Quoted in M. Roustan, *The Pioneers of the French Revolution*, trans. Frederic Whyte (Boston: Little, Brown, 1926), p. 183.

53. Goodman, "Governing the Republic of Letters," pp. 185–6.

54. Roustan, *The Pioneers*, p. 193.

55. Dena Goodman makes this point eloquently, in "Enlightenment Salons," p. 339.

56. Tinker, *The Salon and English Letters*, p. 31.

57. Bernard Le Bouvier Fontenelle, *Conversations on the Plurality of Worlds*, trans. H. A. Hargreaves (Berkeley: University of California Press, 1990).

58. Ibid., p. 12.

59. On the history and meaning of the phrase "public opinion," see my *Numbered Voices: How Opinion Polls Shape American Politics* (Chicago: University of Chicago Press, 1993) or Paul Palmer, "The Concept of Public Opinion in Political Theory," in *Essays in History and Political Theory in Honor of Charles Howard McIlwain*, ed. C. Wittke (New York: Russell & Russell, 1964).

60. Lionel Gossman, *Medievalism and the Ideologies of the Enlightenment: The World and Work of La Curne de Sainte-Palaye* (Baltimore: Johns Hopkins University Press, 1968), p. 61.

61. Also see Thomas E. Crow, *Painters and Public Life in Eighteenth-Century Paris* (New Haven, CT: Yale University Press, 1985), pp. 121–2; and Robert S. Tate, *Petit de Bachaumont: His Circle and the Mémoires Secrets* (Geneva: Institut et Musee Voltaire, 1968).

62. Tinker, *The Salon and English Letters*, p. 30.

63. Martin, *The Rise of French Liberal Thought*, pp. 110–11.

64. Ibid., p. 104–5.

65. Bodek, "Salonières and Bluestockings," p. 185–6.

66. Diderot, *Dialogues*, pp. 194–5.

67. Carole Pateman, *The Sexual Contract* (Stanford, CA: Stanford University Press, 1988), p. 96.

68. Jean-Jacques Rousseau, *Emile*, trans. Barbara Foxley (London: J. M. Dent, 1969), pp. 371–2.

69. I take the phrase "status conferral" from Paul Lazarsfeld and Robert Merton,

"Mass Communication, Popular Taste, and Organized Social Action," in *The Communication of Ideas*, ed. Lyman Bryson (New York: Harper and Bros., 1948).

70. See, for example, Daniel Gordon, "Philosophy, Sociology, and Gender in the Enlightenment Conception of Public Opinion," David Bell, "The 'Public Sphere' and the World of Law in Eighteenth-Century France," and Sarah Maza, "Women, the Bourgeoisie, and the Public Sphere: Response to David Bell and Daniel Gordon," all in *French Historical Studies* (Fall 1992): 935–53. Also see Dena Goodman, "Public Sphere and Private Life: Toward a Synthesis of Current Historiographical Approaches to the Old Regime," *History and Theory* 31 (1992): 1–20.

71. On conceptualizing power, and the debate over its definition, see Steven Lukes, *Power* (New York: New York University Press, 1986).

72. See Landes, *Women and the Public Sphere*, p. 139; Barbara C. Pope, "Revolution and Retreat: Upper-class French Women after 1789," in Carol Berkin and Clara Levett, eds., *Women, War, and Revolution* (New York: Holmes & Meier, 1980), p. 218.

73. Jane Abray, "Feminism in the French Revolution," *American Historical Review* 80 (1975): 54.

74. Pope, "Revolution and Retreat," p. 219.

75. Madame Roland, *The Memoirs of Madame Roland*, trans. E. Shuckburgh (London: Barrie & Jenkins, 1989), p. 58. Also see Gita May's excellent biography of Roland, *Madame Roland and the Age of Revolution* (New York: Columbia University Press, 1970).

76. Pope, "Revolution and Retreat," p. 221.

77. Emmet Kennedy, *A Cultural History of the French Revolution* (New Haven, CT: Yale University Press, 1989), p. 26.

3. RACE DISCRIMINATION, MASS MEDIA, AND PUBLIC EXPRESSION

1. The name "Bronzeville" was used regularly by the *Chicago Defender* to describe the black neighborhood on the city's South Side. St. Clair Drake and Horace Cayton also used the term extensively in their classic study of Chicago, *Black Metropolis: A Study of Negro Life in a Northern City* (New York: Harcourt, Brace & World, 1945), to describe the area on the South Side bounded by Cottage Grove and Wentworth Avenues on the east and west, and 12th and 71st Streets on the north and south. Drake and Cayton used the name Bronzeville because they believed residents of the community pre-

ferred it. They explained that, "The expression 'Bronze' when counterposed to 'black' reveals a tendency on the part of Negroes to avoid referring to themselves as 'black.' And, of course, as a descriptive term, the former is even more accurate than the latter, for most Negroes *are* brown." See ibid., p. 385.

2. Ibid., p. 58; On black migration to Chicago see James Grossman's *Land of Hope: Chicago, Black Southerners, and the Great Migration* (Chicago: University of Chicago Press, 1989) and Allan H. Spear, *Black Chicago: The Making of a Negro Ghetto, 1890–1920* (Chicago: University of Chicago Press, 1967).

3. Carl Sandburg, "Southern Negroes Taught 'City Ways,'" *Chicago Daily News*, July 15, 1919, p. 5.

4. Drake and Cayton, *Black Metropolis*, pp. 214–62.

5. See ibid., p. 382; Spear, *Black Chicago*, p. 12; or Gunnar Myrdal, *An American Dilemma: The Negro Problem and Modern Democracy* (New York: Harper & Brothers, 1944), p. 1127.

6. Drake and Cayton, *Black Metropolis*, pp. 379–80.

7. Spear, *Black Chicago*, p. 26.

8. Ira Katznelson, *Black Men, White Cities: Race, Politics, and Migration in the United States, 1900–30, and Britain, 1948–68* (London: Oxford University Press, 1973), p. 103. Although a discussion of black politics in Chicago during this period is beyond the scope of this book, there are several excellent works on the subject. See for example Harold F. Gosnell's classic study, *Negro Politicians: The Rise of Negro Politics in Chicago* (Chicago: University of Chicago Press, 1935) and James Q. Wilson's *Negro Politics: The Search for Leadership* (New York: Free Press, 1960). Charles Branham has written a very thorough history of black politics in Chicago, with an emphasis on the development of a black "submachine" on the South Side. See *The Transformation of Black Political Leadership in Chicago, 1864–1942* (Ph.D. diss., University of Chicago, 1981).

9. Frederick G. Detweiler, *The Negro Press in the United States* (Chicago: University of Chicago Press, 1922), pp. 1–31. *The Defender* is still published today, making it one of the more resilient African-American papers. On the history of the black press in America see also Maxwell R. Brooks, *The Negro Press Re-Examined: Political Content of Leading Negro Newspapers* (Boston: Christopher House, 1959); Lee Finkle, *Forum for Protest: The Black Press During World War II* (Rutherford: Associated University Presses, 1975); Henry La Brie III, ed., *Perspectives of the Black Press: 1974* (Kennebunkport, ME: Mercer House Press, 1974); Vishnu V. Oak, *The Negro Newspaper* (Westport, CT: Negro Universities Press, 1948); and Armistead S. Pride, *A Register and History of Negro Newspapers in the United States* (Ph.D. diss., Northwestern University, 1950). Although *The Defender* was a national newspaper in the early decades of this century, it exhib-

ited some of the characteristics of the generic community newspaper. On community papers, see Morris Janowitz, *The Community Press in an Urban Setting*, 2nd ed. (Chicago: University of Chicago Press, 1980).

10. Abbott quoted in Roi Ottley, *The Lonely Warrior: The Life and Times of Robert S. Abbott* (Chicago: H. Regnery Company, 1979), p. 81.

11. Ibid., p. 298. Circulation figures for *The Defender* may underestimate the number of readers, though, because in the 1920s blacks often shared newspapers or read them aloud in houses and shops. See Detweiler, *The Negro Press in the United States*, pp. 7–8.

12. See Grossman's *Land of Hope: Chicago, Black Southerners, and the Great Migration*, which illustrates the critical role of the *Defender* in the migration. Also see Katherine A. Bitner, "The Role of the Chicago Defender in the Great Migration of 1916–1918," *Negro History Bulletin*, 48 (Jan.–Dec. 1985), pp. 20–6.

13. Quoted in Ottley, *The Lonely Warrior*, p. 170

14. Consuelo Caldwell Young, "An Objective Reader Interest Study of *The Chicago Defender Newspaper*," M.A. Thesis, Northwestern University, 1943.

15. Drake and Cayton, *Black Metropolis*, p. 80.

16. Ottley, *The Lonely Warrior*, p. 296.

17. See Andrew Buni, *Robert L. Vann of The Pittsburgh Courier: Politics and Black Journalism* (Pittsburgh: University of Pittsburgh Press, 1974).

18. Enoch P. Waters, *American Diary: A Personal History of the Black Press* (Chicago: Path Press, 1987), p. 70. In 1954 *The Defender* published an article by James Knight, the first mayor of Bronzeville, who was elected in 1932. Yet *The Defender* itself did not sponsor the elections until 1934; *The Chicago Defender*, November 27, 1954, p. 5.

19. *The Chicago Defender*, September 15, 1934, p. 5. The "Miss Bronze America" contest was introduced in 1924 and may have been the *Defender*'s response to the "Miss America Pageant," which began in 1921.

20. Ibid., September 12, 1936, p. 1.

21. Ibid., October 19, 1940, p. 18.

22. Ibid., October 14, 1939, p. 1.

23. Ibid., November 25, 1944, p. 1

24. Ibid., February 14, 1959, p. 12.

25. Ibid., September 26, 1936, p. 19.

26. Ibid., October 30, 1937, p. 4.

27. Ibid., November 1, 1937, p. 10.

28. Ibid., August 29, 1936, p. 5.

29. Ibid., September 19, 1936, p. 2.

30. Drake and Cayton, *Black Metropolis*, p. 428.

31. *The Chicago Defender,* November 2, 1940, p. 22.

32. On modern political journalism see W. Lance Bennett, *News: The Politics of Illusion* (New York: Longman, 1988); Doris Graber, *Mass Media and American Politics,* 4th ed. (Washington, DC: Congressional Quarterly Press, 1993). On the history of American journalism, see Edwin Emery and Michael Emery, *The Press and America: An Interpretive History of the Mass Media,* 5th ed. (Englewood Cliffs, NJ: Prentice-Hall, 1984); and Michael Schudson, *Discovering the News: A Social History of American Newspapers* (New York: Basic Books, 1978).

33. See *The Chicago Defender,* September 30, 1944, p. 5; October 7, 1944; November 18, 1944, p. 6; November 18, 1944, p. 10.

34. Ibid., October 9, 1948, p. 3; November 6, 1948, p. 33.

35. Ibid., October 30, 1948, p. 19.

36. Ibid., January 22, 1955, p. 16

37. Ibid., August 22, 1936, p. 1.

38. *Chicago Tribune,* November 17, 1937, p. 8.

39. Vernon Jarett, telephone interview with author, November 5, 1991.

40. Dr. Clementine Skinner, telephone interview with author, November 6, 1991.

41. John Sengstacke, telephone interviews with author, March 18, 1991 and November 11, 1991.

42. Dempsey Travis, telephone interview with author, November 7, 1991.

43. *The Chicago Defender,* January 16, 1937, p. 9.

44. Ibid., May 15, 1937, p. 7.

45. Ibid., May 1, 1937, p. 3.

46. Ibid., January 23, 1937, p. 24.

47. Ibid., April 17, 1937, p. 28.

48. Ibid., January 30, 1937, p. 14.

49. Emile Durkheim, *The Elementary Forms of the Religious Life: A Study in Religious Sociology,* Joseph Swain, trans. (London: George Allen & Unwin. 1915), pp. 219–20.

50. *The Chicago Defender,* September 12, 1936, p. 4.

51. Ibid., October 3, 1936, p. 1. Voting was so casual that one could vote as often as he or she liked. George Jones, a local merchant, told *The Defender* that he voted eight or ten times in 1937 to "give all the boys a play." See *The Defender,* September 18, 1937, p. 1.

52. Myrdal, *An American Dilemma,* p. 485. Although works describing the history of black suffrage abound, some recent books are Jack Bass and Walter DeVries, *The Transformation of Southern Politics: Social Change and Political Consequences since 1945* (New York: Basic Books, 1976); J. Morgan Kousser, *The Shaping of Southern Politics: Suffrage Restriction and the Establishment of the*

One-Party South, 1880–1910 (New Haven, CT: Yale University Press, 1974); Steven F. Lawson, *Black Ballots: Voting Rights in the South, 1944–1969* (New York: Columbia University Press, 1976); and Lawson, *In Pursuit of Power: Southern Blacks and Electoral Politics, 1965–1982* (New York: Columbia University Press, 1985).

53. Gosnell, *Negro Politicians*, p. 374.

54. Ibid., pp. 18–19.

55. See *The Chicago Defender*, September 11, 1948, p. 3; ibid., December 4, 1954, p. 1.

56. Ibid., September 17, 1938, p. 5.

57. For a vivid description of social life in Bronzeville in the 1930s, see Waters, *An American Diary*, pp. 68–89.

58. Waters, *An American Diary*, p. 70. *The Defender* claimed that the Bronzeville mayor idea was copied by seventeen other cities. See *The Defender*, January 8, 1938, p. 1. Mentions were made of the "mayors" of other black communities – a "race mayor of Dallas," a "Derbytown Mayor" in Louisville, a "Bronzeville" mayor of Evanston, Illinois, and mayors of Harlem and Detroit. See *The Defender*, March 27, 1937, p. 7; January, 23, 1937, p. 8; and January 4, 1941, pp. 1–2; November 20, 1954, p. 2.

59. John Sengstacke, telephone interview with author, March 18, 1991.

60. *The Chicago Defender*, December 11, 1954, p. 4.

61. Ibid., November 27, 1954, p. 2.

62. Ibid., February 7, 1959, p. 2.

63. *The Defender* has never been indexed so there may be mentions of the contest during the 1960s, but none were located. During the 1930s and 1940s, by comparison, *The Defender* provided election coverage in every issue during the fall – usually on the front page.

64. In 1952, for example, *The Defender* introduced a contest for "America's Most Popular Woman," and published elaborate contest rules and clip-out ballots in the paper each week for several months. See *The Defender*, March 29, 1952, p. 2.

65. Operation PUSH, led at the time by Rev. Tyrone Crider, began a boycott of NIKE products in the summer of 1990. Crider claimed that NIKE failed to invest in the black community and its businesses, despite the great profits they reap from selling footwear to African-Americans. See *The Chicago Tribune*, August 14, 1990, p. 1.

66. Wilson, *Negro Politics*, p. 297–8. John Sengstacke confirms this hypothesis, saying that the Bronzeville race became unnecessary after the 1930s and 1940s. Since black politicians like Dawson became increasingly powerful as spokesmen for the community, the mayor of Bronzeville was no longer a crit-

ical role. Sengstacke says that the race became a popularity contest by the late 1950s; telephone conversation with author, March 18, 1991.

67. The daily circulation for *The Defender* was 30,675 in 1960 and sank to 27,611 in 1989. See *Directory of Newspapers and Periodicals* (Philadelphia: N. W. Ayer and Sons, 1960), p. 254; and *Gale Directory of Publications* (Detroit: Gale Research, Inc., 1989), p. 402. On the general decline of the black press, see Alan Bussel, "Evolution and Revolution: The Search for New Forms," in La Brie, ed., *Perspectives of the Black Press: 1974*, pp. 141–52.

68. *The Chicago Defender*, October 23, 1943, p. 3.

69. See Sally Moore and Barbara Myerhoff, *Secular Ritual* (Amsterdam: Van Gorcum, 1977), for a review of anthropological and sociological perspectives on nonreligious ritual.

70. The Bronzeville Town Hall was proposed by Warren DeJohnette, a realtor. He envisioned a building that would "assist established social welfare organizations with Negro community problems" and serve as a meeting place as well. See *The Defender*, January 8, 1955, p. 16.

71. Lukes, "Political Ritual and Social Integration," p. 302.

72. Orville H. Platt, "Negro Governors," in *Papers of the New Haven Colony Historical Society* (New Haven, CT: 1900), pp. 318–19. See also Sterling Stuckey, *Slave Culture: Nationalist Theory and the Foundations of Black America* (New York: Oxford University Press, 1987).

73. Joseph P. Reidy, "'Negro Election Day' and Black Community Life in New England, 1750–1860," *Marxist Perspectives*, 1 (Fall 1978), p. 109.

74. Ibid., p. 113.

75. Sengstacke, interview with author, March 18, 1991.

76. Waters, *American Diary*, p. 70.

4. POLITICAL MARGINALITY AND COMMUNICATION IN GREENWICH VILLAGE, 1911–1918

1. Long after I finished my research on intentional outsiders, I found an interesting book by the German scholar Hans Mayer on the same subject. See his fascinating discussion of women, Jews, and homosexuals as outsiders in literature in *Outsiders: A Study in Life and Letters* (Cambridge, MA: MIT Press, 1982).

2. Rebecca Zurier's book, *Art for the Masses: A Radical Magazine and Its Graphics, 1911–1917* (Philadelphia: Temple University Press, 1988), is one of the most recent looks at *The Masses*. I am greatly indebted to her fascinating and comprehensive study of the magazine, and as my notes indicate, I draw on many

of her insights in this chapter. Readers interested in *The Masses* should refer to Zurier's work for details about the production and impact of the publication. Another excellent and thorough study is Leslie Fishbein's *Rebels in Bohemia: The Radicals of The Masses, 1911–1917* (Chapel Hill, NC: University of North Carolina Press, 1982). Margaret Jones has also contributed to the historical literature about *The Masses* – particularly the female writers. See her *Heretics and Hellraisers: Women Contributors to the Masses, 1911–1917* (Austin, TX: University of Texas Press, 1993). Since this chapter focuses exclusively on *The Masses*, I have not provided much in the way of historical context, particularly the social, political, and economic changes that characterized the early twentieth century (e.g., labor movements, immigration, antiwar sentiment, etc.). Readers interested in the period might begin with Alan Dawley's *Struggles for Justice: Social Responsibility and the Liberal State* (Cambridge, MA: Harvard University Press, 1991).

3. I use "communication network" in this chapter to refer to the interlocking relationships among artists and writers living in the small New York City neighborhood of Greenwich Village from the turn of the century through World War I. There are methodologies in the social sciences for conducting "network analyses" that enable one to rigorously map such relationships. Those approaches are usually employed to study contemporary communicative behavior, however, because there is rarely enough evidence to conduct these sorts of analyses on historical communities. On network analysis in general, see Everett Rogers and Donald Kincaid, *Communication Networks: Toward a New Paradigm for Research* (New York: Free Press, 1981). A very interesting study using historical network analysis is Doug McAdam's *Freedom Summer: The Idealists Revisited* (New York: Oxford University Press, 1988).

4. James Playsted Wood, *Magazines in the United States* (New York: The Ronald Press, 1971), p. 407.

5. Art Young, *On My Way: Being the Book of Art Young in Text and Picture* (New York: Horace Liveright, 1928), p.275.

6. Floyd Dell, *Homecoming* (New York: Farrar & Rinehard, 1933), p. 278.

7. See *The Masses* 1 (July 1911): 18.

8. Floyd Dell, *Homecoming*, p. 251.

9. Art Young, *On My Way*, p. 281.

10. N. W. Ayer and Sons' *American Newspaper Annual and Directory* reported the following circulation figures for *The Masses* in their annual volumes:

1911	No figures available
1912	No figures available
1913	10,000
1914	10,000

1915	14,000
1916	14,500
1917	17,000

11. Young, *On My Way*, p. 277.

12. Zurier, *Art for the Masses*, p. 66.

13. See Robert Humphrey, *Children of Fantasy: The First Rebels of Greenwich Village* (New York: John Wiley, 1978) and also Mabel Dodge Luhan, *Movers and Shakers* (New York: Harcourt, Brace and Company, 1936).

14. An exception is *The Comrade*, a serious literary magazine with a socialist bent. See Daniel Aaron, *Writers on the Left: Episodes in American Literary Communism* (New York: Harcourt, Brace & World, 1961), pp. 18–19.

15. *The Masses* 1 (March, 1911): 3.

16. *The Masses* 3 (March, 1913): 2.

17. *The Masses* 1 (October, 1911): 12. Although many find this picture amusing and charming, Rebecca Zurier argues that by including a note on why the picture isn't a joke (squalid living conditions aren't funny), the editors undercut the humor of it: "By cranking up the didactic machinery to announce each instance of humor, the editors in effect killed their chances of appealing to readers through wit," *Art for the Masses*, p. 125.

18. *The Masses* 1 (April 1911).

19. *The Masses* 1 (February, 1911): 3.

20. Art Young, *Art Young: His Life and Times* (New York: Sheridan House, 1939), p. 272.

21. I draw here on Zurier's analysis of the AP case; see *Art for the Masses*, pp. 44–6.

22. Eastman, *Enjoyment of Living* (New York: Harper & Brothers, 1948), pp. 548–559.

23. Ibid., p. 555.

24. Zurier, *Art for the Masses*, p. 127.

25. Eastman, *Enjoyment of Living*, p. 555.

26. Quoted in Zurier, *Art for the Masses*, p. 138.

27. Quoted in ibid., p. 143.

28. *The Masses* 1 (May 1911): 14.

29. Ibid., p. 12.

30. *The Masses* 2 (December, 1912): 3.

31. *The Masses* 1 (February, 1911): 17.

32. *The Masses* 1 (July, 1911).

33. See Granville Hicks, *John Reed: The Making of a Revolutionary* (New York: Macmillan, 1936), pp. 96–104.

34. Ibid. The "pageant" was meant to raise money for the workers, and although

a spiritual success, it did not produce any profits at all. The workers were sorely disappointed with the results of the production, but Reed had already left for Italy by the time the workers found out about the financial disaster.

35. *The Masses* 3 (June, 1913): 14.
36. *The Masses* 3 (February, 1913): 6.
37. Eastman, *Enjoyment of Living*, p. 55.
38. Dell, *Homecoming*, pp. 46–8.
39. See, for example, *The Masses* 1 (December, 1911): 3.
40. *The Masses* 1 (August, 1911): 16.
41. *The Masses* 1 (November, 1911): 4.
42. *The Masses* 7 (April 1917): 37.
43. Fishbein, "Introduction," *Art for the Masses*, p. 6.
44. In *Enjoyment of Living*, Eastman writes, "There was no Freudian psychology in America then [the early years of the twentieth century] – no "mother complex" or "complex" at all, no understanding of the role of infantile fixations or conflicts of unconscious motives. The term neurosis was little known" (p. 196).
45. *The Masses* 9 (June, 1917): 5.
46. *The Masses* 9 (April, 1917): 8.
47. *The Masses* 9 (June, 1917): 23.
48. *The Masses* 9 (April, 1917): 11.
49. *The Masses* 9 (July 1917): 9.
50. *The Masses* 9 (September, 1917): 3. On the finer legal points of *The Masses'* legal problems, see Zechariah Chafee, *Freedom of Speech* (New York: Harcourt, Brace and Company, 1920).
51. *The Liberator* 1 (June, 1918): 11.
52. Young, *Art Young*, p. 336.
53. Quoted in Zurier, *Art for the Masses*, p. 64.
54. Zurier, *Art for the Masses*, pp. 64–5.
55. Eastman wrote of *The Masses* and *The New Masses*, "It would be hard to invent two vehicles of expression more radically contrasted. Not only my experimental philosophy, antipractical theory of art, and constant militance against dogma, but the zest for obstreperous truth-telling which actuated all the leaders of the old crowd distinguish the two ventures completely. Dissimulation was tabu in our gang; jesuitism an arch-enemy; loyalty to an organization treason to the truth; to put over a 'party line' unthinkable" (*Enjoyment of Living*, p. 415).
56. Dell, *Homecoming*, p. 272.
57. *The Masses* 1 (July, 1911): 18.
58. *The Masses* 9 (April, 1917): 35.

59. *The Masses* 1 (February, 1911): back cover.
60. *The Masses* 1 (August, 1911): 18.
61. *The Masses* 1 (July, 1911): 19.
62. Quoted in Zurier, *Art for the Masses*, p. 50.
63. I am thinking here about Steven Lukes's definition of ritual discussed in Chapter 1. See his "Political Ritual and Social Integration," *Sociology* 9 (May 1975): 289–308.
64. Eastman, *Enjoyment of Living*, p. 441.
65. Quoted in Zurier, *Art for the Masses*, p. 46.
66. *The New York Times*, November 7, 1917, p.20.
67. *The New York Times*, November 20, 1917, p. 4.
68. *The New York Times*, April 16, 1918, p. 8.
69. *The New York Times*, April 19, 1918, p. 11.
70. On the importance of *The Masses* case for First Amendment law, see Anthony Lewis, *Make No Law: The Sullivan Case and the First Amendment* (New York: Random House, 1991).
71. Quoted in Ronald Steel, *Walter Lippmann and the American Century* (New York: Vintage, 1980), p. 82.
72. Sue Walton (Chair, Libertarian Party of Illinois), interview with author, Evanston, IL, June 30, 1992.

5. CONTEMPORARY OUTSIDERS

1. For statistics about third-party candidacies, see the *Congressional Quarterly Guide to U.S. Elections* (Washington, DC: Congressional Quarterly, 1985). For figures about Ross Perot's candidacy, and analysis of his electoral support, see *The New York Times*, November 5, 1992, pp. A2 – B4.
2. Throughout this chapter, I use "libertarian" to describe a philosophical system, and "Libertarian" to describe formal party activity and members. Libertarian activists also make a distinction between "small l" libertarians, who believe in the philosophy, yet have not joined the party.
3. George Will, "Libertarians? No, U.S. Needs a Legitimate Fourth Choice," *Chicago Sun-Times*, July 9, 1992, p. 38. Will's comments are particularly interesting, since so many of his views are shared by the Libertarians, and one would think he would be more sympathetic to them.
4. These data are from a 1982 telephone survey of 654 Californians, conducted by California Survey Research, located in Van Nuys, CA. The study is entitled, "Californians View the Libertarian Party," and can be ordered from the researchers.

5. See Hesseltine, *Third-Party Movements in the United States*; Stephen Rockwood et al., *American Third Parties Since the Civil War: An Annotated Bibliography* (New York: Garland, 1985); or Daniel Mazmanian, *Third Parties in Presidential Elections* (Washington, DC: The Brookings Institution, 1974).

6. For example, see David Berman, "Environment, Culture, and Radical Third Parties: Electoral Support for the Socialists in Arizona and Nevada, 1912–1916," *Social Science Journal* 27 (1990): 147–58.

7. See Steven Rosenstone, Roy Behr, and Edward Lazarus, *Third Parties in America: Citizen Response to Major Party Failure* (Princeton, NJ: Princeton University Press, 1984).

8. One exception is J. David Gillespie's recent textbook on third parties, *Politics at the Periphery: Third Parties in Two-Party America* (Columbia: University of South Carolina Press, 1993). Gillispie's is a near-encyclopedic collection of information about third parties in America, from the nineteenth century to present. His focus is largely descriptive, and his brief theoretical discussion draws largely from the mainstream literature in political science, so it is a fine exemplar of conventional research in that field. Chapter Seven of *Politics at the Periphery* contains a small-scale personality study of third-party activists.

9. Samuel Eldersveld, *Political Parties: A Behavioral Analysis* (Chicago: Rand McNally, 1964) and *Political Parties in American Society* (New York: Basic, 1982). For a list of studies of political activism and social movements, see the excellent review and bibliography by Doug McAdam, John McCarthy, and Mayer Zald, "Social Movements," in *Handbook of Sociology*, ed., Neil Smelser (Newbury Park, CA: Sage, 1988), pp. 695–737.

10. Eldersveld, *Political Parties in American Society*, p. 191.

11. Ibid., p. 187.

12. On mainstream party recruiting, see Robert Huckfeldt and John Sprague, "Political Parties and Electoral Mobilization: Political Structure, Social Structure, and the Party Canvass," *American Political Science Review* 86 (March 1992): 70–86.

13. The other researcher was Jill Edy, a doctoral student, who conducted half of the interviews reported here. She and I worked together to standardize, as best we could, our approach to the different topics in the interview protocol.

14. Sue Walton, head of the LPI, gave us a list of activists whom she believes are particularly dynamic and interesting. The group was chosen intentionally to be diverse, because we wanted to speak with a variety of different sorts of activists. The interview contained only open-ended questions, and was meant to serve as a starting point for conversation. Certain questions were skipped or added depending upon who the informants were, and how they viewed their role in the party.

15. Sue Walton, former state chair of the Libertarian party of Illinois, provided the figures for national membership. Conversation with the author, August 13, 1992.

16. The 1976, 1980, and 1984 figures are from the *Congressional Quarterly's Guide to U.S. Elections* (Washington, DC: Congressional Quarterly, 1985), pp. 364–66. The 1988 figure is from *The Statistical Abstract of the United States: 1991* (Washington, DC: U.S. Bureau of the Census, 1991), p. 250. The 1992 figure was reported in the *Libertarian Party News* (December 1992) 7:9. This issue, available from the national Libertarian office in Washington, DC, also contains Libertarian vote totals in state races for all fifty states.

17. James Harris, "Third Parties Out," *The Nation* 251 (November 12, 1990), p. 549. The figures about ballot access are also from Harris' article.

18. In David Bergland, *Libertarianism in One Lesson* (Costa Mesa, CA: Orpheus, 1986), pp. 24–5.

19. Readers should consult the Bergland book or the LP party newsletters for more issue stands. Some of the more academically oriented books favored by Libertarians are Milton Friedman's *Capitalism and Freedom* (Chicago: University of Chicago Press, 1962); F. A. Hayek's *The Road to Serfdom* (Chicago: University of Chicago Press, 1980); Robert Novak's *Anarchy, State, and Utopia* (New York: Basic, 1974); and Thomas Sowell's *The Economics and Politics of Race* (New York: William Morrow, 1983).

20. Bergland, *Libertarianism in One Lesson*, pp. 14–17.

21. Ibid., p. 15.

22. On the decline of trust in government, see Paul Abramson, *Political Attitudes in America: Formation and Change* (San Francisco: W. H. Freeman, 1983), pp. 193–240.

23. See Dennis King's study, *Lyndon LaRouche and the New American Fascism* (New York: Doubleday, 1989).

24. A few Libertarians have had some limited success in getting their letters to the editor published by Chicago newspapers. Christopher Maxwell, corresponding secretary of the LPI, had two letters published by the *Chicago Sun-Times* and one published by the *Chicago Tribune* in July of 1992 alone.

25. See John Green and James Guth, "The Sociology of Libertarians," *Liberty* 1 (September/October 1987): 5–12.

26. This is an odd, rather biased sample of activists, since it was drawn from a list of contributors: People without high-paying occupations, or little extra income to donate to the party, had no chance of being selected for the survey.

27. In excerpts from the interviews reproduced in this chapter, I have added punctuation and also some bracketed explanatory notes. This was done sim-

ply to improve the syntax of informants' comments: I was very careful not to alter, in any way, the substance of their remarks.

The interview protocol we used was fairly lengthy. Beyond standard demographic questions, and queries about their media use, we talked extensively with informants about their political afilliations, reasons for joining the party, and how the party has changed their views. We also asked about their participation in Libertarian activities – protesting, attending meetings, making speeches, recruiting, petition drives, etc. – in order to get a sense of the level of their involvement. Finally, we asked an array of questions about their views of the party's effectiveness, use of media, coverage by the media, and informal social networks created through the party. The complete protocol is available from the author.

The interviews for this study were conducted on the telephone, and later transcribed for analysis. I had conducted ten earlier, in-person interviews with Libertarians, which helped me to formulate questions for the phone interview and enabled me to understand the group's goals. The results of my face-to-face interviews are not included in this chapter.

28. David Bergland, *America's Libertarian Heritage: The Politics of Freedom* (Costa Mesa, CA: Orpheus, 1991).

29. Marshall Fritz, a Libertarian and the president of Advocates for Self-Government, a libertarian organization, claims that his pet project is finding libertarian celebrities who are unaware of the party. He wrote in a recent newsletter: "Entertainers and others in the public eye can have a huge influence on the political and social agenda. . . . If you know of any celebrities (in any field) who seem like they could be libertarians, tell me." *The Liberator* 6 (April/May/June 1990): 9.

30. *The Illinois Libertarian* 16 (January, 1990): 1.

31. Milt Rosenberg, of WGN in Chicago, has had many Libertarians on his radio program. On September 9, 1992, for example, he interviewed the Libertarian presidential candidate on his popular evening show, "Extension 720."

32. Among these "think tanks" are the Ludwig von Mises Institute in Washington, DC, the Heartland Institute in Chicago, and the CATO Institute, also in Washington.

33. As I mentioned earlier, there has been some historical work on third parties – the Free Soil, American, and Progressive parties, for example.

34. Samuel Eldersveld, in his book on political parties, uses the phrase "third party threats." Ironically, third parties have not been particularly threatening to the two major parties, which have remained quite robust since the turn of the century. See Eldersveld's *Political Parties in American Society*, pp. 39–42.

6. CONCLUSION

1. Marx did not himself coin the phrase "projective consciousness," but describes this specifically human trait in *Capital*. I borrow it from the Marxist scholar, John McMurtry. See his innovative reading of Marx's major works, *The Structure of Marx's World-View* (Princeton, NJ: Princeton University Press, 1978), pp. 22–34.

2. See my discussion of Lukes's definition of ritual in Chapter 1.

3. Dell's correspondence is archived in the Newberry Library in Chicago, and Eastman's can be found at the Lilly Library at Indiana University in Bloomington.

4. This is Benedict Anderson's idea, introduced in Chapter 1.

5. Quoted in Dena Goodman, "Governing the Republic of Letters: The Politics of Culture in the French Enlightenment," *History of European Ideas* 13 (1991): 185.

6. See the excellent discussion by St. Clair Drake and Horace Cayton, *Black Metropolis: A Study of Negro Life in a Northern City* (New York: Harcourt, Brace & World, 1945).

7. Benjamin Barber, *Strong Democracy: Participatory Politics for a New Age* (Berkeley: University of California Press, 1984), p. 232. On communication and community, also see John Dewey's classic, *The Public and its Problems* (Athens, OH: Swallow Press, 1954); and James Carey's essay, "A Cultural Approach to Communication," *Communication* 2 (1975): 1–22.

8. The Libertarian complaints about standard survey questions are compelling (leftists have these same problems), but there is some irony in these charges: Any public opinion researcher would be appalled by their "Fritz Quiz," since the questions are both leading and badly organized. Although contemporary survey research is problematic on a number of levels, as Bourdieu, Blumer, and others have pointed out, Libertarians disregard even the most fundamental tenets of survey research methodology.

9. See Bourdieu's, "Public Opinion Does Not Exist," in *Communication and Class Struggle*, ed. A. Mattelart and S. Siegelaub (New York: International General, 1979) and my application of his ideas to the Clarence Thomas Supreme Court nomination battle, "Surveys in the Public Sphere: Applying Bourdieu's Critique of Opinion Polls," *International Journal of Public Opinion Research* 4 (1992): 220–99.

10. One recent, important exception is William Gamson's *Talking Politics* (New York: Cambridge University Press, 1992).

11. The most influential book on symbols in American political studies is Murray

Edelman's *The Symbolic Uses of Politics* (Urbana: University of Illinois Press, 1985).

12. The most provocative discussion of the relationship between information and geography is still Harold Innis's *The Bias of Communication* (Toronto: University of Toronto Press, 1964).

Bibliography

Aaron, Daniel. 1961. *Writers on the Left: Episodes in American Literary Communism.* New York: Harcourt, Brace & World.

Abramson, Paul. 1983. *Political Attitudes in America: Formation and Change.* San Francisco: W. H. Freeman.

Abray, Jane. 1975. Feminism in the French Revolution. *American Historical Review* 80: 43–62.

Anderson, Benedict. 1991. *Imagined Communities: Reflections on the Origin and Spread of Nationalism.* London: Verso.

Baker, Jean. 1983. *Affairs of Party: The Political Culture of Northern Democrats in the Mid-Nineteenth Century.* Ithaca, NY: Cornell University Press.

Barber, Benjamin. 1984. *Strong Democracy: Participatory Politics for a New Age.* Berkeley: University of California Press.

Bass, Jack, and Walter DeVries. 1976. *The Transformation of Southern Politics: Social Change and Political Consequences Since 1945.* New York: Basic Books.

Becker, Howard. 1963. *Outsiders: Studies in the Sociology of Deviance.* Glencoe, NY: The Free Press.

Bell, Colin, and Howard Newby. 1972. *Community Studies: An Introduction to the Sociology of the Local Community.* New York: Praeger.

Bell, Roderick, David Edwards, and R. Harrison Wagnes. 1969. *Political Power: A Reader in Theory and Research.* New York: The Free Press.

Bellah, Robert, et al. 1985. *Habits of the Heart: Individualism and Commitment in American Life.* New York: Harper & Row.

Beniger, J. R., and Susan Herbst. 1990. "Mass Media and Public Opinion: Emergence of an Institution." In *Change in Societal Institutions,* eds. M. Hallinan, D. Klein, and J. Glass. New York: Plenum.

Bennett, W. Lance. 1988. *News: The Politics of Illusion.* New York: Longman.

Bentley, Arthur. 1967. *The Process of Government.* Cambridge, MA: Harvard University Press.

Bergland, David. 1986. *Libertarianism in One Lesson.* Costa Mesa, CA: Orpheus.

Berkin, Carol R., and Clara M. Lovett, eds. 1980. *Women, War, and Revolution.* New York: Holmes & Meier.

Berman, David. 1990. Environment, Culture and Radical Third Parties: Electoral Support for the Socialists in Arizona and Nevada, 1912–1916. *Social Science Journal* 27: 147–58.

Bitner, Katherine A. 1985. The Role of the *Chicago Defender* in the Great Migration of 1916–1918. *Negro History Bulletin* 48 (Jan.–Dec.): 20–6.

Blumer, Herbert. 1948. Public Opinion and Public Opinion Polling. *American Sociological Review* 13: 542–54.

Bodek, Evelyn Gordon. 1976. Saloniéres and Bluestockings: Educated Obsolescence and Germinating Feminism. *Feminist Studies* 3: 185–99.

Bourdieu, Pierre. 1979. "Public Opinion Does Not Exist." In *Communication and Class Struggle*, eds. A. Mattelart and S. Siegelaub. New York: International General.

Branham, Charles. 1981. The Transformation of Black Political Leadership in Chicago, 1864–1942. Ph.D. diss., University of Chicago.

Bridenthal, Renate, and Claudia Koonz, eds. 1977. *Becoming Visible: Women in European History.* Boston: Houghton Mifflin.

Brooks, Maxwell R. 1959. *The Negro Press Re-Examined: Political Content of Leading Negro Newspapers.* Boston: Christopher House.

Brown, Judith. 1986. *Immodest Acts: The Life of a Lesbian Nun in Renaissance Italy.* New York: Oxford University Press.

Brubaker, Rogers. 1984. *The Limits of Rationality: An Essay on the Social and Moral Thought of Max Weber.* London: George Allen & Unwin.

Buni, Andrew. 1974. *Robert L. Vann of the Pittsburgh Courier: Politics and Black Journalism.* Pittsburgh: University of Pittsburgh Press.

Calhoun, C. J. (Craig). 1980. Community: Toward a Variable Conceptualization for Comparative Research, *Social History* 5: 105–29.

———. 1992. ed. *Habermas and the Public Sphere.* Cambridge, MA: MIT Press.

Canfield, James. 1984. *A Case of Third Party Activism: The George Wallace Campaign Worker and the American Independent Party.* Lanham, MD: University Press of America.

Carey, James. 1975. A Cultural Approach to Communication, *Communication* 2: 1–22.

Chafee, Zechariah. 1920. *Freedom of Speech.* New York: Harcourt, Brace and Company.

Charlotte, Catherine (Lady Jackson). 1880. *The Old Régime: Court, Salons, and Theatres.* London: Richard Bentley.

Chodorow, Nancy. 1978. *The Reproduction of Mothering: Psychoanalysis and the Sociology of Gender*. Berkeley: University of California Press.

Clergue, Helen. 1971. *The Salon: A Study of French Society and Personalities in the Eighteenth Century*. New York: Burt Franklin.

Cohen, A. P. 1982. *Belonging: Identity and Social Organisation in British Rural Cultures*. Manchester: Manchester University Press.

———. 1985. *The Symbolic Construction of Community*. London: Tavistock Publications.

Crow, Thomas E. 1985. *Painters and Public Life in Eighteenth-Century Paris*. New Haven, CT: Yale University Press.

Dawley, Alan. 1991. *Struggles for Justice: Social Responsibility and the Liberal State*. Cambridge, MA: Harvard University Press.

Dell, Floyd. 1933. *Homecoming*. New York: Farrar & Rinehard.

D'Epinay, Madame. 1930. *Memoirs and Correspondence of Madame D'Epinay*. Translated by E. G. Allingham. London: George Routledge.

Detweiler, Frederick G. 1922. *The Negro Press in the United States*. Chicago: University of Chicago Press.

Dewey, John. 1954. *The Public and its Problems*. Athens, OH: Swallow Press.

Diderot, Denis. 1927. *Dialogues*. Translated by Francis Birrell. London: Routledge.

Drake, St. Clair, and Horace Clayton. 1945. *Black Metropolis: A Study of Negro Life in a Northern City*. New York: Harcourt, Brace & World.

Dreyfus, Hubert, and Paul Rabinow. 1983. *Michel Foucault: Beyond Structuralism and Hermeneutics*. Chicago: University of Chicago Press.

Durkheim, Emile. 1915. *The Elementary Forms of the Religious Life: A Study in Religious Sociology*. Translated by Joseph Swain. London: George Allen & Unwin.

———. 1947. *The Division of Labor in Society*. Translated by George Simpson. New York: The Free Press.

Eastman, Max. 1948. *Enjoyment of Living*. New York: Harper & Brothers.

Edelman, Murray. 1985. *The Symbolic Uses of Politics*. Urbana: University of Illinois Press.

Eldersveld, Samuel. 1964. *Political Parties: A Behavioral Analysis*. Chicago: Rand McNally.

———. 1982. *Political Parties in American Society*. New York: Basic.

Emery, Edwin, and Michael Emery. 1984. *The Press and America: An Interpretive History of the Mass Media*. 5th ed. Englewood Cliffs, NJ: Prentice-Hall.

Entman, Robert M. 1989. *Democracy Without Citizens: Media and the Decay of American Politics*. New York: Oxford University Press.

Evans, Sara M. 1989. *Born for Liberty: A History of Women in America*. New York: Free Press.

Felski, Rita. 1989. *Beyond Feminist Aesthetics: Feminist Literature and Social Change.* Cambridge, MA: Harvard University Press.

Ferguson, Russell. 1990. "Introduction." In *Out There: Marginalization and Contemporary Cultures,* eds. Russell Ferguson, Martha Gever, Trinh Minh-ha, and Cornel West. Cambridge, MA: MIT Press.

Finkle, Lee. 1975. *Forum for Protest: The Black Press During World War II.* Rutherford, NJ: Associated University Presses.

Fishbein, Leslie. 1982. *Rebels in Bohemia: The Radicals of The Masses, 1911–1917.* Chapel Hill, NC: University of North Carolina Press.

Fontenelle, Bernard Le Bovier. 1990. *Conversations on the Plurality of Worlds.* Translated by H. A. Hargreaves. Berkeley: University of California Press.

Foucault, Michel. 1976. *Power/Knowledge: Selected Interviews and Other Writings 1972–1977.* ed. Colin Gordon. New York: Pantheon.

———. 1990. *The History of Sexuality,* vol. 1. Translated by R. Hurley. New York: Vintage.

Fraser, Nancy. 1989. *Unruly Practices: Power, Discourse, and Gender in Contemporary Social Theory.* Minneapolis: University of Minnesota Press.

———. 1992. "Rethinking the Public Sphere: A Contribution to the Critique of Actually Existing Democracy." In *Habermas and the Public Sphere,* ed. C. J. Calhoun. Cambridge, MA: MIT Press

Friedman, Milton. 1962. *Capitalism and Freedom.* Chicago: University of Chicago Press.

Gamson, William. 1975. *The Strategy of Social Protest.* Homewood, IL: Dorsey.

———. 1992. *Talking Politics.* New York: Cambridge University Press.

Gillespie, J. David. 1993. *Politics at the Periphery: Third Parties in Two-Party America.* Columbia: University of South Carolina Press.

Ginsberg, Benjamin. 1986. *The Captive Public: How Mass Opinion Promotes State Power.* New York: Basic.

Gitlin, Todd. 1980. *The Whole World is Watching.* Berkeley: University of California Press.

Goldenberg, Edie. 1975. *Making the Papers: The Access of Resource-Poor Groups to the Metropolitan Press.* Lexington, MA: Lexington Books.

De Goncourt, Edmond, and Jules De Goncourt. 1972. *The Woman of the Eighteenth Century: Her Life, From Birth to Death, Her Love and Her Philosophy in the Worlds of Salon, Shop and Street.* Freeport, NY: Books for Libraries Press.

Goodman, Dena. 1989. Filial Rebellion in the Salon: Madame Geoffrin and Her Daughter. *French Historical Studies* 16: 28–47.

———. 1989. Enlightenment Salons: The Convergence of Female and Philosophic Ambitions. *Eighteenth-Century Studies* 22: 328–50.

———. 1991. Governing the Republic of Letters: The Politics of Culture in the French Enlightenment. *History of European Ideas* 13: 183–99.

———. 1992. Public Sphere and Private Life: Toward a Synthesis of Current Historiographical Approaches to the Old Regime. *History and Theory* 31: 1–20.

Gosnell, Harold F. 1935. *Negro Politicians: The Rise of Negro Politics in Chicago.* Chicago: University of Chicago Press.

Gossman, Lionel. 1968. *Medievalism and the Ideologies of the Enlightenment: The World and Work of La Curne de Sainte-Palaye.* Baltimore: Johns Hopkins University Press.

Graber, Doris. 1993. *Mass Media and American Politics.* 4th ed. Washington, DC: Congressional Quarterly Press.

Graham, Ruth. "Loaves and Liberty: Women in the French Revolution." In *Women, War and Revolution,* eds. Carol R. Berkin and Clara M. Lovett. New York: Holmes & Meiet.

Green, John, and James Guth. 1987. The Sociology of Libertarians. *Liberty* 1(Sept.–Oct.): 5–12.

Grimshaw, William. 1992. *Bitter Fruit: Black Politics and the Chicago Machine, 1931–1991.* Chicago: University of Chicago Press.

Grossberg, Lawrence, Cary Nelson, and Paula Treichler. 1992. *Cultural Studies.* New York: Routledge.

Grossman, James. 1989. *Land of Hope: Chicago, Black Southerners, and the Great Migration.* Chicago: University of Chicago Press.

Gusfield, Joseph. 1975. *Community: A Critical Response.* New York: Harper & Row.

Habermas, Jürgen. 1974. The Public Sphere: An Encyclopedia Article. *New German Critique* 1 (Fall): 49–54.

———. 1989. *The Structural Transformation of the Public Sphere.* Translated by Thomas Burger. Cambridge, MA: MIT Press.

Hall, Stuart, and Tony Jefferson, eds. 1976. *Resistance Through Rituals: Youth Subcultures in Post-War Britain.* London: Hutchinson.

Hallin, Dan. 1986. *The "Uncensored War": The Media and Vietnam.* New York: Oxford University Press.

Hallin, Dan, and Paolo Mancini. 1984. Speaking of the President: Political Structure and Representational Form in U.S. and Italian Television News. *Theory and Society* 13: 829–50.

Hause, Steven, and Anne Kenny. 1984. *Women's Suffrage and Social Politics in the French Third Republic.* Princeton, NJ: Princeton University Press.

Hayek, F. A. 1980. *The Road to Serfdom.* Chicago: University of Chicago Press.

Hebage, Dick. 1979. *Subculture: The Meaning of Style.* London: Methuen.

Herbst, Susan. 1993. *Numbered Voices: How Opinion Polling Has Shaped American Politics.* Chicago: University of Chicago Press.

————. 1993. Mass Media and Public Opinion: Citizens' Constructions of Political Reality. *Media, Culture and Society* 15: 437–54

————. 1992. Gender, Marginality, and the Changing Dimensions of the Public Sphere. *Communication Research* 19: 381–92.

Herbst, Susan and James R. Beniger. 1994. "The Changing Infrastructure of Public Opinion." In *Audiencemaking*, eds. D. Charles Whitney and James Ettema. Newbury Park, CA: Sage.

Hertz, Deborah. 1978. Saloniéres and Literary Women in Late Eighteenth-Century Berlin. *New German Critique* 14: 97–108.

Hesseltine, William. 1962. *Third-Party Movements in the United States*. New York: D. Van Nostrand Company.

Hicks, Granville. 1936. *John Reed: The Making of a Revolutionary*. New York: Macmillan.

Hinckley, Ronald H. 1991. Public Opinion and the Persian Gulf War. Paper read at annual meeting of the American Association for Public Opinion Research, May 16–19, Phoenix, AZ.

hooks, bell. 1981. *Ain't I a Woman: Black Women and Feminism*. Boston: South End Press.

Huckfeldt, Robert, and John Sprague. 1994. *Citizens, Politics, and Social Communication: Information and Influence in an Election Campaign*. New York: Cambridge University Press.

Hufton, Olwen. 1971. Women in Revolution 1789–1796. *Past and Present* 53: 90–108.

Hume, David. 1987. *Essays, Moral, Political, and Literary*. Indianapolis: Liberty Classics.

Humphrey, Robert. 1978. *Children of Fantasy: The First Rebels of Greenwich Village*. New York: John Wiley.

Innis, Harold. 1964. *The Bias of Communication*. Toronto: University of Toronto Press.

JanMohamed, Abdul, and David Lloyd. 1990. *The Nature and Context of Minority Discourse*. New York: Oxford University Press.

Janowitz, Morris. 1980. *The Community Press in an Urban Setting*. 2nd. ed. Chicago: University of Chicago Press.

Jones, Margaret. 1993. *Heretics and Hellraisers: Women Contributors to the Masses, 1911–1917*. Austin, TX: University of Texas Press.

Jones, Shirley. 1979. "Madame de Tencin: An Eighteenth-Century Woman Novelist." In *Woman and Society in Eighteenth-Century France: Essays in Honour of John Stephenson Spink*, eds. Eva Jacobs, W. H. Barber, Jean H. Bloch, F. W. Leakey, and Eileen Le Breton. London: Athlone.

Kaplan, Steven Laurence. 1979. *La Bagarre: Galiani's "Lost" Parody.* Netherlands: Martinus Nijhoff.

Katz, Elihu. 1987. Communications Research Since Lazarsfeld. *Public Opinion Quarterly.* 51 (Winter): S25–S45.

Katznelson, Ira. 1973. *Black Men, White Cities: Race, Politics, and Migration in the United States, 1900–30, and Britain, 1948–68.* London: Oxford University Press.

Kennedy, Emmet. 1989. *A Cultural History of the French Revolution.* New Haven, CT: Yale University Press.

Kors, Alan. 1976. *D'Holbach's Coterie: An Enlightenment in Paris.* Princeton, NJ: Princeton University Press.

Kousser, J. Morgan. 1974. *The Shaping of Southern Politics: Suffrage Restriction and the Establishment of the One-Party South, 1880–1910.* New Haven, CT: Yale University Press.

La Brie, Henry III. 1974. ed. *Perspectives of the Black Press: 1974.* Kennebunkport, ME: Mercer House Press.

Landes, Joan. 1988. *Women and the Public Sphere in the Age of the French Revolution.* Ithaca, NY: Cornell University Press.

Latour, Anny. 1970. *Uncrowned Queens.* Translated by A.A. Dent. London: J. M. Dent.

Lawson, Stephen F. 1985. *In Pursuit of Power: Southern Blacks and Electoral Politics, 1965–1982.* New York: Columbia University Press.

———. 1976. *Black Ballots: Voting Rights in the South, 1944–1969.* New York: Columbia University Press.

Lazarsfeld, Paul, and Robert Merton. 1948. "Mass Communication, Popular Taste, and Organized Social Action." In *The Communication of Ideas,* ed. Lyman Bryson. New York: Harper and Bros.

Levy, Gay, Harriet Branson Applewhite, and Mary Durham Johnson, eds. 1979. *Women in Revolutionary Paris, 1789–1795, Selected Documents.* Urbana: University of Illinois Press.

Lewis, Anthony. 1991. *Make No Law: The Sullivan Case and the First Amendment.* New York: Random House.

Lippmann, Walter. 1925. *The Phantom Public.* New York: Harcourt, Brace.

———. 1965. *Public Opinion.* New York: The Free Press.

Lofland, John. 1966. *Doomsday Cult: A Study of Conversion, Proselytization, and Maintenance of Faith.* Englewood Cliffs, NJ: Prentice-Hall.

Lougee, Carolyn. 1976. *Le Paradis des Femmes: Women, Salons, and Social Stratification in Seventeenth-Century France.* Princeton, NJ: Princeton University Press.

Lough, John. 1991. Lemonnier's Painting, "Une Soirée Chez Madame Geoffrin en 1755." *French Studies* 45: 269–78.

Luhan, Mabel Dodge. 1936. *Movers and Shakers.* New York: Harcourt, Brace and Company.

Lukes, Steven. 1986. *Power.* New York: New York University Press.

———. 1975. Political Ritual and Social Integration. *Sociology* 9: 289–308.

———. 1974. *Power: A Radical View.* London: Macmillan.

McAdam, Doug. 1988. *Freedom Summer: The Idealists Revisited.* New York: The Ronald Press.

McAdam, Doug, John McCarthy, and Mayer Zald. 1988. "Social Movements." In *Handbook of Sociology,* ed. Neil Smelser. Newbury Park, CA: Sage.

McGerr, Michael E. 1986. *The Decline of Popular Politics: The American North, 1865–1928.* New York: Oxford University Press.

McMurtry, John. 1978. *The Structure of Marx's World-View.* Princeton, NJ: Princeton University Press.

Martin, Kingsley. 1954. *The Rise of French Liberal Thought: A Study of Political Ideas from Bayle to Condorcet.* New York: New York University Press.

May, Gita. 1970. *Madame Roland and the Age of Revolution.* New York: Columbia University Press.

Mayer, Hans. 1982. *Outsiders: A Study in Life and Letters.* Cambridge: MIT Press.

Maza, Sarah. 1992. Women, the Bourgeoisie, and the Public Sphere: Response to David Bell & Daniel Gordon. *French Historical Studies* 17 (Fall): 935–50.

Mazmanian, Daniel. 1974. *Third Parties in Presidential Elections.* Washington, DC: The Brookings Institution.

Mills, Stephanie. 1991. Salons and Beyond: Changing the World One Evening at a Time. *The Utne Reader* 44 (March/April): 68–78.

Moi, Toril. 1986. *Sexual/Textual Politics: Feminist Literary Theory.* London: Methuen.

Moore, Sally, and Barbara Myerhoff. 1977. *Secular Ritual.* Amsterdam: VanGorcum.

Morris, Aldon, and Carol McClurg Mueller. 1992. *Frontiers in Social Movement Theory.* New Haven: Yale University Press.

Myrdal, Gunnar. 1944. *An American Dilemma: The Negro Problem and Modern Democracy.* New York: Harper & Brothers.

Nathans, Benjamin. 1990. Habermas's 'Public Sphere' in the Era of the French Revolution. *French Historical Studies* 16 (Spring): 620–44.

Neuman, W. Russell. 1991. *The Future of the Mass Audience.* New York: Cambridge University Press.

Novak, Robert. 1974. *Anarchy, State, and Utopia.* New York: Basic.

Oak, Vishnu V. 1948. *The Negro Newspaper.* Westport, CT: Negro Universities Press.

Ottley, Roi. 1979. *The Lonely Warrior: The Life and Times of Robert S. Abbott.* Chicago: H. Regnery Company.

Page, Benjamin, and Robert Shapiro. 1991. *The Rational Public: Fifty Years of Trends in Americans' Policy Preferences.* Chicago: University of Chicago Press.

Palmer, Paul. 1964. "The Concept of Public Opinion in Political Theory." In *Essays in History and Political Theory in Honor of Charles Howard McIlwain,* ed. C. Wittke. New York: Russell & Russell.

Park, Robert, et al. 1925. *The City.* Chicago: University of Chicago Press.

Parker, Andrew, et al. 1992. *Nationalisms and Sexualities.* New York: Routledge.

Pateman, Carole. 1988. *The Sexual Contract.* Stanford, CA: Stanford University Press.

Pearson, Judy Cornelia. 1985. *Gender and Communication.* Dubuque, IA: William C. Brown.

Platt, Orville H. 1900. "Negro Governors." In *Papers of the New Haven Colony Historical Society.* New Haven, CT.

Pride, Armistead S. 1950. A Register and History of Negro Newspapers in the United States. Ph.D. diss., Northwestern University.

Reidy, Joseph P. 1978. 'Negro Election Day' and Black Community Life in New England, 1750–1860. *Marxist Perspectives* 1 (Fall): 102–17.

Rockwood, Stephen, et al. 1985. *American Third Parties Since the Civil War: An Annotated Bibliography.* New York: Garland.

Rodgers, Daniel T. 1987. *Contested Truths: Keywords in American Politics Since Independence.* New York: Basic Books.

Rogers, Everett, and Donald Kincaid. 1981. *Communication Networks: Toward a New Paradigm for Research.* New York: Free Press.

Roland, Madame. 1989. *The Memoirs of Madame Roland.* Translated by E. Shuckburgh. London: Barrie & Jenkins.

Rosenstone, Steven, Roy Behr, and Edward Lazarus. 1984. *Third Parties in America: Citizen Response to Major Party Failure.* Princeton, NJ: Princeton University Press.

Rousseau, Jean-Jacques. 1985. *The Confessions of Jean-Jacques Rousseau.* Translated by J. M. Cohen. New York: Penguin.

———. 1969. *Emile.* Translated by Barbara Foxley. London: J. M. Dent.

Roustan, M. 1926. *The Pioneers of the French Revolution.* Translated by Frederic Whyte. Boston: Little, Brown.

Ryan, Mary. 1990. *Women in Public: Between Banners and Ballots, 1825–1880.* Baltimore: Johns Hopkins University Press.

Schudson, Michael. 1978. *Discovering the News: A Social History of American Newspapers*. New York: Basic Books.

Sibley, David. 1981. *Outsiders in Urban Society*. Oxford: Basil Blackwell.

Smart, Barry. 1985. *Foucault, Marxism, and Critique*. London: Routledge & Kegan Paul.

Sowell, Thomas. 1983. *The Economics and Politics of Race*. New York: William Morrow.

Spear, Allan H. 1967. *Black Chicago: The Making of a Negro Ghetto, 1890–1920*. Chicago: University of Chicago Press.

Spivak, Gayatri. 1988. "Can the Sabaltern Speak." In *Marxism and the Interpretation of Culture*, eds. Cary Nelson and Lawrence Grossberg. Urbana: University of Illinois Press.

Steegmuller, Francis. 1991. *A Woman, a Man, and Two Kingdoms: The Story of Madame d'Epinay and the Abbé Galiani*. New York:Alfred A. Knopf.

Steel, Ronald. 1980. *Walter Lippmann and the American Century*. New York: Vintage.

Stuckey, Sterling. 1987. *Slave Culture: Nationalist Theory and the Foundations of Black America*. New York: Oxford University Press.

Swanson, David, and Dan Nimmo. 1990. *New Directions in Political Communication: A Resource Book*. Newbury Park, CA: Sage.

Tallentyre, S.G. [Evelyn Beatrice Hall]. 1901. *The Women of the Salons and Other French Portraits*. London: Longman, Green, and Co.

Tate, Robert S. 1968. *Petit de Bachaumont: His Circle and the Mémoires Secrets*. Geneva: Institut et Musee Voltaire.

Tilly, Charles. 1983. Speaking Your Mind Without Elections, Surveys, or Social Movements. *Public Opinion Quarterly* 47: 461–78.

Tinker, Chauncey Brewster. 1915. *The Salon and English Letters*. New York: Macmillan.

Tönnies, Ferdinand. 1955. *Community and Association*. Translated by C. Loomis. London: Routledge & Kegan Paul.

Turner, Victor. 1969. *The Ritual Process*. Ithaca, NY: Cornell University Press.

Villa, Dana. 1992. Postmodernism and the Public Sphere, *American Political Science Review* 86: 712–21.

Waters, Enoch P. 1987. *American Diary: A Personal History of the Black Press*. Chicago: Path Press.

Weber, Max. 1978. *Economy and Society: An Outline of Interpretive Sociology*, eds. Guenther Roth and Claus Wittich. Berkeley: University of California Press.

Weinreb, Ruth Plaut. 1993. *Eagle in a Gauze Cage: Louise D'Epinay Femme de Lettres*. New York: AMS Press.

West, Cornel. 1990. "The New Cultural Politics of Difference." In Russell

Ferguson, et al., *Out There: Marginalization and Contemporary Cultures.* Cambridge, MA: MIT Press.

Wilson, James Q. 1960. *Negro Politics: The Search for Leadership.* New York: Free Press.

Wood, James Playsted. 1971. *Magazines in the United States.* New York: The Ronald Press.

Young, Art. 1928. *On My Way: Being the Book of Art Young in Text and Picture.* New York: Horace Liveright.

————. 1939. *Art Young: His Life and Times.* New York: Sheridan House.

Young, Consuelo Caldwell. 1943. An Objective Reader Interest Study of *The Chicago Defender Newspaper.* Master's thesis, Northwestern University.

Zurier, Rebecca. 1988. *Art for the Masses: A Radical Magazine and Its Graphics, 1911–1917.* Philadelphia: Temple University Press.

Index